THE APPEARANCE OF JUSTICE

THE APPEARANCE OF JUSTICE

☆ ☆ ☆

John P. MacKenzie

Charles Scribner's Sons / New York

Copyright © 1974 John P. MacKenzie

Library of Congress Cataloging in Publication Data

MacKenzie, John P.
      The appearance of justice.
      Includes bibliographical references.
      1. Judges—United States. 2. Judicial ethics—
United States. I. Title.
KF8775.M25   347′.73′2034   73-1374
ISBN 0-648-13805-0

Quotation from Robert Frost on p. 153 from
"A Semi-Revolution" from *The Poetry of
Robert Frost*, edited by Edward Connery
Lathem. Copyright 1942 by Robert Frost.
Copyright © 1969 by Holt, Rinehart and
Winston, Inc. Copyright © 1970 by Lesley
Frost Ballantine. Reprinted by permission of
Holt, Rinehart and Winston, Inc.

To Amanda

CONTENTS

INTRODUCTION

There are countries in the world where the courts are so reviled and ridiculed, held in such contempt, so "sold out" by common acknowledgment, that the thought of resort to the judiciary for the settlement of important conflicts has been a bad joke for generations. Courts in the United States at all levels are freshly experiencing some of the same sensations of public discontent, by no means solely from radicals who say they would do away with the system entirely. Minorities such as the blacks, the browns, and the poor, and majorities such as women, all have expressed dissatisfaction with the legal system as they have sought to enter it and partake of American justice. Nor are the disadvantaged the only groups putting pressure on the judiciary. Probably the strongest challenges to the capability of the legal order now come from the business community and the newly aroused consumer and average citizen. Americans of all stations are therefore concerned with whether the courts and judges are good enough, and we have all become increasingly aware of their shortcomings.

These challenges compound the stress that is built into the American system of government, which in its genius separates the powers. To a certain extent we set the branches at war with one another, but we also require them to make mutual accommodations. One of our national hopes has always been that with the help of this arrangement we have a strong and independent judiciary, but the process of preserving its independence while upgrading its performance is not a smooth one.

The judiciary is at once a fragile and a powerful institution. The courts are often deemed "the least dangerous branch," the weakest of the three, with no power of their own. The football referee doesn't wear a helmet or shoulder pads; but he doesn't need them, because the warring teams agree that he will not be annihilated for "calling them as he sees them." In the American system the judge, especially the federal judge, is the referee but he is also much more. He helps to set national policy in the way he deals with executive actions, legislative enactments, and the citizens who come before him for justice. The executive can propose a law, Congress can enact it; but only the courts can say whether it is constitutional and, perhaps more important though less dramatic, only the courts have final say whether the law will be generously or grudgingly construed and enforced.

Without armies to carry out their judgments, courts are dependent on the consent of the governed no less than the other branches to make their pronouncements law. When the image of the judiciary is tarnished, the moral authority of the courts is critically undermined. The appearance of partiality, whether based on the judge's apparent economic self-interest, his class or race prejudices, or simple carelessness about the concerns of citizens and the public, is the greatest threat that confronts our judges. A judiciary that is sufficiently armored with a good reputation for integrity can withstand other threats, including what many consider to be the attempts of other branches to intimidate or take it over with appointees bent on doing their bidding.

Against a yardstick of the highest ethical and behavioral standards, how does the American federal judiciary measure up? Until the indictment of Judge Otto Kerner of the U.S. Seventh Circuit Court of Appeals in 1971, it had been many years since a member of the judiciary was impeached or removed, indicted or convicted, despite politically motivated attacks on Justice William O. Douglas and an unsatisfying clearance in the House of Representatives. However, one justice, Abe Fortas, resigned in 1969 rather than fully explain his nonjudicial dealings. The ethical sensitivity of his first proposed replacement, the otherwise widely respected Clement Haynsworth, was tested and found wanting by the United States Senate. *His* proposed replacement, G. Harrold Carswell, was rejected chiefly for lack of qualifications for the job. The embodiment of mediocrity, insolence, inattention to principle or precedent, and want of judicial temperament, Carswell brought into question the entire system of picking federal judges, since he had been nominated and confirmed for a federal district court and had been elevated to a circuit court of appeals. Finally in 1970, Harry A. Blackmun qualified for the High Court after a confirmation hearing that showed that he, at least, had long understood better than most of his fellow judges the need for the strictest personal code.

The lower federal courts, where most lawyers agree "the power really is," were far from exempt from scandal and controversy. The Fifth U.S. Circuit Court of Appeals, which earned an honored place in history for its civil rights record in the 1950s and 1960s, found itself hip deep in oil holdings at about the time Haynsworth was being judged and while the organized bar was starting to work on a new set of judicial ethics. Some of the top federal judges in Tennessee, one of them a prime candidate for the Supreme Court, turned out to be insiders of business dealings with members of their bar and were embarrassingly connected with litigation in their courts. The federal judges in Oklahoma City, a place that had bred scandal in the state judiciary, showed an amazing lack of awareness about conflicts of interest by both lawyers and judges in handling one of the nation's major bankruptcies.

Meanwhile proceedings in federal courts were becoming nearly as disordered as the streets. Some defendants and their lawyers made guerrilla theater out of their trials, but frequently they shared responsibility for disruption and confusion with the judge. It is fair to say that the disorderliness at the 1968 Spock trial, which was not physically disruptive, was entirely the fault of the presiding judge. In the Chicago Seven conspiracy trial, it is probably not possible to pass judgment, if it matters, on "who started" the tragic disorders; but it is clear that the judge was a freewheeling participant and not the cool arbiter, even under provocation, that the times urgently required.

The disruptive behavior and reputations of Panthers, New

Leftists, and others, as well as their lawyers, played a curious and disproportionate role in shaping the judiciary's response to what had become a crisis of confidence in the integrity of the courts. In the minds of prominent judges and many leaders of the American Bar Association, the attacks made on the judicial system by the alienated ruled out one of the classic purifying techniques: full public disclosure of the outside interests of a public official. The black-robed brotherhood, the tight fraternity of judges, feared that the William Kunstlers of this world would use the disclosed financial data for further assaults on their reputations.

The response to scandal and disorder took a tortured course. First, Earl Warren was determined to leave the judiciary in a better state than he had suddenly found it in the spring of 1969. He rammed through a temporary code of judicial conduct with limited disclosure of judges' financial dealings. But no sooner had he retired than the counterreaction began, sometimes led and sometimes followed by the new chief justice, Warren Earl Burger.

The ABA, deeming its fifty-year-old ethical standards out of date (in some ways the Canons of Judicial Ethics were actually quite modern and adequate; the trouble lay more with the violators), created a committee to revise them. Rather than continuing at least to experiment with the Warren reforms, the Judicial Conference of the United States rolled them back to await the product of the private group. It was a major, if temporary, lending of public power to a private organization. Even Congress stood by to see what the ABA and the judges would do. The intricate machinery of the judicial lobby, the Judicial Conference, began to grind. Subtle changes in the proposed code evolved, reflecting new concerns of the judges that they would come under some kind of supervision.

It may safely be said that neither the attempts of some influential judges to make the problem go away nor the organized bar's effort to write a code acceptable to the judges will settle matters. This is because the friction over ethics is in large part due to the public's rising expectations about the conduct of its officials. It is also because the legal problems of the coming decade, such as pollution and consumer protection, may require even more sensitivity and a purer judicial system than the past two decades with their civil rights and civil liberties emphasis.

This account of how we arrived at this juncture and these proposals for where we should go from here spring not from disrespect for the federal judiciary, but on the contrary, from a deeply felt respect and admiration for the American judicial system in all its independent greatness. In general, this is an attempt to treat the ethical issues on their merits rather than in political terms, to the extent that they can be divorced from politics. Thus there will be less concern about the political or ideological impact of the Fortas, Douglas, Haynsworth, and other cases than about the correctness of the conduct that came into controversy. The aim is to be nontechnical, even when lawyers and judges have managed to make things appear highly complex, but not to oversimplify and not to do an injustice to the vast majority of judges who sincerely seek better answers for difficult questions. The focus is almost entirely on the federal system, in part because the ethical tone of the federal courts and the Supreme Court has been so seriously deficient—despite conditions much more favorable to justice than prevail in most state systems—that one can only assume the truth of reports indicating a far worse climate in the state courts.

It goes without saying—and it will not be said repeatedly in this book—that the majority of American federal judges are able, honest, and desirous of doing the right thing. It also need not be repeated that the ethical and behavioral considerations in this book are not the whole of judging. Admittedly some of the notions already advanced in this introduction are by no means generally accepted among those considered experts in the field; the fuller explanations that follow may yet leave them unconvinced. For example, many issues described here in terms of ethics and proper judicial behavior are not viewed as such by many who have studied the problem closely. But the conduct of our judges is too important to be left to the experts. Finally but importantly, this book attempts to make clear that the public, whose interest is the goal of the entire system of justice, need not be left out of the reform process but can inform itself and help the American judiciary find its way.

1

☆ ☆ ☆

ENTANGLEMENTS

"[T]he lines of separation drawn by the Constitution between the three departments of the government . . . being in certain respects checks upon each other, and our being judges of a court in the last resort, are considerations which afford strong arguments against the propriety of our extra-judicially deciding the questions alluded to, especially as the power given by the Constitution to the President, of calling on the heads of departments for opinions, seems to have been *purposely* as well as expressly united in the *executive* departments."

Chief Justice Jay and associate justices
to President Washington, 1793

"I cannot and I will not be an instrument by which the separation of powers specified in our Constitution is called into question."

Justice Abe Fortas, at hearings on his
nomination to be chief justice, 1969

Separation of powers—that bedrock principle of constitutional government, that admired doctrine, that distinctive off-spring of American political genius—has been conspicuously dishonored throughout history. It has been violated with style and flourish, as when the first chief justice, John Jay, negotiated a treaty with Britain while holding judicial title, or when John Marshall, in the course of delivering the charter of judicial supremacy in *Marbury* v. *Madison*, judged the legality of commissions he had signed as a cabinet official. In small ways also, the

principle of divided government functions has been traduced as
presidents have asked judges and justices to perform executive
chores and the judiciary has complied.

Despite its legitimate ancestors, the disregard for separation of
powers is often seen as illegitimate action in modern times. The
infractions have occurred randomly through history and have
crossed political and ideological lines, giving no party a monop-
oly on virtue or vice. But something seems to have happened to
the public's view of such practices. Whether or not the average
American thinks in terms of political theory, many Americans
seem to have brought to bear a general sense of the fitness of
things, no longer tolerating the infractions. Using its ethical
sense, the public has stirred public figures to revive their respect
for the governmental principle. The Jay precedent is not good
law and will not justify the executive tasks performed by a Justice
Abe Fortas. This chapter recalls some of the chores that justices
have done for presidents, in international diplomacy and in
domestic politics, as well as some of the political mischief that
some jurists have spun for themselves, before examining from the
standpoint of judicial ethics the Fortas–Lyndon Johnson relationship as it emerged during Fortas's bid to become chief justice.

The principle and its companion system of checks and
balances are designed to keep power scattered among the
legislative, executive, and judicial operatives in government so
that it will not slip into the hands of a few mighty people. For the
judicial branch, a special corollary with a force of its own comes
into play: the demand for an independent judiciary, evidenced in
the Constitution by more secure tenure for members of the
Supreme Court and lower federal judges. Without such special
solicitude for independence, the Constitution seems to say, the
powers are not really separated, the branches do not truly check
each other, and of course the citizenry has no refuge from
arbitrary rule.

The idea of neutrality and impartiality in a judge is an ancient
one—witness the Justinian Code, which admonished that "no
man shall be a judge of his own cause"—while refined and
applied concepts of tripartite government are relatively modern.
But increasingly the judge's impartiality as a matter of ethical

fairness and the judge's independence in the American constitutional system serve vital, overlapping functions: maintaining the purity of the judicial decision-making process and instilling, perpetuating, and renewing public confidence in the integrity of government. Historic Supreme Court rulings in 1927, 1955, and 1972 found the same violation of constitutional due process of law in these three situations: a justice of the peace whose compensation rose or fell depending on the number of guilty verdicts he rendered (1927); a judge not financially interested in the outcome of a case but who sat as a "one-man grand jury," performing the executive function of prosecutor, the judicial function of presiding officer, and the popular jury function of finding the facts and ascertaining guilt (1955); and the part-time judge who, while not standing to gain income from his guilty verdicts, could use traffic fines to pad the town treasury for which the judge, wearing his hat as mayor, had responsibility (1972). In each case the situation was unfair to the individual defendant caught in its toils and in each case the Supreme Court set aside convictions. The Court stated the idea well in the 1955 decision:

> Every procedure which would offer a possible temptation to the average man as a judge . . . not to hold the balance true between the State and the accused, denies the latter due process of law. Such a stringent rule may sometimes bar trial by judges who have no actual bias and who would do their very best to weigh the scales of justice equally between contending parties. But to perform its high function in the best way "justice must satisfy the appearance of justice."

With these concepts of ethics and independence in mind, let us look at some of history's departures from them before examining the Fortas controversy in closer detail.

☆

Although the Founding Fathers were emphatic enough about the urgent need for divided government, it may be that the original understanding of constitutional separation of powers did not even come close to condemning the sort of extracurricular entanglements that have become so controversial in more modern times. Consider Chief Justice Jay, who helped write the

Federalist Papers and demonstrated early that he understood the division of labor concept. It was Jay's letter for the Court that courteously but firmly rejected the request of President Washington for legal advice on pressing matters of state. On Washington's behalf, Secretary of State Jefferson had written Jay a beguiling plea for assistance on legal questions "of considerable difficulty," complications growing out of the revolutionary war, matters critical to the young nation's ability to get along in the world "and of great importance to the peace of the United States." The president, with all his problems and a bit out of his depth on these legal matters, would be "much relieved," according to the request, if the justices would make themselves available to give counsel on issues more congenial to judges than executives, though not susceptible to quick resolution through litigation. Replying with regard to "the lines of separation, drawn by the Constitution between the three departments, of the government," Jay wrote:

These being in certain respects checks upon each other, and our being Judges of a Court in the last resort, are considerations which afford strong arguments against the propriety of our extra-judicially deciding the questions alluded to, especially as the power given by the Constitution to the President, of calling on the heads of departments for opinions, seems to have been *purposely* as well as expressly united in the *Executive* departments. We exceedingly regret every event that may cause embarrassment to your Administration, but we derive consolation from the reflection that your judgment will discern what is right, and that your usual prudence, decision and firmness will surmount every obstacle to the preservation of the rights, peace, and dignity of the United States.

Yet Jay, having thus established his credentials in 1793 as a separationist as well as a diplomat in dealing with the president who appointed him, was soon to take leave from the bench for diplomatic tasks. Eight months later, in February 1794, he presided at his last Supreme Court session. In April he accepted Washington's appointment as special ambassador to England to negotiate a treaty deemed vital at the moment. The nomination of a justice for such a post "was not received favorably in the Senate," historian Charles Warren records, but it was confirmed on a party line vote of eighteen to eight after the failure of a resolution declaring that "to permit Judges of the Supreme Court to hold at the same time any other office of employment emanating from the holden [*sic*] at the pleasure of the Executive is contrary to the spirit of the Constitution, and as tending to expose them to the influence of the Executive, is mischievous and impolitic."

Politics were never far from the scene. Although the treaty put to rest fears of another flare-up with England by securing British evacuation of their forts in the Northwest, Republicans condemned it as a treasonous Federalist sellout. "You must expect to be mauled by the sons of bluntness," a Supreme Court colleague told Jay, "one of the kinds of reward which good men have for their patriotism."

Not until June 1795, after his return to the United States, did Jay formally abandon his judicial office. His reason was not, as one by hindsight might suppose, that diplomacy and judging had not mixed, but rather that Jay had been elected governor of New York after a campaign conducted by others during his absence abroad. (Jay had been a passive and losing candidate for the same post in 1792, also while holding the nation's highest judicial office.) To replace him, President Adams nominated John Rutledge of South Carolina, who had served as an associate justice from 1789 to 1791 but who left the Court to head the judiciary of his own state. Rutledge promptly talked himself out of Senate confirmation with a verbal tirade—against the Jay Treaty—delivered from the bench in a charge to a grand jury while sitting as a circuit court judge. It is clear that Rutledge's rejection by a fourteen to ten vote in December 1795 was the result of what he said, not the fact that he had said it; the Senate's Federalist majority was displeased not with the jurist's extrajudicial venture into politics, but with his politics. The next nominee, Oliver Ellsworth of Connecticut, was confirmed easily enough; but he soon undertook a diplomatic task of his own, a mission to France to seal America's postrevolutionary relationship with that country. The traveling broke his health, and he felt compelled to resign in December 1800. Associate Justice William Cushing, who had run for governor of Massachusetts in

1794 while on the Court, declined Adams's offer of promotion. Adams, a lame duck president who still hoped to perpetuate his party's influence on the Court, then nominated Jay for another time as chief justice. Like Adams, Jay had been defeated in the Jeffersonian Republican landslide, and he was leaving the New York governorship after having served two three-year terms. Despite all his comings and goings, a complaisant Senate confirmed Jay on December 19, a day after the nomination was made. The only trouble was that the president had failed to check in advance with his nominee, who declined the commission. Only then did Adams nominate his secretary of state, John Marshall, putting an end to the game of musical chairs and, of course, ushering in a judicial era.

Viewed from an observation point two centuries distant, this series of events is breathtaking. One can only wonder what national leaders today would attempt such maneuvers, much less succeed at any of them. These extrajudicial adventures are among the precedents that are rallied whenever a judge's moonlighting activities are questioned, and they are indeed among the precedents purported to mark some of the outer limits of permissible judicial behavior. Were these not the Founding Fathers? Is not their example to be emulated today or is there nothing fixed in constitutional practice?

One answer is that times really have changed; if these activities be precedents, they are bad ones. Although duly impressed with the versatility of eighteenth-century men, we are not persuaded today that there is a shortage of talent to do our work. The Founding Fathers were men who moved easily from colonial governments to revolutionary councils into confederations and constitutional conventions and from there to membership in the national Congress, the courts, the cabinets, the presidency—often in search of their own identities and roles even as the young nation was doing the same. Then, too, government in that day was much more a closed corporation of men who knew each other. Suffrage was restricted; United States senators were elected by state legislatures; every five slaves were tallied as three citizens for population purposes. The Supreme Court was not then a full-time or much-desired job. This is not a part of our history that guides us by its ethical example; it is a part that dramatizes how different we have become.

☆

Justices have done other work of importance for presidents. The chores have ranged from the arbitration of boundary disputes to the Pearl Harbor investigation by Justice Owen J. Roberts, the Nuremberg assignment of Justice Robert H. Jackson, an aborted Moscow mission for Chief Justice Fred M. Vinson, and the most conspicuous off-the-bench assignment of all, the chairmanship of the Warren Commission.

The history of ethics at the highest judicial level is a jagged one. Attempts to trace it do not produce a coherent pattern or anything like a recognized policy among the justices. If the next few pages fail to rationalize their conduct, it is in part because of its great variety and the individualism of the men who have sat in the Supreme Court. Yet perhaps one rule, if it could be called that, should be noted. Depicted here are examples, for the most part, of unusual behavior on the high bench. Of the one hundred justices who have served, an overwhelming majority have stuck to the business of judging and have avoided the extracurricular ventures of the few. In addition, it bears repeating that a pattern does exist of rising public expectations about judicial conduct over this long span of years.

The Nuremberg war crimes trials were the occasion for an odd confusion of roles: Justice Jackson was the chief prosecutor, while the top federal prosecutor, Attorney General Francis Biddle, was a judge. Jackson took the job with enthusiasm because it promised "relief from the sense of frustration at being in a back eddy with important things going on in the world." He felt "a sense of duty to respond to the President's request," but that was "secondary" to the chance to implement world peace and carry the law to new frontiers. "That was a challenge. Another thing was that I had always loved advocacy and trial work, and this was about the most important trial that could be imagined. To represent the government in an international trial, the first of its kind in history, was a challenge that no man who loved advocacy would pass up willingly."

Other justices have shared Justice Jackson's appetite for more important pursuits despite having achieved the pinnacle of the law, membership on the Supreme Court of the United States, perhaps more acutely during a time of war or rumors of war. Justice Felix Frankfurter, famed for his own involvement in presidential matters, wrote Roosevelt in 1941 of the anxiety of his "baby Brother," Frank Murphy, who sat next to him on the bench, to serve the nation. In the midst of a very involved oral argument, Murphy told Frankfurter, "I wonder if the President knows how bad things are in the Philippines. . . . No one in the United States knows that problem as well as I do, and I know how to handle it." He would not go there permanently, but, he said, "while I love the work of the Court, I do want to serve my country, and I'd be glad to go out there for a few months, and then on the way back to Mexico, which also needs attention." Murphy proceeded to accept a reserve commission in the army, to the consternation of Chief Justice Stone who feared that such actions "might strain the balance between civil and military authority" when issues of military power reached the Court, as they quickly did. Justice Murphy disqualified himself in the 1942 case of the German saboteurs, but a law clerk later recalled the impression that Stone felt some damage had been done, that he believed every member of the Court had a duty to avoid compromising the *Court's* position. Even jurists who remain on the home front are more likely in times of national peril to "go to war" in their jurisprudence, often suppressing an inclination to rule against the executive and thus add to its burdens.

Those burdens often prompt presidents to make the most of any national crisis in their efforts to obtain needed assistance. Earl Warren, a lifelong politician who had forsaken nonjudicial activities as soon as he entered the Supreme Court building in 1953, fell victim to the cry of emergency in 1964 when President Johnson persuaded him to head the investigation of the murder of President Kennedy. Undoubtedly Warren's presence on the commission did lend credibility to its report, but the Court may have lost some of its own reputation for independence in the exchange.

A crisis atmosphere made possible an earlier, more massive

raid on the judiciary when five members of the Supreme Court sat on the fifteen-man commission named to settle the presidential election of 1876 between Rutherford B. Hayes and Samuel J. Tilden. Whether the use of Justices Samuel F. Miller, William Strong, and Joseph P. Bradley, Republicans, and Stephen J. Field and Nathan Clifford, Democrats, served to produce a satisfactory result can be determined easily. A simple poll of schoolchildren and their teachers would probably disclose that the verdict of the commission remains as unsatisfying by hindsight as it was at the time. The presence of five justices along with the five senators and five representatives did nothing to improve acceptance, nor did the fact that Justice Bradley, the swing voter, supported his vote with a judicial-type opinion. The very selection of Bradley as the "impartial" member of the commission carried with it the assumption that the four other justices were split evenly along strict party lines before considering the evidence, a sad commentary indeed on the impartiality of the Court's members.

Restless judges playing great games of statecraft in pursuit of the "national interest" may be more than meddlesome and unethical—they may blunder in over their heads. The conduct of members of the Supreme Court while the *Dred Scott* case was pending provides one of history's most familiar and sorriest examples of justices who were not "kept strictly to their own department."

It was partly a matter of a president who was happy to be taken off the political hook, willing to use or be used by the judiciary, acting in concert with jurists playing amateur politicians. The episode took place during the three-week period just before and just after the inauguration of President James Buchanan in 1857. The method chosen by a majority of the Court to "settle the agitation" over the power of Congress to prohibit slavery in the territories was the use of dictum—language unnecessary to the decision in the case and at least technically outside the province of judges to utter. This classic case, of course, involved the claim of Scott, a slave who was transported from a slave state to a territory and back again, that he was entitled to his freedom. The case could have been resolved against Scott on the limited ground that his citizenship, and thus his right to be in court suing for anything at all, was determined according to the law of the slave state to which he had returned and where he sued. This was, in fact, the decision of the Court at its conference on February 15, 1857, held in customary secrecy. The writing of the limited opinion was assigned to Justice Samuel Nelson of New York. However, Justice John McLean of Ohio, a man who had openly avowed his presidential ambitions while on the highest bench, and Justice Benjamin R. Curtis of Massachusetts made clear to their colleagues that they intended to dissent broadly, holding in Scott's favor in all respects and declaring their belief that the Missouri Compromise, by which Congress in 1820 had prohibited slavery in the territories, was fully constitutional. The five southern members of the Court—Chief Justice Roger B. Taney of Maryland and Justices Peter V. Daniel of Virginia, James M. Wayne of Georgia, John Catron of Tennessee, and John A. Campbell of Alabama—were in a position to outnumber the two dissenters on the broad issue and they decided to do so. That left Nelson and Robert C. Grier of Pennsylvania as the only justices committed to the initial majority position. On February 19, Justice Catron wrote to Buchanan asking him to "drop Grier a line" telling his fellow Pennsylvanian how helpful it would be for the country, "how necessary it is, and how good the opportunity is, to settle the agitation by an affirmative decision of the Supreme Court, the one way or the other." Grier, his colleague told the president-elect, "has no doubt about the question on the main contest," Scott's lawsuit, "but has been persuaded to take the smooth handle for the sake of repose." Justice Catron intimated that the Court was now on the verge of deciding the broad issue and he evidently hoped the decision would be by the widest possible majority. He went on to advise Buchanan that he could safely say in his inaugural address that the Supreme Court would decide the matter soon enough; he need not comment further. Buchanan promptly wrote Grier who on February 23, saying he had the concurrence of the chief justice and Justice Wayne in his action, wrote back, laying out the entire decision and judicial lineup as it stood and remained. He told Buchanan he had come

over to the point of view of the southern justices: "A majority
including all the Judges south of Mason and Dixon's line
agreeing in the result, but not in their reasons—as the question
will be thus forced upon us, I am anxious that it should not
appear that the line of latitude should mark the line of division
in the Court." The opinions would not be delivered until March
6, two days after the inauguration. "We will not let any others of
our brethren know anything about *the cause of our anxiety* to
produce this result, and though contrary to our usual practice,
we have thought it due to you to state to you in candor and
confidence the real state of the matter." In his March 4
inaugural address, Buchanan laid the slavery issue aside as "a
judicial question which legitimately belongs to the Supreme
Court of the United States before whom it is now pending, and
will, it is understood, be speedily and finally settled. To their
decision, in common with all good citizens, I shall cheerfully
submit."

History records how spectacularly the Court failed to "settle
the agitation," but that is not our main issue. Nor is this the
occasion to criticize the writing of dictum, a practice tradition-
ally denounced by "sound" jurists but employed by judges of all
shades of opinion when it suits them. The suggestion here is that
the unfortunate course of action the Court chose is not to be
considered apart from the intriguing methods by which they
went about it. The Supreme Court always has a range of options
open to it—indeed a far wider range in the twentieth century
than it had in the mid-nineteenth—and will always be challenged to use its power wisely. In the exercise of such power, the
suggestion is that freedom from such contaminants as correspondence with the White House will help immeasurably to keep
justices focusing on what wisdom demands.

As already mentioned, this transgression of the separation of
powers principle may be of a piece with the breach of general
proprieties. In the opinion of historian Charles Warren, writing
in the 1920s, a letter such as Grier wrote to Buchanan

would not at the present time be regarded as one of strict propriety; but
at the time it was written, it was not an infrequent occurrence for the

Judges to impart, in confidence, to an intimate friend or relative the probable outcome of a pending case. Judge Curtis had so written to his uncle, as to this very case, during the previous year; Judge Story frequently indulged in the habit; and it seems to have been regarded as a proper practice, provided the seal of secrecy was imposed.

In the *Dred Scott* example the "seal of secrecy" was imposed by those members of the Court who corresponded with the president—indeed, they kept their secret from their brethren on the Court, to say nothing of the general public. Only the leader of a coordinate branch of government was told and he, of course, was most discreet.

The relationship between Frankfurter and Roosevelt, always known to be extremely close, embarrassed the admirers of both men beyond expectations when their correspondence was published in 1968. Apparently no subject was off limits for Frankfurter, who bombarded FDR with advice (Roosevelt was more discreet in his replies) on congressional relations, tax policy, the economy, neutrality and lend-lease, war making, and whatever else occurred to the justice's wide-ranging intellect. To take only one example, one can only imagine the public response today if it were known that a Supreme Court justice had written to the president, as Frankfurter wrote FDR on February 26, 1941, that Roosevelt had just written and published an "admirable letter on wire-tapping—limiting its uses to the strictest possible area, and then only under utmost safeguards," which the justice said was one of the things he had just read about that "rejoice my heart." In those days, it might be said in Frankfurter's defense, judicial review of executive wiretapping policy seemed quite remote and the danger of compromising a Supreme Court case may have seemed slight. But this only leaves one to wonder why a justice would concern himself with this executive action.

Testifying in 1969 about the impact of the published correspondence, Dean Acheson, who had been Frankfurter's constant morning walking companion, told the Senate that the "intimate and notorious friendship" of the justice and president "did harm to the public reputation of both the Court and the Justice." While he knew that Frankfurter was not in the president's pocket, "I cannot expect those who did not know him to share this opinion," Acheson said. The letters, he added, "never should have been written, preserved or published."

Harlan Fiske Stone, first as associate justice under Taft and Hughes and later as chief justice, hammered out his own views on executive entanglements on the anvil of hard experience. He was not reluctant to counsel President Hoover, with whom he had worked in the Coolidge cabinet, on a number of executive appointments, though he declined service on Hoover's national crime commission. He became wary, however, of President Roosevelt.

In 1939 Roosevelt, after inviting Stone and Frankfurter for an evening's cruise on the Potomac, dropped the word to newsmen that consultation with two Supreme Court justices had fortified his view that it was proper to let the army and navy incur debts for barracks for new recruits despite Congress's refusal to appropriate funds. Stone resolved never again to go on a "social" cruise with FDR. He told his wife to be ready with a prior engagement out of town if another invitation should come. Stone's reaction has been taken as an indication that he partly blamed himself for having been put in such a position.

It was after Roosevelt had named him chief justice that Stone delivered the classic statement of why a justice should reject presidential invitations to step off the bench long enough to help out on something politically sensitive—and a classic method by which a seasoned and self-possessed jurist can handle the matter without giving offense.

"My dear Chief," FDR had written to Stone in July 1942, "I have a problem in this rubber matter, as you know. It is extremely difficult for me, with a million other problems mostly military and naval on my hands. . . ." Could Stone give a little of his own time to resolve the dispute over how the nation should handle its synthetic rubber production—"merely a helping hand, a summary, and a verbal suggestion or recommendation" from an impartial outside source like "your good self"? Roosevelt said he hated "even to break in on your vacation for a few days, and I hope you will forgive me for turning to you in time of need. I think it is wholly ethical work for the Chief Justice!"

Holding in check his own irritation, Stone carefully drafted a reply and told Roosevelt three days later that despite the incentives of "personal and patriotic considerations," the most anxious and painful reflection had led him to conclude that he could not properly undertake the assignment. Apart from the "generally recognized consideration that it is highly undesirable for a judge to engage actively in public or private undertakings other than the performance of his judicial functions," there was the certainty of political attack on his findings. "A judge, and especially the Chief Justice, cannot engage in political debate or make public defense of his acts." His judicial work has the built-in defense of the legal record upon which it is based, but when he performs executive or legislative tasks the jurist "is without those supports. He exposes himself to attack and indeed invites it, which because of his peculiar situation inevitably impairs his value as a judge and the appropriate influence of his office."

Stone cited the Jay and Ellsworth diplomatic missions as precedents that subsequent chief justices had fortunately not followed. "I console myself," he concluded apologetically, "by the assurance that there are others, *not judges,* more capable than I, of doing this particular task, on whose disinterestedness and patriotism you and the public can rely." Stone had set a worthwhile precedent of his own. Although both the president and the chief justice denied the episode when word reached the newspapers and the actual correspondence remained secret for several years, there was widespread editorial praise for the man who had said no to FDR.

As a chief justice trying to keep the Court functioning, Stone rued Roosevelt's inability to find elsewhere someone to head the Pearl Harbor investigation that was conducted under Justice Owen J. Roberts. When Justice James F. Byrnes began to spend more time at the White House, the chief began to miss him also and was relieved when Byrnes resigned to become FDR's "assistant president" in title as well as fact. "I am sorry to lose you from the Court," he told Byrnes, "but I'm glad you can make up your mind whether you want to be a judge or something else." Byrnes, who reported in his autobiography that the chief justice "applauded my efforts," needed no arm twisting from Roosevelt. Two days after Pearl Harbor, Byrnes recalled,

I reminded him that after twenty-four years of service in Congress, nearly all of it on appropriations committees studying the work of the departments, I had acquired a lot of information about the government that might enable me in wartime to perform greater service than upon the Court, and if he ever concluded I could be of more value elsewhere, I hoped he would call upon me. He did not delay in doing so.

Truman did not consult Stone before recruiting Jackson for Nuremberg, and this lack of consideration only heightened the chief justice's resentment at the increased administrative burdens thrust on him because there were fewer justices to do the work. He rejected entirely the notion that justices were part of a presidential manpower pool, and he objected to the trials themselves on their own merits, calling the German proceedings a "high-grade lynching party" that dispensed victors' retribution under color of international law.

Then there were the justices who either lobbied extensively with the White House and Congress or were so politically prominent that they became political candidates. David Davis, a close adviser to Lincoln, left the Supreme Court when he was elected a U.S. senator from Illinois. Preeminent among the lobbyists was William Howard Taft, the former president who, entering the chief justiceship at the age of sixty-two, had no desire for further political office but who felt too much at home in Washington not to dabble in statecraft.

Within two weeks of his appointment, Taft and the attorney general, in a visit to the White House, commented at President Harding's request on his war veterans bonus message. Taft came away with the satisfying feeling that he had helped improve the message. Although he resisted presidential raids on the Court's time, as when President Hoover sought a judicial chairman for what became the Wickersham Commission on Law Observance and Enforcement, Taft was the aggressor in his relations with the White House and Congress. When it came to staffing the judiciary from top to bottom, a friend recalled in a eulogy, Taft "let no merely technical canon of propriety prevent him from

using his influence in what he thought was the right direction."
His boldness with Congress reached a high point in 1926 when
he summoned the chairmen and ranking members of both
judiciary committees to advise them of the desires of the Judicial
Conference of the United States.

He did not confine himself to lobbying for legislation that was
securely within his province as the leading figure of the
American judiciary, nor did he confine himself to orthodox
methods even when operating within that realm. He once put his
official limousine and chauffeur at the disposal of a key
congressman with the unsubtle reminder that the most important
legislation he sought, the reform of the Supreme Court's jurisdiction, ought to be pushed along more rapidly. The American Bar
Association's 1924 judicial canons, written under his chairmanship, were by no means confining. A judge "may well contribute
to the public interest by advising those having authority to
remedy defects of procedure, of the result of his observation and
experience," said canon 23, because of his "exceptional opportunity to observe the operation of statutes." But the canon
emphasized that judicial competence ran to "especially those
[statutes] relating to practice" and ascertaining "whether they
tend to impede the just disposition of controversies." Taft rode
roughshod over the canons' injunctions against political activity;
as biographer Alpheus T. Mason concluded from a survey of his
papers, "Taft's lobbying has no precedent in Supreme Court
annals." To be sure, there was much legislative and executive
involvement that had to be considered entirely proper, such as
the lobbying campaign—it required a campaign, though Taft's
predecessor, Chief Justice Edward Douglas White, had considered it unbecoming to spearhead it—to provide the highest court
with separate and equal housing outside the Capitol building.
Indisputably, Taft indeed had "exceptional opportunity to
observe the operation" of the federal laws that governed the
Court's own procedure, and he was duty-bound to advise
Congress of what he considered its deficiencies.

Of all the raids on the Supreme Court for personnel, the most
conspicuous was the GOP nomination of Charles Evans Hughes
and the justice's resignation in 1916 to run for president. Many

previous justices had hankered for such a political opening. Salmon Chase so lusted for the White House during and after the Civil War that he did not care which political party offered him the nomination. Stephen J. Field sought the Democratic nomination in 1880. William O. Douglas was "available" for vice-president in 1944. Many would covet the presidency again, but the only time such a race was actually run was with Hughes, that eminent figure of judiciousness, as the candidate. That action, coupled with Hughes's successful return to the Court in 1930, is another in a series of precedents for the most wide-ranging extrajudicial ventures at the highest level. It is fortunate that, as Taft prophesied in urging Hughes to accept the nomination, the 1916 situation was "so exceptional" that raiding the bench for political leadership has not become an accepted twentieth-century practice.

☆

Of all the episodes of judicial entanglement with the executive branch, perhaps none provoked such national concern as the involvement of Associate Justice Abe Fortas with the administration of Lyndon B. Johnson, an involvement that became central to the 1968 battle over confirmation of Fortas as chief justice.

Few could have predicted that the seeds were being sown for tragedy when, in July 1965, President Johnson invaded the Supreme Court to show Justice Arthur J. Goldberg the possibilities of even greater heights—not merely the chance to do justice, as Goldberg thought he was doing on the highest court in the land, but far more: the opportunity to lead the way to world peace at the United Nations. At the moment it did not seem a matter of urgency that Johnson had reestablished, and Goldberg had ratified, the notion that something higher than the pinnacle of the legal profession was available to a sitting justice and was worthy of the aspiration of a lawyer who had reached that lofty perch. There were rumblings, but not widespread apprehension, that Johnson had begun to manipulate positions on the Court. Goldberg was asked directly at a press conference how he felt about the use of the Court as a manpower pool. His reply emphasized that he was resigning from the Court, not taking on an extrajudicial assignment. What mattered, he said, was this opportunity to be of national service, since the president placed some confidence in his ability as a negotiator.

A similar "call to duty" soon brought Fortas to the Supreme Court. For three days after Goldberg announced his resignation, Johnson tried without success to enlist his confidant and lawyer of twenty-five years as a justice. Goldberg himself visited the law offices of Arnold, Fortas & Porter without persuading Fortas to leave his lucrative and influential private practice. Then on July 28, 1965, LBJ called Fortas over to the White House, telling him he was delivering a statement on Vietnam. When Fortas arrived, the president told him he was sending fifty thousand troops to Vietnam and Abe Fortas to the Supreme Court. Swept up in this manner, Fortas accepted. "I did not seek the post of Justice of the Supreme Court of the United States," Fortas told the Senate Judiciary Committee three years later. "That was not part of my life plan. . . . I dislike being in the position of rejecting a call by the President of the United States to public service. . . . He nevertheless, as is well known, insisted that I do this—that it was my duty to do it."

It became clear that Johnson was not about to carry out the Truman dictum that a president loses a friend when he appoints a justice. It became equally clear that Fortas did not want to change his life-style with its White House entree, although he was aware that the appointment was a threat to that style. Moreover, Fortas did not in fact change but continued to answer the calls to duty. He also served with considerable distinction as an associate justice, though with a blend of idealism and materialism that may cloud history's judgment. From the outset of his four terms on the Court, Fortas was a fully qualified member who needed no long breaking-in period to catch on to the Court's work. He aligned himself with the liberals on most of the philosophically divisive issues before the Court, and when he wrote opinions in support of these views they were crafted and articulate. He established beachheads, if not landmarks, for the enlargement of juvenile justice. He found deep religious and moral values in the constitutional protection against self-incrimination and he enunciated those principles with feeling and effect. He parted with his liberal colleagues in business cases, and as

Fortas saw it, the difference between himself and them was that he was a realist while his friends on the Court lacked the know-how of "business realities." This throwback to his immensely successful Washington law practice carried over into his attitude toward the war.

Fortas was a hawk about the Vietnam war—doubtless out of conviction, but it was impractical to be otherwise. His war advisory role became increasingly public, and as it did, he corrected reporters who failed to classify him with the hawks around Johnson. According to columnist Joseph Alsop, "The long bombing pause of Christmas, 1965, was bitterly opposed by [Clark] Clifford and his fellow White House adviser Justice Abe Fortas." Opposition to Johnson's Asian policies was not a quality that would get one ahead in Washington and outspoken opposition might disqualify a candidate for the Supreme Court itself. In the spring of 1967 I asked the late Thurman Arnold, Fortas's former law partner, for his guess on the nominee to replace retiring Justice Tom C. Clark, or, since he disclaimed any particular inside knowledge on this subject, what sort of person Johnson might select as his second High Court nominee. This was Arnold's characteristically pungent reply: "I can tell you who it's *not* going to be. It's not going to be one of your Eastern law professors who's against the Vietnam war!" The nominee, Thurgood Marshall, was publicly uncommitted about the war. In contrast to Marshall, Fortas went so far as to upbraid a businessman friend for a statement to the press deploring the economic consequences of the war, giving his friend advice "because he was my friend" that produced a clarifying statement less embarrassing to the Johnson administration.

On the domestic side, Fortas was said to be in consultation with the White House on a host of important matters, but he publicly confirmed only one: that during the Detroit riots of August 1967 he was with the president and was one of the men among whom the executive order sending federal troops into the burning city was "circulated" before delivery. Johnson was amazed that anyone should challenge the message as blatantly political and overly technical saying, according to *Time* magazine, "I had the best constitutional lawyer in the United States

right here, and he wrote that." Fortas conceded only that he saw
the draft, which was enough in itself to cause wonder. To those
who had misgivings about the propriety of this, it was no
consolation that previous justices had been friendly with presidents; they had not been associate justices nominated for
promotion to the center seat on the Supreme Court at a time
when so many of the compromising facts were *known* to the public
so that the public and the Senate were called upon to register
approval or disapproval.

More difficulties developed for Fortas at the intersection of the
nation's international and domestic strife—the realm of civil
liberties. In what he described as an act of conciliation, Fortas
published in May 1968, the month before his nomination for
chief justice, a slim paperback volume called *Concerning Dissent
and Civil Disobedience.* The pamphlet's 128 pages covered a wide
range of controversial subjects connected with the permissible
and impermissible forms of dissent in a free society. Not
surprisingly, the book touched on many highly volatile issues,
including some that were before the Court or were bound to
come before the Court in one form or another. The author set
forth a body of beliefs and a philosophy of dissent with which
many reasonable men could agree.

But he also uttered statements smacking of prejudgment in
some of the touchiest areas. At a time when alleged flag
desecration was before the Court in an appeal of a criminal
conviction in New York, Fortas's book declared, "Laws forbidding the burning or desecration of the national flag have existed
for many years, and it is hardly likely that anyone would
seriously contest their constitutionality or legality." At a time
when young men were attacking the draft laws for failure to
allow for conscientious objection to a particular war, the book
held that selective conscientious objection "is hardly consistent
with the basic theory of organized society." While draft resisters
and their lawyers were attempting in the lower courts to adopt as
their own the principles Justice Jackson had elicited from the
Nuremberg tribunal, Supreme Court Justice Fortas was announcing that the Nuremberg defense was unavailable to them.
It may indeed have been true that the notion derived by the

peace movement from the war crimes trials—that all citizens share responsibility for their nation's "war crimes" and therefore have a moral obligation to disobey war orders—was inapplicable as a defense of selective service violations. But it was not an idea that was ripe for judgment, or prejudgment, from a justice of the Supreme Court.

Abstract pronouncements on general legal propositions are as detrimental in the context of a contemporary pamphlet as the oft-criticized practice of writing advisory opinions (of the sort requested unsuccessfully by George Washington or rendered gratuitously in the *Dred Scott* case). Judges tend to admire their own written words and form attachments to them. When justices indulge in extrajudicial discussion of issues likely to arise before the Court, they run the risk "of deepening their convictions without widening their experience." One analyst of the problem observed that Fortas apparently felt safe discussing publicly or writing about certain issues of war and peace, social unrest, and civil disobedience in the belief that these matters would not come before the courts. But here he miscalculated and ran the unacceptable risk of prejudging not only the merits of the issues, but also the question of whether such issues were appropriate for the judiciary's handling.

Senate confirmation proceedings for Supreme Court nominees have often been disgraceful and partisan affairs. Especially since the school desegregation decision of 1954, which moved Deep South senators to use the process to vent their anger at the Court, the Senate has disgraced itself with its shabby treatment of the men whose qualifications they have been privileged to judge. A single senator can delay confirmation for months, as did Senator William Langer when Earl Warren was nominated. A few members, armed with the Senate's rules and acting in the Senate's name, can bring down ridicule upon everyone concerned, as when the conservative Wall Street lawyer John Harlan was opposed as an "internationalist." Presidential recess appointments, under which a nominee may sit for as long as a congressional session subject to rejection or refusal to confirm, have proven unwise and a source of senatorial mischief, as when William J. Brennan, Jr., was quizzed closely on subjects about which he had already written opinions for the Court. Happily, recess appointments, while still available, have become rare. Thurgood Marshall was catechized with half a hundred scholarly and historical questions read by Senator Strom Thurmond, the South Carolina Dixiecrat-turned-Republican, who did not know the answers to most of them himself. The questions were designed to embarrass the nominee, commit him to embarrassing positions, or dramatize Thurmond's charge that the Court had strayed in its civil rights decisions.

These senatorial instincts were at play in 1968 when the Fortas nomination for chief justice was sent to the Senate; the political fever of the season aggravated the situation. Symbolically, both the Democratic and GOP national conventions interrupted consideration of the nomination. The tone was set by the ambitious Robert P. Griffin, Republican of Michigan, a freshman senator who was soon to clash with the Republican Senate leader, Everett M. Dirksen of Illinois, over leadership matters. Griffin promptly identified the obvious defect of the nomination: that it smacked of "cronyism." Reinforcing the appearance of cronyism was Johnson's selection of Homer Thornberry to replace Fortas as an associate justice. Thornberry, the likable and moderate former Texas congressman, had been nominated for a Federal judgeship by President Kennedy at the urging of Vice-President Johnson and was confirmed in July 1963 but was detained in Washington well into 1964 when President Johnson insisted that he needed his friend's help in critical votes on the House Rules Committee. Unlike Fortas, who had to be maneuvered into the judiciary, Thornberry had to prevail upon Johnson, in the face of the president's pleas of national emergencies, to let him finally depart for the court post at Austin. Nor did Johnson forego the opportunity to call upon Thornberry, whose political acumen was the trait Johnson most prized, for advice on White House messages and other matters. Respected and liberal members of the Senate wondered privately how Thornberry could manage the work of the Supreme Court, but it was a moot question unless Fortas could be elevated.

Starting with ammunition thus supplied by the opposition party, Griffin fired his political volleys. The vacancy should not be filled this way, he said, because the Senate should confirm only the nominee of the winner of the November election. He denounced "lame duck" nominations and cited sixteen examples of men nominated to the Supreme Court by a president during his last year in office. The Senate had wisely decided to deny confirmation to nine of the nominees. (John Marshall had been one of the seven confirmed.)

Although Griffin said he was relying on a Senate principle in his "lame duck" argument, he was also describing a political process by which an incumbent president who will not succeed himself has great difficulty putting his nominations over. Griffin's analysis made no allowance for the character of the nominee or other variables. For example, the Senate's unusual rejection of one of its own, the highly partisan though able Senator George E. Badger, came after the 1852 election for which incumbent President Millard Fillmore had failed to win the nomination of his own party. It was one of three nominations the luckless Fillmore tried to make stick for the same vacancy. John Tyler accounted for three of the others before leaving office in 1845, but a fourth nominee, Samuel Nelson, won confirmation in Tyler's last month as president. Griffin argued,

If there are some who believe, even for purely political reasons, that the opportunity to make such nominations at this particular point in time should be reserved for the new President soon to be elected by the people, there is ample precedent for such a position. It should surprise no one that such a political maneuver has been met head-on by a political response from within the Senate. Indeed, it would signal a failure of our system if there were no reaction to such a blatant political move.

Raising the level of discourse several notches, Griffin subsequently challenged the Senate Judiciary Committee to come to grips with published reports of Fortas's entanglements with the Johnson administration. Griffin's testimony, the opening salvo by opponents of the nomination as the Judiciary Committee began its hearings, met with the scorn of Dirksen, the ranking minority member, who called it "frivolous, diaphanous—you know what that means, don't you—gossamer—you know what that means, don't you—argument that just does not hold water." The Senate waited, with intense interest, to see what the nominee would say.

But the nominee tried immediately to reserve room for "a constitutional problem" about discussing the work of the Court. This was in keeping with concern for the Court's independence, especially in view of the open hostility to the Court displayed by some senators; but immunity from some questioning about it was not available to Fortas, since he was a candidate for promotion and the Senate was entitled to some examination of his previous work. This put Fortas at a disadvantage, which was aggravated by his need to plead a special form of privilege—a species of executive privilege—about White House dealings that also aroused the senators' interest. Proud though he was to have been of service to the troubled president, Fortas repeatedly asked to be excused from answering some questions—not in the interest of judicial independence, but rather to preserve the *executive's* interest in confidential communications.

Volunteering nothing that had not already appeared in the press, Fortas admitted to attending White House conferences on matters that were impressive in that they indicated presidential confidence but were compromising for a justice. His attendance was limited to "matters that are very perplexing and that are of critical importance to the President," such as "stages in the fantastically difficult decisions about the war in Vietnam" and "in that critical and desperate situation" when Detroit was torn by riots. Fortas admitted that he had seen Johnson's message ordering federal troops into Detroit before it was delivered but said he did not "approve" it. "The President does not ask my approval," he testified.

Fortas explained his function this way:

In every situation where I have been called to the White House for this purpose, so far as I can recall, my function—the President runs conferences, as I am sure all of you know—my function has been to listen to what is said. . . . The President always turns to me last, and he then expects me to summarize what has gone on. And that is about the way it is, Senator, and that is the way it works.

Senator Sam J. Ervin, Jr., the North Carolina Democrat

whose experience as a state supreme court justice and whose willingness to speak for hours on any legal subject gained him a reputation as the Senate's constitutional scholar-in-residence, then embarked upon one of his patented surveys of recent deplorable constitutional developments. Case by case, for nearly five hours over two days, he recited the evidence and the Supreme Court's unprecedented and unjustified rulings as he saw them; and case by case Fortas politely declined comment. Fortas analogized his situation to that of a member of Congress who was immune from being called to answer "in any other place" for any speech or debate in the legislature. A corollary of legislative immunity, which protects congressmen and senators from court action for conduct in the line of duty, would be that the Senate should reciprocate and show similar courtesy and forbearance toward a member of the judiciary, Fortas suggested.

Whatever right the Senate might have to inquire into the Supreme Court's past decisions in such a situation, relations between the judiciary and legislature reached what must have been an all-time low on July 18, 1968, when Senator Thurmond, without interference from Chairman Eastland, berated the nominee for more than two hours about decisions the senator did not like, not restricting his tirade to cases in which Fortas had been involved. The most dramatic moment came when Thurmond, his voice even but with hatred in his eyes, demanded to know the justice's views about the case of *Andrew Mallory* v. *United States*, decided in 1957 by a unanimous Supreme Court in an opinion by Justice Frankfurter. Said Thurmond:

This was a case in which the defendant voluntarily confessed to a serious crime, a serious assault, in fact, rape. He was convicted by the trial court, 12 men who heard his testimony, and the trial judge who heard it. They concluded the confession was voluntary. They concluded that all the details he had set out in that confession—he set out himself were true and correct. There is no question, no issue about the confession being voluntary. There was really no question that he committed the crime. But when it went to the Supreme Court, they reversed the case and the man went free. *Why did he go free?* A criminal, a convict, a guilty man, who committed a serious rape on a lady in this city. Simply because the Court said they held him a little too long before arraignment.

Do you believe in that kind of justice? Don't you think the main purpose of the courthouses, of the judges, of the jury is to go to the heart of a case and render justice, to convict them when they are guilty, and turn them loose when they are free, and not let technicalities control the outcome? And isn't that what happened in that case?

Fortas replied, "With the greatest regret, I cannot respond to that, because of the constitutional limitation."

"Mallory!" the Senator intoned. "I want that name to ring in your ears. Mallory!"

Fortas, who had appeared prepared for almost anything but this assaultive, personal discourtesy to himself and to his office, registered amazement. His eyes shifted to the committee's center chair, but a slouching Eastland did not look up from whatever he was reading.

"Mallory," said Thurmond,

a man who raped a woman, admitted his guilt, and the Supreme Court turned him loose on a technicality. And who I was told later went to Philadelphia and committed another crime, and somewhere else another crime, because the courts turned him loose on technicalities. Is not that type of decision calculated to encourage more people to commit rapes and serious crimes? Can you as a Justice of the Supreme Court condone such a decision as that? I ask you to answer that question.

After a long pause, Fortas said,

Senator, because of my respect for you and my respect for this body, and because of my respect for the Constitution of the United States, and my position as an Associate Justice of the Supreme Court of the United States, I will adhere to the limitation that I believe the Constitution of the United States places upon me and will not reply to your question as you phrased it.

In the crowded Senate Caucus Room, only Thurmond seemed to have missed what seemed the devastating impact of this soft answer.

"Can you suggest any other way in which I can phrase that question?" he persisted.

"That would be presumptuous," replied Fortas. "I would not attempt to do so."

Fortas's testimony, which spanned four uncomfortable days, was something of a brilliant display of a lawyer's powers and techniques. Not content to sit mute while Thurmond romped through the Court's decisions as Ervin had done, the witness repeatedly ventured partial replies, enough to indicate that he disagreed with his interrogator but not enough to expose himself to cross-examination, then apologized for going too far. Asked by Thurmond whether one of his dissents was "an example of translating a personal preference into a constitutional requirement," Fortas replied, "I most certainly would not—but I should not say that. I must stand on the constitutional position. I cannot respond to that, Senator." Said Thurmond, "I thought you did respond," to which Fortas replied, "I am sorry. It was an inadvertence."

But the testimony suffered from a profound defect. It simply was not believable on the sensitive subject of proprieties. Though Fortas had suffered abuse, it was unclear when he left the stand who had done more damage to the principle of separation of powers, the nominee or his detractors. The very polish of the virtuoso performance revived the image of the poised Washington infighter and arranger, the man of influence, rather than the man of legal distinction that Fortas indisputably was. On paper, the nomination still commanded the floor votes of a Senate majority, including a solid squadron of liberals in both parties. But more realistically, it was a dwindling majority, not the supermajority that is so often required when southern Democrats and conservative Republicans, acting under Senate rules conducive to delay, are in the way. Importantly, morale sagged among Fortas's liberal supporters, with the Vietnam component of the controversy sapping their will. Precious time was lost when the pro-Fortas majority failed to muster a quorum for the last Judiciary Committee meeting before Congress recessed for the national party conventions in August.

By the time the Senate reassembled after Labor Day, more troubles had accumulated. A magazine article casually mentioned that an LBJ speech writer had turned over his draft of the 1966 State of the Union address to Fortas and Clark Clifford, who by now was secretary of defense, for rewriting. Senator

Gordon Allott, Republican of Colorado, produced a strand of evidence that Fortas had handled part of the White House legislative work of helping to draft a bill authorizing Secret Service protection for presidential candidates. And a telephone tip led opponents to investigate a major extrajudicial job Fortas had held during the previous summer: leader of an advanced seminar on law and society at American University. The State of the Union matter on its face ran counter to Fortas's testimony that he had made "full disclosure" of his White House involvements by confirming that he helped on critical Vietnam matters and the Detroit riot. The report that a version of the candidate protection legislation had been cleared with Fortas undermined the nominee's insistence that he had been called in on major matters only.

Liberals, many of them feeling betrayed, fell silent on the ethical issue, reserving what fervor they had to express outrage at Thurmond's harangue or Griffin's plans for a filibuster. One distinguished law professor who had counted himself a Fortas supporter was typical in attitude, if more picturesque in speech, when he explained why he would not comment on the ethical questions. "Who wants to be allied with Strom Thurmond? With me it's a matter of personal hygiene." Another said simply that a candid discussion of ethics and cronyism would "provide ammunition for the wrong people." Opponents made a halfhearted effort to recall Fortas to the witness chair and to obtain the testimony of Defense Secretary Clifford and other witnesses. When Clifford and other administration officials asked not to be pressed to testify—stopping somewhat short of invoking executive privilege—the committee did not pursue them. Opponents had no need at this point to attempt to compel their appearance: the burden had shifted to Fortas. The nominee became persuaded that the delays must cease, the record must be closed, and the Senate must be moved to act promptly, and that these considerations outweighed any desire to issue further denials. Finally on September 17 the nomination was wrested from the committee by an eleven to six favorable vote. Most of the majority report consisted of a catalog of judicial moonlighters from Jay to Taft and a denunciation in advance of the looming filibuster on the

Senate floor. The dissenting views blended ethical and ideological arguments in by-now familiar proportions, including bitter complaints about Supreme Court obscenity rulings.

Anxious to bring matters to a head so that Congress could get back to some serious election year campaigning, Senate leadership brushed aside other business and brought up the nomination on September 25. "Filibuster" is too strong a word for what developed; actually, it was a succession of spiritless monologues nominally addressed not even to the merits of the nomination but to the parliamentary issue of whether the matter should be made the pending Senate business. The talkathon lasted less than a week.

Dirksen, the mercurial minority leader who had prospered over the years from cooperation with Lyndon Johnson, defected and announced he would not vote for cloture. He cited Fortas's vote in the case of *Witherspoon* v. *Illinois*, which threatened to require (and two years later did require) setting aside the death sentence meted out to Chicago mass murderer Richard Speck. With Fortas joining the majority, the Court had ruled that no death sentence could be carried out at the behest of a jury from which all potential jurors had been removed automatically because they indicated opposition to capital punishment. The decision was hardly extreme, though it could provoke an emotional response especially if misinterpreted. The Court did not say that no juror with reservations about capital punishment could be excluded from the jury box, and it left room for screening out jurors whose scruples prevented their ever voting for a conviction in a capital case. If the Speck verdict would have to be set aside, it would be only because Illinois prosecutors had profited unfairly from the power to exclude any scrupled jurors.

It was especially ironic that Dirksen learned of the political implications of the *Witherspoon* decision from Chief Justice Roy J. Solfisburg, Jr., of the Illinois Supreme Court, who was to resign within a year while under investigation for misconduct, and that Dirksen did not consult Albert E. Jenner, Jr., of Chicago, with whom he had worked on judicial matters in the past. Jenner, who had represented William C. Witherspoon in the Supreme Court by assignment, could have put the case in a more favorable light if Dirksen had been interested. But Dirksen, who was up for reelection, was feeling home pressures, though his opponent never came close to unseating him, and his GOP soldiers were deserting him. Although Griffin was beginning to squirm because of his forced association with more seasoned filibusterers like Thurmond, he scented victory in a battle that had begun as a lonely outcry and was transformed into an effective challenge to his party's Senate leadership.

When the roll was called on the first day of October, fifty-four senators voted for cloture and forty-three voted to continue talking—a bare majority and an enormous fourteen votes shy of the needed two-thirds of those present and voting. A day later, Fortas threw in the towel. He wrote the president asking that his name be withdrawn because further efforts toward confirmation would only harm the Court more through continued "attacks which have been sometimes extreme and entirely unrelated to responsible criticisms." Johnson, decrying the unprecedented defeat of a nomination through filibuster, complied. On October 10, after the Court's new term had opened with Fortas still sitting as an associate justice, Johnson announced that in the prevailing climate he would not send another name to the Senate. Warren, now committed to ending his active career, would continue to serve as chief justice, his notice of retirement still in the hands of the chief executive, be he Lyndon Johnson, Hubert Humphrey or—most likely—his ancient political enemy, Richard Nixon.

In the course of resisting the rhetorical question of Senator Thurmond, Fortas had summed up his side of the problem: "I cannot and I will not be an instrument by which the separation of powers specified in our Constitution is called into question." One of the many facets of tragedy, for the nation no less than the nominee, was that the principle itself was discredited and diminished by his conduct. One heard it asked over and over again, Why shouldn't the president be able to call in a justice? Must a president forsake all friendships when he appoints a justice? How can anyone deny the president, with all the troubles he faces, the best help available? Two years after his fall from office, Fortas held the same view he had always held. He told an interviewer:

In my view if the President of the United States asks a Justice of the Supreme Court or a barber or a priest for advice he should give it to him. With one exception, which is, of course, you don't discuss anything with the President of the Court's business. If I had it to do all over again I'd do it the same way. In the first place you *can* tell if it's going to come to the Supreme Court. Issues come to the Court refined, polished and sharpened. But suppose you are wrong—you can disqualify yourself.

But Supreme Court justices are not interchangeable with priests and barbers when it comes to the separation of powers or the need for judicial independence. Aside from that, Fortas in fact did not disqualify himself when the Court heard and decided the flag-burning case; rather he delivered a dissent from the reversal of the conviction of a decorated black war veteran who had set fire to his flag when he heard an erroneous report that James Meredith had been killed in a Mississippi ambush. Fortas in fact did not step aside in induction cases or cases challenging the president's power to send men overseas to fight an undeclared war in Asia.

In such cases disqualification is often inadequate in any event. A petitioner whose last recourse is the Supreme Court needs the votes of four justices to win review—not a majority of the justices voting, but the affirmative votes of four members of the Court. The petitioner deserves a fair chance for nine uncommitted men of whom he must interest four in his case. Unsurprisingly, Fortas, in common with many other legal thinkers who had less of a stake in the war issue, clung to the view that "the Supreme Court ought not to rule on this life-and-death decision for the nation." Granted, the scale of conflict can reach a point where a congressional declaration of war is demanded to continue it. "Logically, maybe yes. But if you formally declare war, then treaty obligations come into play and a whole series of complicating factors." For a sizable body of Americans, mostly young Americans, the *Court* had an obligation to "rule on the war." Many such persons, deeply persuaded that a war so evil must also be unconstitutional, were not concerned about the outcome of judicial review; to them the act of taking up a full-scale review would have been a significant victory in itself for those trying to force confrontations with the war at every opportunity. For such

Americans, whether one agrees with them or not (this writer is far from certain that the war would be ruled illegal), nine justices, unfettered, unentangled with the executive branch, is the minimum number.

This of course does not mean that all nine justices must sit no matter how many of them should, for some reason, disqualify themselves. If a justice is disqualified, the desirability of a full court cannot justify his sitting and only an emergency could ever justify it. The way to pursue the desirable goal of a full court is for each jurist to keep his disqualifying activities to a minimum. The best way to do that, given the unpredictability of how legal issues will arise, is to stick to the business of judging and avoiding ventures into war making and off-the-bench expressions, however well intended, on public controversies.

One may say that the Fortas views expressed in his short book were no more prejudicial to a person appealing a flag-burning conviction than the same views would have been if expressed in a concurring or dissenting opinion in a case decided by the Court. But the commitment made in the course of deciding cases may be both desirable and unavoidable. The setting of an actual court case tends to limit the jurist to expressions of opinion relevant to the evidence. The danger of prejudice is heightened when a judge, indulging his preconceptions without necessarily broadening his understanding and without being confined to the facts of a specific case, publicly discusses issues that he has not yet confronted as a judge—a judge who has heard both sides.

In assessing the wisdom and ethics of Fortas's relationship with President Johnson, it must be remembered that the justice did not merely consult with the president, as on occasion other justices may have done discreetly and privately. He sat in on the councils of war and domestic crisis. He met with *groups* of men in the company of the president. The meetings were secret, but his presence there was open and notorious. "The President always turns to me last," said Fortas in seeking to minimize his role in executive matters before the Judiciary Committee. "Always"—whenever they would meet, which is to say they met more than once and met with some regularity. "Turns to me"—not used to turn, but *turns*, and presumably would continue to turn until the expiration of his term, despite rising sensitivities. "Last"—the last in a group of men, not in some occasional, quiet, one-on-one confrontation of the kind Justice Louis D. Brandeis had had with President Woodrow Wilson. Fortas was, therefore, equivalent to a White House staffer. That he merely "summarized" the options open to the president on the basis of the statements of others hardly disparaged the importance of the staff function.

"When the legislative and executive powers are united in the same person or body," Montesquieu said in 1748,

there can be no liberty, because apprehension might arise lest the same monarch or senate should enact tyrannical laws, to execute them in a tyrannical manner. Again, there is no liberty, if the judiciary power be not separate from the legislative and executive. Were it joined with the legislative, the life and liberty of the subject would be exposed to arbitrary control; for the judge would then be the legislator. Were it joined to the executive power, the judge might behave with violence and oppression. There would be an end of everything, were the same man or the same body, whether of the nobles or the people, to exercise those three powers, that of enacting the laws, that of executing the public resolutions, and of trying the cases of individuals.

There was reason to hope, in the spring of 1969, that the lesson of entanglements had been learned. In explaining his choice of Warren E. Burger as the new chief justice, President Nixon put noticeable stress on the absence of any relationship that could be dubbed "cronyism." Because of the Fortas matter, he told newsmen, he had determined that the appointee should not be a personal friend or a political friend. He wanted a cordial but arm's-length relationship with the chief justice, who henceforth would be his own man. Mr. Nixon considered it vitally important that the Court's members all knew they were absolutely independent of the executive and legislative branches of government.

2

☆ ☆ ☆

THE PRICE OF INDEPENDENCE

"Well, I believe in the independence of the judiciary. I am for mother and I am for home. But even that, like everything else, can be carried too far. There is a kind of tyranny in the idea that you look neither to the right nor the left."

Chief Judge David L. Bazelon, United States Court of Appeals for the District of Columbia Circuit, before the Senate Judiciary Subcommittee on the Separation of Powers, April 7, 1970

"The judge must not only be independent—absolutely free of all influence and control so that he can put into his judgments the honest, unfettered and unbiased judgment of his mind, but he must be so freed of business, political and financial connections and obligations that the public will recognize that he is independent. It is of supreme importance, not only that justice be done, but that litigants before the court and the public generally understand that it is being done and that the judge is beholden to no one but God and his conscience."

Judge John J. Parker, "The Judicial Office of the United States," 1949

How free from improper outside pressures or distracting influences are our judges? How independent do we really want them to be?

We seem to want our judges to be free from improper influences from other branches of government, whether brought about by outside political pressures against the judges' will or, as in the Fortas case, with the acquiescence and sometimes the initiative of the judge. Americans want their judges to be immune from popular clamor so that they can do justice in the cases before them based on evidence rather than sentiment. Losing litigants may wish a judge partook more fully of worldly wisdom or common sense, but broadly the demand for an impartial, unflappable arbiter is uppermost. We want our judges to behave properly—as *we* view what is proper—and to display "good behavior," to use the Constitution's own phrase, observing certain boundaries of propriety for which the jurist is in turn granted tenure in the federal system.

But how can we make sure that judges behave themselves? How can we compel them to engage only in conduct that enhances their independence, without curbing that independence as we do so? These questions beget related questions. For one, what power does society have to discipline its independent judges? For another, how and when should society's power be exercised, especially when there is uncertainty over what that power is?

Uncertainty there indisputably is. The historical and constitutional debate about the scope of disciplinary powers is anything but stilled. The learned have written volumes on the subject; judges have argued about it and have rendered scattered decisions thereon; Congress has debated it—all inconclusively. Uncertainty is not all bad in our constitutional system; clarity is not an end in itself when the objective is maximum freedom for each while preserving the rights of others. Nevertheless, there is often cause to lament that the norms of a judge's propriety are not established, even as we accept the fact that the lines of ultimate power are not sharply drawn.

The full range of theory on the scope of the power to discipline or remove judges and justices was covered in the congressional attack on Associate Justice William O. Douglas, whose behavior occupies the bulk of this chapter. To Representative Gerald Ford of Michigan, the Republican leader in the House, the popular chamber had the power and the right to impeach, and the

Senate to convict, a member of the Supreme Court on any basis they chose. An impeachable offense, he told the House on April 15, 1970, "is whatever a majority of the House of Representatives considers it to be at a given moment in history; conviction results from whatever offense or offenses two-thirds of the other body considers to be sufficiently serious to require removal of the accused from office." Under this theory, it is every man for himself, no standards for the legislator, and no defense for the jurist.

Douglas's lawyers and his defenders within Congress contended that judges are not so helpless against unbridled political whim. Representative Paul N. McCloskey, Jr., the liberal California Republican, argued for a precise constitutional limitation in the standard to be applied by Congress. He offered a criterion by which, not surprisingly, the charges against Douglas were insufficient on their face, thus warranting their dismissal without further ado. His standard, for which a special subcommittee of the House Judiciary Committee showed considerable sympathy, was that the expansive phrase "high crimes and misdemeanors" in the Constitution means that the misconduct must either be judicial misconduct—abuse of judicial power—or conduct that constitutes a crime. "There is no basis for impeachment on charges of *non*-judicial misconduct which occurs off the bench and does *not* constitute a crime," McCloskey contended.

As a matter of naked power, Ford's view is correct enough since the impeachment process is unreviewable. No member of Congress need justify his votes to a "higher court"—though his constituents may demand explanations. The fault with Ford's view is that it is too nakedly stated to be acceptable to legislators of two stripes: the fair-minded and the pretentious. The fair-minded would demand for members of a coordinate branch at least some of the elements of due process they would expect if a legislator were on trial, safeguards that have been enjoyed increasingly by more and more Americans who come within the toils of the law. Due process of law at a trial certainly implies that a judge ordinarily will not invent the crime as he goes along.

The pretentious would at least want to clothe their vote in reasoning more respectable than Congressman Ford's formulation.

There are more practical objections to a theory of limitless impeachment power. In order to function as a legislature without constant diversions to keep watch over the judiciary, Congress itself might prefer to be at least nominally bound by some definition of "impeachable offense" and reject Ford's definitionless theory. The cumbersomeness of the impeachment machinery, which some have decried, is itself an impediment to the freewheeling use of the power, and one of the most formidable obstacles is the burden of actually persuading two-thirds of the Senate at the end of the long process. Since that body, by a tradition we shall observe a little more closely later, usually takes the initiative in federal judicial nominations, it is unlikely to tolerate an easy removal standard by which any senator's protégé is taken from the bench. In addition, the vices of Congress's members, their unwillingness until recently to come to grips with their own standards of conduct, also have served to protect sitting judges from ethical attack of impeachment proportions.

There is a subsidiary debate over the power, or lack of it, to remove or otherwise discipline judges or justices by methods other than impeachment. Some say a certain amount of power over federal district judges already resides in the eleven federal circuit courts of appeals. Each is authorized by Congress to sit as a judicial council to supervise the business and promote the efficiency of the inferior courts.

A test of this power was staged in the Supreme Court in the case of Judge Stephen S. Chandler of the United States District Court at Oklahoma City at about the same time the fight over Justice Douglas was warming up in Congress. Chandler, fully as flamboyant as Douglas but far less accomplished, had engaged for years in bitter in-house fighting with his fellow members of the district court and with members of the reviewing Tenth U.S. Circuit Court of Appeals. According to an unpublished study by the staff of the House Judiciary Committee, the conflicts were rooted in politics and personalities, but they took the form of disputes over the assignment of cases and the distribution of judicial patronage. The Judicial Council of the Circuit, the active appellate judges minus one who disqualified himself because of the ferocity of his personal encounters with Chandler, did not seek to remove the judge from office. Rather, it removed most of the office from the judge—his share of the case load. Chandler was never formally accused or tried for conduct less than "good behavior" but was thus disciplined in an order that said he was "unwilling or unable" to discharge his duties fully. The judiciary was divided on the Chandler case, many judges saying that something simply had to be done about the cantankerous individual judge, though many others were apprehensive about the assertion of power by some lifetime judges over other lifetime judges.

Although Chandler's plea to the Supreme Court for relief languished on the docket for five years before being heard, no answer issued from the high bench. When Chief Justice Burger delivered the Court's response on June 1, 1970, the result was that five of the eight sitting justices felt that Chandler was not entitled to an answer because of the curious twists and turns the case had made as the judge and his adversary judges jockeyed and maneuvered for tactical advantage. One justice, the irrepressibly fastidious John Marshall Harlan, concurred on the ground that Chandler was fully entitled to an answer but that the answer was no. And two justices, Douglas and Hugo L. Black, sharply dissented, calling the entire episode a foolish venture in the unconstitutional exercise of power to "ride herd" over independent judges. "It is time we put an end to the monstrous practices that seem about to overtake us," said Douglas. The net result was that while the circuit council won no clear victory, it survived as an institution to wield its power on another day until or unless tested again. As a practical matter, the councils emerged with a conditional license to govern but a warning that they must be careful how they governed. The power existed, somewhere between the managerial authority to make case assignments and the ultimate power of removal, to take significant action against a federal judge's will.

Another vexing question, raised belatedly in the case of Judge Otto Kerner, is whether a federal judge who has not been impeached is accountable in the criminal courts for crimes committed either before or during his time on the bench. Kerner was convicted of both: taking a bribe while governor of Illinois and, while a judge, lying to a grand jury investigating the bribery. Kerner appealed both sets of convictions, contending that a sitting federal judge must be impeached before being prosecuted. The view of the Justice Department in the Nixon administration, first reflected in legal advice from Assistant Attorney General William H. Rehnquist to Attorney General John N. Mitchell during the Fortas investigation in 1969, was that there was no constitutional barrier to prosecution of sitting judges.

Some maintain that if adequate powers to discipline judges short of impeachment do not yet exist, it would be completely within the power of Congress under the Constitution to create machinery such as a judicial body endowed with authority to conduct removal proceedings. Broadly and perhaps too simply stated, the argument runs this way: The power to impeach is not the entire power to remove; that is, while the Constitution gives to the House "the sole power of impeachment" and to the Senate "the sole power to try impeachments," there are other ways of removing an errant judge. Since members of the federal bench "hold their offices during good behavior," there must be such a thing as "bad behavior" sufficiently serious to warrant removal by some means other than impeachment. Since English judges were subject to removal both by legislative impeachment and by a judicial writ, the Constitution's framers, with their heritage of law evolved by the judges in England, did not rule out nonimpeachment removal. Moreover, by this view, what goes on strictly within the judicial branch of government does not imperil the separation of powers. Therefore Congress, which has the power both to create the lower federal courts and to tell them what kind of cases to try, could establish courts to try a judge's fitness for office or could enable existing courts to do so.

Such arguments have considerable force and appeal, especially for those seeking broad-spectrum treatment for judicial ill health. But these arguments need not be developed in detail here in view of the political situation where the necessary power lies,

in Congress. In particular, powerful senior members of the
Senate Judiciary Committee have been solidly against such
ideas. Chairman James O. Eastland, Democrat of Mississippi,
clearly deemed this kind of legislation of doubtful constitutionality and of unproven necessity. Senator Sam J. Ervin, Jr., North
Carolina Democrat, chairman of the Judiciary Subcommittee on
the Separation of Powers, published thick volumes of reports
developing counterarguments to related disciplinary bills offered
in the late 1960s by Senator Joseph D. Tydings, Democrat of
Maryland. Senate politics are subject to change, but after
Tydings's six-year drive to "improve" judicial machinery in this
and other areas, the only major change was that the senator
failed to win reelection in 1970; the thrust for this kind of reform
was defeated with him. The Nixon administration did express its
support for the Tydings proposals but William H. Rehnquist,
assistant attorney general in charge of the Justice Department's
Office of Legal Counsel, gave no indication that the executive
branch would press for them. Tydings and the Justice Department did collaborate in 1970 to include a fitness and removal
commission in omnibus legislation restructuring the courts of the
District of Columbia, but this was accomplished under the theory
that those courts were akin to state courts and were not clothed
with the same independence guaranteed to conventional federal
courts under the Constitution.

To Senator Ervin, the judicial independence and the separation of powers were threatened as fully by strictly judicial
machinery for removal as by any other method; in fact, in his
view, Congress has no right to "delegate" its own removal powers
to the judges. Even before his defeat, Tydings saw his reform
proposals put on the shelf at least temporarily to await the
attempts of the federal bench to "put its own house in order" in
the wake of all the ethical fracases of the period. Even if more
legislators should someday become convinced of the desirability
of such legislation, there will surely be Ervins and Eastlands in
the way, armed with theories of equal weight and always
commanding formidable political support. The federal judiciary
itself has proved in the past, and could prove again, a powerful
lobby against restrictive legislation.

One seasoned politician-judge, Robert W. Hemphill of the U.S. District Court for South Carolina, told Senator Ervin why judges suspect new pieces of judicial reform machinery such as a commission to police the conduct of judges. "Once a commission is created," the former congressman explained, "it has to find something to do. A staff is assembled, whose first determination is a perpetuation of their existence, and the creation of a climate of usefulness." To Hemphill, "The Senate is America's watchdog in assuring proper screening before elevation to the federal bench."

The existence of uncertainties and power vacuums does not mean that the judiciary is hermetically sealed from outside attack. Judges who stray too far from ordinary or accepted practices generate an equal, opposing, and effective public and political reaction. Whether society suffers because of such inhibiting attacks on supposedly independent judges or justices is still a question.

Each challenge to the independence of the judiciary has unique features of its own, but it ought to be remembered, before examining the case of Justice William O. Douglas, that he was widely and rightly recognized as an American original. The nation has had activist justices; it has had justices whose firm philosophy, tenure, and skill have influenced the course of American judicial history; it has had justices whose talents were not cabined by the demands of their office. But Douglas combined these features, and more. He summoned forth, in intensity and depth, a full range of emotions and legal opinions about his behavior both on and off the bench.

To many Americans the militantly independent Justice Douglas has made a priceless contribution, both on and off the bench, to the causes of civil liberties, civil rights, economic justice, and world peace. His outside writings—an average of one book a year since 1950—and his speeches no less than his votes and written opinions have instilled pride in constitutional values. His ceaseless drive to bring together people of different nations and backgrounds, his constant efforts to launch educational campaigns to compete with communism in developing nations, and his willingness to glamorize peace in the world as well as conservationism and other values at home—all this, in the view of the justice's admirers, towers above any nit-picking criticism of this or that minor fault.

But to many other Americans, Douglas embodied the judicial tyranny of elitism and highhanded behavior both on the bench and off. His activities that were subject to question were not only irritants but also opportunities for retaliation. If a critical mass of seeming improprieties could be gathered, Douglas could be made to answer for them and an investigation by Congress could be justified.

Just as Fortas was the willy-nilly instrument of his own downfall because of conduct that cost him the chief justiceship, so Douglas brought upon himself a drastic curtailment of the independence he prized. This brilliant, colorful, and exasperating man, often so incisive and insightful in his judicial opinions but so erratic and frail in his dealings elsewhere, hurt the Supreme Court and himself by the way he exercised to the fullest his personal right to independence.

If Congressman Ford had set out with only the limited goal of severely reducing Douglas's effectiveness, he could pronounce his campaign a success. Within a week of the Senate's rejection of G. Harrold Carswell's nomination to the Supreme Court, on April 15, 1970, Ford began to paper the congressional landscape with multiple accusations, setting in motion what became an impeachment inquiry by a unit of the House of Representatives. Inauspiciously for Ford, he billed it in part as the appropriate congressional response to the Carswell defeat. In fact, Ford's staff had been preparing the case for months, hesitating to launch the attack during the nomination struggles of 1969 and early 1970. As a result the charges, when hurled in public, were sufficiently grounded in fact so that they could not all be dismissed out of hand even if they could not ultimately be proved. One direct consequence was that Douglas disqualified himself in important cases, often to the discomfiture of the entire Court and the detriment of the liberal result Douglas would have supported. For months on end the entire Court was embarrassed by the possibility that one of their members could be impeached; there was reason to be confident that this would not eventuate, but there was no basis to be absolutely certain, given the assertiveness of Congress over recent nominees and the depth of the anger of a vocal minority of ardent conservatives in the House.

Whether or not Ford and his colleagues fully realized it, they seemed to work at least a temporary change in the justice's behavior. This very model of independence found it politic to attend the 1969 and 1970 conventions of the American Bar Association, forsaking the western wilds for torrid summer meetings in Dallas and St. Louis—a remarkable occurrence and a little sad. He also wrote opinions that gratuitously emphasized his personal commitment to "law and order"—opinions of value in civil liberties literature but probably not the same opinions he would have written had he not been personally under attack. The justice, in short, was not himself.

So frequently did Douglas disqualify himself during the height of Congress's investigation that he stirred comment that he was being especially and perhaps unnecessarily concerned over proprieties. But Douglas's circumspection did not curb the critics. When Douglas took himself out of the *I Am Curious (Yellow)* obscenity case on April 27, 1970, Congressman Ford called it a tacit admission that Douglas should have disqualified himself in another case for which he was under criticism, the Court's January 26, 1970, action denying review, over Douglas's dissent, to publisher Ralph Ginzburg. Ginzburg, who was seeking to overturn a libel judgment won by Senator Barry M. Goldwater for an article published in one of his magazines, was also the publisher of a magazine article by Douglas, and many joined Ford in believing it was at least odd that the justice had missed the ethical point. To a degree Douglas was damned if he did disqualify himself and damned if he didn't, but of course it was far preferable in these circumstances to suffer the publicity and criticism that went with the prudent course of disqualification.

One major source of his disqualification was the justice's own need for skilled counsel to defend himself. Volunteer or enlisted help came from sympathetic lawyers, including former law clerks, whose ability had won them partnerships in major law firms in the litigation-generating cities of New York, Los Angeles, and Washington. These law firms in turn handled major litigation typical of the sort that finds its way to the Supreme

Court. The proprieties certainly dictated that the cases of those law firms, which could be presumed to benefit all their members in some degree, were cases in which Douglas should not sit, and though it brought anguish, he did not.

One such case was a monumental railroad rate case of a scale entertained by the Supreme Court only once or twice in a decade. The case affected important interests of haulers and shippers of the nation's freight. With Douglas out of the case, the Court on December 8, 1970, deadlocked four to four. The consequence was that the shipper customers of the railroads lost an important battle with the carriers, because a tie vote in the Supreme Court affirms the decision of the lower court without setting a legal precedent. The legal principle over which the parties had waged an expensive battle remained unsettled until they mounted yet another lawsuit. In this case, if one assumes that Douglas would have cast the deciding vote in favor of the users of the railroads, the railroads were the undeserving beneficiaries of circumstance. It happened that the law firm representing the railroads was Covington & Burling, Washington's largest, and that one of the firm's partners was helping Douglas in his personal defense, thus forcing the justice out of the case. Disqualifications of this sort are widely regretted, but ordinarily they are regarded as nobody's fault. It has become fairly elementary to state that ethics require a judge to minimize the number of times he must disqualify himself, but Justice Douglas presumably could not have avoided the need for counsel in his own defense.

Another close case involved the celebrated attempt to exhibit the film *I Am Curious (Yellow)* in Maryland. Douglas's disqualification resulted in a four to four tie, upholding lower court decisions against the film and affirming the power of the state's embattled board of censors. Clearly it was a result Douglas would deplore and would have averted had he been able to cast a vote. Grove Press was the American distributor of the explicitly sexy Swedish movie. Grove Press was also the publisher of the *Evergreen Review*, which in April 1970 printed excerpts from Douglas's new book, *Points of Rebellion*, some of which were offensive in both content and form to Congressman Ford. To many persons familiar with the case, the disqualification was clearly warranted because of the justice's business relationship, temporary though it was, with Grove Press, but Douglas and his lawyers disclaimed this as an explanation for his action. Instead, they told the special investigating subcommittee, it was part of Douglas's policy of staying out of cases "where sharp public controversy makes it unseemly for him" to sit.

Any doubt of Douglas's view of the obscenity case on its merits could have been resolved by reference to the opinion he had delivered on December 15, 1969, dissenting as the Court removed a federal restraining order against prosecution of the same movie's exhibitors in Boston. The anticensorship message was vintage Douglas but the highly personal tone was uncharacteristically personal and defensive. Douglas wrote that he disagreed with rulings in favor of censorship, "but not because, as frequently charged, I relish 'obscenity.' I have dissented before and now because I think the First Amendment bars all kinds of censorship." Censorship, he said, "is a relatively new arrival on the American scene, propelled by dedicated zealots to cleanse all thought." To Douglas the Bill of Rights favored free expression with no exception for "obscenity, however defined. That does not mean that 'obscenity' is good or that it should be encouraged. It only means that we cannot be faithful to our constitutional mandate and allow any form or shadow of censorship over speech and press." The opinion was written before negotiations began for publishing the *Evergreen* excerpts from his book but while he was very much under fire though not yet the subject of a congressional investigation. The opinion was unusual, not because it explained Justice Douglas's constitutional theory of immunity from government censorship—he had explained his views for years in volume upon volume—but rather because the justice felt the need to justify his actions to others, again something of a sad comedown for this ultimate individualist.

The theme of refusal to disqualify oneself because of conflict of interest is a recurring one in the final report of the special House Judiciary Subcommittee that exonerated Douglas in December by a vote of four to one, after more than six months of political wrangling and secret investigation. A fascinating story unfolds from a study of the subcommittee's 924 pages: the story of Douglas's involvement with Los Angeles businessman Albert Parvin and Parvin's personal foundation. It is not an easy story to follow from the report, partly, it seems, by careful design. In a very real sense the report, prepared under the protective eye of the chairman of the full Judiciary Committee, Emanuel Celler, was indeed the "whitewash" of Douglas his critics claimed it was. Documentation and narrative were sprinkled arbitrarily through the thick volume in a way that inevitably made it difficult to read. It was almost as though the compilers feared that evidence gathered and printed in one section of the report in Douglas's favor might be employed against him somewhere else. Repeatedly in the course of dismissing charges against Douglas because they failed to amount to impeachable offenses, the majority went so far as to indicate that the questioned conduct was in no respect blameworthy even under conventional ethical precepts. Thus they committed—in reverse —Representative Ford's error of equating unethical behavior with impeachable conduct. The cause of clearer ethical standards might have been better served by a report concluding that Douglas was indiscreet—but that while indiscreet he was in no way dishonest.

What emerges from the report is a pattern of prodigious outside activities by the justice, not only in the cause of world peace but also in the interest of keeping the Parvin Foundation from coming apart as the result of government tax investigations, Parvin's questionable use of foundation assets, and the force of outside criticism, both press and congressional. If the record is complete—and certainly it is voluminous and by far the most complete account currently available—it gives fresh insight into the world as seen from the eyes of this apparently aloof justice. Most importantly, despite the sympathetic light it sheds on the foundation controversy as viewed from Douglas's perspective, the record displays a history of entirely too much preoccupation with matters extraneous to the business of judging in the nation's highest court.

No witness to Douglas's work on the Court in the years since his appointment in 1939 could doubt that he had energy to burn for outside interests. On the bench during oral argument he seemed impatient or totally distracted from the arguments of plodding counsel. Whether Douglas was riffling through legal briefs, preparing his own resume of the opinion he might write in the case, or just answering his mail the spectator never knew; but it seemed certain that nothing said by the lawyer at the podium captured his attention for very long nor was it very new, especially for a justice who was entering his fourth decade of hearing cases that were descended from cases he had seen many times through the years. Month after month, Douglas would dispose of his opinions ahead of his brethren, often with brilliance as well as speed but frequently with a dash and a flair that lawyers found merely sloppy. Ceaselessly he pressed the Court to take on more and more of the cases brought before them by petitioners, denying the widely held claims of justices and the bar that the Court often took on more than it could handle efficiently. He constantly finished his term's work early, and without waiting for the rest of the Court to catch up, he would take off for the western hills. Beyond question, sheer brilliance accounted for much of Douglas's speed on his job. Another factor conducive to speed was his habit of assuming absolutist, uncompromising positions on issues of recurring concern to the Court, so that he would not or did not need to consume long hours in the collegial exercise of persuading, accommodating, or being persuaded.

Douglas would have been president of the United States in 1945 if—and a big if it was—the Democratic National Convention of 1944 had chosen him for vice-president instead of Harry S. Truman. The frequency with which he was mentioned for posts from the presidency down was at least indicative of the range of his ambition and capabilities. If he had time to spare, he also had a world full of interests to explore in that spare time.

So, while offers like Albert Parvin's do not come to each of us every day, it may not have greatly surprised Douglas to receive a letter in July 1960 from this successful West Coast businessman, a total stranger, who had read the justice's latest book, *America Challenged*, and wanted to take up its cause of better global understanding.

It is my desire to endow a trust or foundation for the sole purpose of promulgating and promoting better relations amongst nations through education. As foundations go these days this will be rather a modest one, but could inspire others more copious. It will to begin with consist of some 2 to 2½ million dollars in stocks and interest bearing notes. These could produce a minimum annual income of $100,000. . . .

Parvin would be highly honored if Douglas would help establish and direct this work, for which the justice would be reimbursed for expenses and paid an annual fee or salary.

The record does not show what reservations Douglas might have had about such an outside activity, but apparently he had none. The Parvin Foundation was swiftly established, with the legal help of Parvin's own attorneys, and it embarked upon a program of fellowships for foreign students to spend a year at Princeton University learning the American system of government. The original trustees included Douglas, the foundation's president; Parvin, its vice-president; federal judge William J. Campbell of Chicago, an old friend of Parvin's; Robert F. Goheen, president of Princeton; Robert M. Hutchins, Douglas's mentor on the Yale law faculty, former president of the University of Chicago, and president of the Fund for the Republic, of which Douglas was also a director. Idolized by Parvin and increasingly an intimate personal friend of the businessman as well, Douglas clearly could dictate the terms of his compensation. He chose to be paid $12,000 a year, which despite Parvin's protest that it was inadequate included expenses and a $2,400 annual premium toward a retirement annuity.

Although the directors indicated no uneasiness with the foundation's financial underpinnings, the seeds of future discord were sown early through connections with gambling interests. The principal source of the foundation's endowment had been the sale, earlier in 1960, of Parvin's interest in the Flamingo Hotel in Las Vegas. Parvin, it appeared, had been such a success in his career in the hotel supply and interior decorating business that he often found himself financially interested in the hotels he supplied and redecorated. The Flamingo investment was initially the result of the hotel's inability to pay the bills of Parvin and other creditors. When Parvin sold the hotel, he again became its creditor, giving it a ten-year mortgage. The mortgage, in turn, was converted into the Parvin Foundation's biggest asset. Parvin turned his interest in the mortgage over to the foundation through a trust managed by a bank so that the foundation received the mortgage income without administering either the mortgage or the business operations of the Flamingo. These intricacies are important because of the distance they put between Justice Douglas and the foundation on one hand and the gambling enterprise on the other.

Another odd and never fully explained transaction clouded the picture, but this, too, was done before any Flamingo income passed to the foundation. Whether or not it was known to the foundation's officials other than Parvin, the sale of the hotel was heavily taxed by a major organized crime figure, Meyer Lansky, a man sometimes called the banker for national crime syndicates. Lansky was paid a "finder's fee" of $200,000 for the transaction although, in the dry language of the House subcommittee report, "when Mr. Parvin was interrogated by the Subcommittee staff on June 9, 1970, he stated that Meyer Lansky did not participate in the negotiations for the sale. Mr. Parvin said that the buyers of the Flamingo, after the purchase price had been negotiated, directed that the $200,000 be added."

None of this history, of course, necessarily tainted any of the foundation's work, which proved to be dedicated and quite productive. What did begin to rub off on the foundation, and what aroused increasing interest from the Internal Revenue Service, was Parvin's inability or disinclination to divorce himself from the hotel business, which is to say the casino business, while at the same time taking an active part in the foundation's activities and especially its investments. His disregard for the appearance of propriety caused constant and recurring embarrassment for everyone connected with the foundation.

With some reason, Parvin considered himself an able investor and investment counselor well suited to enhancing the assets of his foundation. As the chairman and sole member of the foundation's finance committee from 1961 until public controversy erupted late in 1966, Parvin was ever on the lookout for investment opportunities for the foundation that were similar to, but more conservative than, the opportunities that came to him as a private businessman. He had what Douglas later described as a "compulsion" to manage the portfolio of the foundation he had sired. Although Parvin vigorously denied that any of his foundation transactions were for his own benefit, such management compulsions typically arouse the curiosity of the federal tax collector because personal and family foundations are so laden with temptations and opportunities for illegal tax avoidance.

With little or no interference from Douglas or any other director, Parvin freely donated blocks of securities of various companies to the foundation, bought stock from the foundation, obtained for the Parvin-Dohrman Co. a $750,000 loan from the foundation, managed a short sale of aircraft stock from the foundation's portfolio, and opened an account with a California savings and loan institution at a critical time in the life of the S&L—just when an influx of capital from a variety of sources was being regarded as an attempt by a group of investors to take it over.

The dry minutes of the foundation disclose, however, that the directors' faith in Parvin had limits. On the same day the board "authorized the opening of an account with the Long Beach Federal Savings & Loan Association," a controversial transaction that was later to cause Douglas slight discomfort as a justice, the minutes tell of Parvin's recommendation that the foundation join him in a venture that would, "in three or four years, probably produce returns which ordinary investment would not produce." Translation: The foundation had a chance to make money speculating. Parvin had put up $1.4 million toward the construction of a building on Chicago's Lake Shore Drive. If the foundation wanted to share equally in his investment, he understood that the Bank of America National Trust and Savings Association would lend the foundation the money needed to buy in. "After some discussion," the minutes state, "and on motion made, seconded and carried, it was resolved that the matter be tabled at this time and be taken under further consideration."

Beginning in 1964, agents of the Internal Revenue Service, as part of a broad investigation of organized crime, searched the records and tax returns of Parvin, the foundation, the Parvin-

Dohrman Co., of which Parvin was a longtime controlling stockholder, and others. It was part of what the IRS called "Operation Complex," an investigation that required forty-one agents and consumed 30,617 man-hours. When the criminal phase of the Parvin investigation terminated favorably to Parvin in April 1967, the Treasury men maintained and increased their interest in its civil aspect with the result that in 1969, just as Douglas was leaving his foundation post, IRS declared its intention to revoke the foundation's tax-exempt status.

A key step along the way was the entry of the Parvin-Dohrman Co. into the Nevada hotel business in July 1966. The foundation's principal income was from the trust-administered mortgage on the Hotel Flamingo in Las Vegas; but now Parvin, the foundation's prime benefactor, was again directly interested in the profitability of the Fremont Hotel and casino on the same Vegas strip. The foundation's holdings in the Parvin-Dohrman Co. were small compared with its basic source of income, but now its relationship to a Nevada gambling enterprise was more direct through its ownership of company stock than it had been through the mortgage interest. Douglas expressed surprise when told of this development by the IRS and the *Los Angeles Times*, which inaugurated a new phase of the foundation's history with a news story on October 16, 1966, headlined "Outside Income of Justice Raises Judicial Ethics Issue" and subheaded "Douglas Gets $12,000 From Foundation Which Derives Some Funds From Las Vegas Gambling Hotel Mortgage." Douglas told reporter Ronald J. Ostrow that he thought the foundation had owned an interest in the Flamingo for only "a brief period, but [which soon was] disposed of by the finance committee." He said he did not serve on the finance committee, which handled all investments and reinvestments. (As already indicated, Parvin *was* the finance committee.) While the newspaper was preparing the article, Douglas had written Parvin on October 6,

An official of the federal government came in to see me to advise me that according to their investigations, the Flamingo Hotel in Las Vegas is a so-called Mafia property. My understanding from our conversations a year or so ago was that the Foundation's interest in any Flamingo stock was liquidated. If it has been and if the Foundation has no other Las Vegas interests, I think that the problem is solved.

Douglas then added, in a low-keyed note of concern,

But in view of the interest and concern here, I thought I should bring this specific matter to your attention, and to see if we could work out a procedure whereby the Foundation stays clear of any Las Vegas interest. This is no reflection on you in any way whatsoever. But it occurred to me that in view of this storm which seems to be brewing, we might adopt even specific instructions for our Finance Committee to stay clear of that particular area.

Although some congressmen sought to link Douglas more closely with organized crime figures, no direct or personal connections ever were proved or, for that matter, responsibly alleged after the impeachment investigation ended. Nevertheless, these loose relationships were close enough for many observers to conclude that a fundamental canon of judicial ethics had been infringed. Canon 4 of the then existing ethical code demanded that "a judge's official conduct should be free from impropriety and the appearance of impropriety." The canon always has been something of a truism, an expression of piety that all would be willing to endorse provided each judge is free to interpret it for himself. Many consider it a meaningless piety, a relic of a more genteel age when civilized persons "knew" what honesty was, something that could be scrapped in favor of more specific and enforceable rules of a faster-moving time.

The problem of judicial propriety arose from the acknowledged facts. There was little to be said in favor of Douglas's foundation arrangement. While the Vegas enterprises were "legitimate"—that is, legal under state law—they were repeatedly and increasingly the target of law enforcement inquiries into whether proprietors were "skimming" profits off the top to evade taxes and whether the skimmings were going to racketeers. A valid and principled claim could be made that Douglas, in his zeal to serve larger causes, had become too closely associated with tainted activities through the foundation and that the Court itself was correspondingly besmirched. In a practical sense, the targets of law enforcement interest happened to be the same sorts of persons who were bringing to the Supreme Court some of the most critical civil liberties issues of the day, such as the scope of the government's power to eavesdrop on suspected lawbreakers and the extent of the privacy rights of guilty and innocent alike. One such figure was prominent gambler Ed Levinson, an employee of Parvin's as an officer of the Fremont, who was simultaneously defending himself against federal charges and suing the United States for invasion of his privacy. His cases were settled far short of the High Court, but the law governing them was being made there as the Court grappled with a new generation of constitutional issues. A gambling enterprise is of course entitled to the full protection of the Constitution, including the presumption of innocence; but its ultimate status before the law must be determined by judges, who must be disinterested not in the Constitution but in the gambling industry.

By foundation standards, Douglas's compensation did not seem unreasonable: $12,000 for the direction of a global enterprise with a budget ten to fifteen times that amount by a gifted person of worldwide reputation. "How can you buy such talent?" Parvin asked his newspaper interviewer. "He does 10 times what a full-time, fully paid president would." However, viewed as a judicial matter, the compensation was excessive, whether "earned" or "unearned." If earned, it represented too much off-the-bench work for hire by a justice with life tenure. If unearned, such a salary would invite suspicion that a judge was in someone's pocket. Either way, the arrangement did not explain itself but rather invited much more searching and irritating inquiry. In dollars-and-cents terms it said something Douglas had been saying and dramatizing for many years: that the Supreme Court of the United States did not fully occupy his talents.

Whether or not Douglas felt the lash of any ethical canon, he showed by his actions during the ensuing months that he considered appearances to be very important indeed. He followed up on his expression of concern to Parvin when the foundation's directors held their first meeting after the *Los Angeles Times* story was published. Douglas was ready at the November 1 meeting to move, and Parvin to second, the motion that the foundation hire independent counsel "to review the Foundation's financial records and to prepare specific recommendations, if such were deemed necessary, to remove any question of strict compliance with federal tax regulations." The question had arisen, Douglas reported to the board, in a visit by IRS agents who had asked for records for examination "in connection with a possible violation of the Foundation's tax exempt status." The special counsel was perhaps the nation's best-known tax attorney, Carolyn Agger, wife of Associate Justice Abe Fortas, who had maintained her highly successful tax practice when her husband went on the bench in 1965.

Parvin stressed in his report to the board that there never had been "any operational connection of any kind" between the foundation and gambling, and that his own attorneys and an accounting firm had found "no irregularities" in any of the foundation's investments or expenditures. The four board members present—Douglas, Parvin, Hutchins, and Harry Ashmore—"unanimously expressed their confidence in Mr. Parvin." Letters came from the absent members, Goheen and Judge Campbell, the Chicago jurist offering his resignation "with the greatest affection" for Parvin personally "and with genuine admiration for the outstanding achievements you have accomplished for the Foundation." (The congressional report does not quote the judge's letter in full or otherwise explain his reasons for resigning.) At the same time the board augmented the "finance committee" to include Ashmore and Hutchins along with Parvin and Los Angeles attorney Harvey Silbert, a Parvin associate, a first step in a long overdue process of reconstruction.

As events demonstrated, Miss Agger was decidedly independent of Parvin, but before accepting the legal assignment she raised the question of whether she was sufficiently independent of Douglas to be effective. Douglas wrote Ashmore a week later that Miss Agger's firm

is going ahead on the Parvin Foundation matter, though she indicated that if the issues became newspaper items, the Foundation might want to get someone more 'independent.' By this I gather she meant that my association with her and her firm has been so long that it might not look well if a knock-down row arose. I think that has no merit, as I have always felt free to sit in all cases her firm brings before the Court, even though one of their staff for years has for a fee handled my tax matters. I told her that if the Foundation were in trouble tax-wise by reason or [*sic*] irregularities we would probably resign anyway.

Thus wary, though outwardly calm about the matter, Douglas set in motion a confrontation between those who were determined to clean up the foundation and those who professed to see nothing to clean up. Miss Agger wrote to Ashmore that the first order of business was to sever Parvin from the portfolio and to make sure the IRS knew that anything questionable was in the process of correction. Apparently the IRS was suspicious of some kind of "prohibited transaction," the use of foundation property for personal purposes. She wrote:

This may or may not have occurred, but apparently the investigating agents believe that it may have. Accordingly, I believe that it would be wise for the Trustees to employ an independent accountant to reaudit the Foundation's records very thoroughly. . . . The pressing problem, at the moment, from the Foundation's viewpoint, is to avoid even the appearance of continued Parvin participation and control, and to do everything to make it plain that the Trustees, other than Mr. Parvin, have assumed complete control of the Foundation.

Ashmore forwarded Miss Agger's letter to Parvin in a letter larded with still more personal reassurances. The legal opinion was addressed solely to meeting the legal problem, he wrote. As to adding members to the finance committee,

there is no question of Bob Hutchins or my having any personal desire to be consulted on the details of Foundation investments. None of us has any doubt about your integrity or your competence; the record speaks eloquently for both. But Miss Agger appears to confirm the view of Douglas and Hutchins (who, we ought not to forget, are pretty good lawyers themselves) as to the steps that may be necessary to insure that we have left no loophole for adverse action by the Internal Revenue Service.

Parvin's injured response was immediate. He wrote back that he did not agree with Miss Agger's advice about divorcing him from foundation finances and telling the IRS. "Honestly, Harry, what is wrong with me?" he asked. "And frankly, what does Miss Agger think I am? I am certain that the financial and investment program of the Foundation, if handled by anyone but me, would result in a loss of income to the Foundation of perhaps $50,000 to $100,000 per year."

As 1966 drew to a close, Ashmore summarized in a letter to Douglas the justice's reasons for believing he could not "continue to be associated with the Foundation as it is now constituted." The four reasons were (1) the likelihood that the IRS would press its investigation despite the absence of evidence of any violation of law and lack of likelihood that any evidence incriminating Parvin would turn up; (2) the connections, however tenuous, between the Parvin-Dohrman Co. and hotels maintaining gambling casinos and its potential as a basis for "political attacks on you in Congress and in the press"; (3) the probability that the foundation's investment management did not meet IRS standards and the IRS's suspicions based on Parvin's continued investment role; and (4) the possibility that IRS might suspend the foundation's tax exemption which could be overcome only by a lawsuit "and even if the legal action succeeded the resulting publicity would be intolerable."

Prudent and sufficient as these reasons might have been for bowing out of the foundation, they were not the reasons Douglas gave his Supreme Court brethren in a memorandum addressed to Chief Justice Warren on October 31, 1966, which began, "In light of some recent vicious press articles concerning me and the Parvin Foundation, I thought you and the Brethren should know what the truth is." Although he complained that his educational venture "has been very much distorted in the press," Douglas did not say that unfair and unfavorable publicity might cause him to leave it. Rather, he said, "as the work and activities of the Foundation increase I am not sure how much longer I can direct its affairs."

The Douglas memorandum detailed the work of the foundation and repeatedly sounded a theme that runs through Douglas's career yet is frequently missed by press and public though not, apparently, by Parvin: the strength of the justice's anticommunism. The foundation's purpose was to help in "combatting the forces of communism at the world level" by bringing future world leaders to America for "exposure to both the theory and the practical operations of a free society" so that "they would return to their own countries with new insight into how the forces of communism could be combatted. We have been very proud of our achievements."

As for criticism of the foundation portfolio, Douglas said,

> Except for minor items, the selection of the portfolio was made solely by Mr. Parvin and was transferred by him to the Foundation as an irrevocable gift. Moreover, the foundation has no connection with the operation of any enterprise whatsoever. Let me also say that there has been no conflict whatsoever between the Foundation and my work on the Court. Historically many Justices have had outside connections or activities—as a trustee or overseer of a college, as a professor of law or as a lecturer or author, as the owner of securities in a corporation. Every single Justice has been meticulous in observing the fundamental principle that he will not sit in a case in which he has a direct or even indirect interest.

The memorandum did not dispose of the prime area of IRS concern as it was then emerging: that is, the possible self-dealing by Parvin which could taint the foundation's educational program by showing that the foundation also served an individual's private interest. The memorandum did, of course, deal with the most immediate public impression of a possible unsavory connection with the underworld.

A few angry congressmen called for Douglas's head, but the news during the following months neglected the foundation's quiet restructuring as it continued along the lines of Miss Agger's advice. Agreement was reached at a December meeting to transfer at least temporarily the functions of the finance committee, including the entire management and control of the portfolio, "to an outside independent financial or educational institution."

A recurring suggestion that the foundation's solution might be to merge with the Center for the Study of Democratic Institutions was discussed and decision deferred. Douglas and others leaned heavily toward this solution but Parvin opposed it, apparently for the same reason he opposed much of what was going on at this time: the fear of a loss of his foundation's identity.

Before the board's next meeting, and quite coincidentally, Douglas delivered two on-the-bench opinions that added an ironic dimension to the controversies surrounding him. One was a partial dissent urging the Court to do more than merely delay the merger of the Pennsylvania and New York Central railroads; the other was a dissenting opinion arguing that judges must not be held totally immune from inquiries into their actions. In the railroad case on March 27, 1967, Douglas said the Interstate Commerce Commission should be ordered to conduct a deeply searching inquisition into the behind-the-scenes financial world implications of the rail combine. "The financial hierarchy of the new cartels must be exposed so the centers of control will be known," he said from the bench. "Who will sit at the switch-board of this great cartel? Where is the power? Who is the king? We don't know." On April 11, Douglas dissented from what he considered an unwarranted extension to judges in state courts of the doctrine of immunity from suit under federal civil rights laws for alleged on-the-bench misdeeds. "The argument that the actions of public officials must not be subjected to judicial scrutiny because to do so would have an inhibiting effect on their work is but a more sophisticated manner of saying, 'The King can do no wrong,' " he said. Judicial immunity sprang from the same theory since the judges were the king's judges, "his delegates for dispensing justice," answerable not to the people but to the king alone.

In these two opinions Douglas, long a champion of free inquiry, of disclosure of corporate activity, and of the accounta-bility of judges and other public officials, was operating at quite a different level from Douglas, the public official and public figure whose off-the-bench activities had become the subject of wide-spread public interest. Even when a private person "is catapulted into the news by events over which he had no control," he wrote in a concurring opinion on January 9, 1967, "such privacy as a person normally has ceases when his life has ceased to be private."

When those realms of corporate power were explored a few years later in an inquest into the bankrupt Penn Central, the staff of the House Banking and Currency Committee found that one of the most ruinous vices of the company's directors was inattention to and rubber-stamping of investment decisions made by others. It was a vice that the Parvin Foundation had indulged in, but only now was the justice turning his attention to it.

When the foundation's board of directors held its next meeting on April 12, 1967, it was in "the office of the President" in Washington, D.C.—that is, in the Supreme Court chambers of the justice. Whether to reassure beneficiaries or for some other unstated reason, the board resolved to maintain commitments to Parvin Fellowships at Princeton and at the University of California at Los Angeles. Parvin was named "a Director for his life or until he resigns." The board unanimously reaffirmed previous approval of the outside investment counsel, Loeb, Rhodes & Co., and designated Douglas, Parvin, and Goheen as the finance committee to work with the investment counsel through Goheen and Treasurer Silbert.

Douglas privately began to express more concern for the appearances of propriety. The approaching international peace and law conference at Geneva, Switzerland, called Pacem in Terris II, already apparently "doomed" because of participation by "high-powered" and hawkish officials of the Johnson administration, was developing ethical problems as well. On May 11, 1967, he wrote Parvin that the foundation should take another look at its pledge of support for the conference scheduled for later that month. He added:

> I put it this way because the Center [for the Study of Democratic Institutions] is spending money lavishly on this Conference, the cost running around half a million dollars. They got all that, of course, from the Swiss group, which is very much under attack. If the Swiss litigation with the federal government continues and is not settled, I doubt very much if I should go on the Center's budget. My strong inclination as of now is to stay home. And certainly I don't want to go on the Parvin Foundation funds, for the reasons I have indicated.

The "Swiss group" meant the high-flying, high-risk Investors

Overseas Services international mutual fund management concern; its president, Bernard Cornfeld; and the IOS Foundation that underwrote most of the conference. The "attack" and the "litigation" were proceedings by the Securities and Exchange Commission, which ultimately moved successfully to exclude IOS from American markets, saving domestic United States investors from the fleecing that others were taking abroad. Douglas, as it turned out, did attend the conference and gave its opening address. Four hundred delegates, many of them luminaries, from seventy nations attended to discuss Vietnam, the Middle East, and divided Germany. The delegates were part of an IOS pattern of "lion hunting" by which Cornfeld's precarious financial operations were bolstered by name-dropping on a large scale. IOS went on from the Pacem II conference to sponsor in September 1968 another extravaganza in Geneva surrounding World Human Rights–Law Day, with Chief Justice Earl Warren among the dignitaries from many lands. For such labors, Cornfeld was rewarded with a longer-lived financial operation and, in December 1969, by an audience with the pope. Much later, he wound up in Swiss jails.

Late in 1968 Douglas entered the home stretch of his involvement with the foundation. Apparently still desirous of pursuing his outside interests through the foundation, he had not yet taken up his own announced option of leaving it. But he did take steps to offset a move by Parvin back into the Nevada hotel business. As the justice's counsel put it in a brief to the Judiciary Committee, Parvin's company, the Parvin-Dohrman Co., proposed to add to its hotel holdings (the Fremont acquisition in 1966 having triggered the internal changes of that year) a company with more hotel interests. When that fact "came to Justice Douglas's attention, he again urged that the stock be sold." The sale of the foundation's 31,000 shares of Parvin-Dohrman stock was not easily accomplished, however, because Securities and Exchange Commission rules barred the foundation from unloading more than 1 percent of the company's shares on the market at any given time. This was because Parvin was, in law, a controlling stockholder who was bound by regulations designed to protect the investing public from certain stock dealings by persons holding a controlling interest in a company. After considerable anguish over the inability to extricate the foundation more efficiently from the expected Las Vegas associations, Parvin, in a characteristically profitable move, sold his controlling interest in the company, leaving the foundation free to dispose of all its Parvin-Dohrman holdings. This should have helped remove some of the friction over policy and philosophy between Parvin and Silbert on one hand and Douglas, Goheen, Hutchins, and Ashmore on the other. But even the unloading of the stock caused friction as Silbert, according to a Douglas letter to Miss Agger, "charged gross neglect on my part" for permitting portions of the stock to be sold too low "when a telephone call to him would have brought the advice not to sell as the stock was going higher." That, Douglas retorted, would have been use of "insider" information, "which would have proved the charge that the Foundation was in the vest pocket of the Parvin interests. We sold without the benefit of 'insiders' information, and I am glad that we did. But the whole Silbert discussion led me to think I was associated with a wholly unethical man and I should withdraw." Checking with Miss Agger, he said he would not resign as officer and director "if it would in any way embarrass the IRS proceeding" with its threat to the foundation's tax exemption. "I have a deep affection for Mr. Parvin and do not wish to hurt him," Douglas said.

Douglas then wrote to Parvin complaining of Silbert's attitude. "If the philosophy of Mr. Silbert expressed at our Board meeting prevails, then we will lose the fiscal agent [the outside investment help], we will lose the IRS suit, and we will face, I fear, a resignation of Directors. . . . These matters must be hammered out and resolved." Miss Agger wrote Douglas that she had been surprised at Silbert's criticism of the justice. "I suspect that he may have acted at the suggestion of Parvin who did not wish to criticize you himself," she said.

Early in March 1969, when Parvin, to Douglas's great relief, was accomplishing the final unloading of all the Parvin-Dohrman shares, the two men exchanged letters that dramatized the gap between them. Parvin said Douglas's worries were "very disturbing" and that Douglas seemed "unduly provoked." Douglas's idea of outside management of the foundation portfolio was no sure-fire solution and might itself cause difficulties with the government, he argued. He went on:

I know of the many past embarrassments and anxieties you have had as a result of being associated with the Foundation. They hurt me deeply. I know, too, how dedicated and faithful you are to the purposes of the Foundation. As long as I remain on its Board, I will not knowingly do anything that would give cause for concern to you or any of the other directors. However, I will not be brainwashed, intimidated and subdued by the chronic accusers and bureaucrats, and as long as I feel I am doing right, I shall fight for that right. . . . To me, more than the Foundation's assets, more than even its principles, your personal image and welfare must predominate. . . .

Douglas began his reply by proclaiming his deep respect for Parvin's integrity, but for which "I would have resigned long ago. The idea advanced at the January 26th meeting that I should have consulted 'insiders' before allowing the fiscal agent to sell any of the Parvin/Dohrman stock was quite a blow. It ran counter to all I knew about 'inside' information and its use. Had I done what Mr. Silbert criticized me for not doing it would have proved the IRS case." The IRS case, said Douglas, "is built on appearances. Donors who create foundations are supposed to keep hands off."

Before Douglas's final meeting with the board there was yet another letter to Parvin, on May 12, 1969. It could have been a last gesture by Douglas, an offer to stay with the foundation, but apparently the terms were unacceptable to the Los Angeles businessman. Writing aboard a plane home from Brazil, Douglas said: "The manufactured case against you and the Foundation is a shocking thing that we must fight to the end and win. But as the issues are formed it may get nastier and nastier. The press has already started on them—Reuters in Rio bearing down hard. The strategy is to get me off the Court, and I do not propose to bend to any such pressure." The proposed solution, a renewal of an old idea, was the merger of the foundation into the Center for the Study of Democratic Institutions, but this time in a separately maintained "Parvin Fund" which would preserve the foundation's old identity but would place the IRS problem "in such small dimensions as to make its solution easy." Although it was the climaxing letter of nearly a decade of voluminous correspondence, it was the first to reach the public as within two weeks Parvin made it available to the *New York Times*. Representative H. R. Gross, the Iowa Republican who makes judicial behavior one of his watchdog preoccupations, promptly inserted the newspaper's account of the letter in the *Congressional Record*, laying stress on sections that made it appear that Douglas was rendering heavy legal advice. To Gross and to many other legislators, rendering legal advice was the equivalent of "practicing law," an impeachable offense. It would have been fairer and more accurate to say that the justice was rendering investment and management advice.

Release of this letter was not the only occasion on which Parvin inflicted injury on Douglas, however unintentionally. In the course of his own divorce litigation, Parvin casually testified that Douglas had "drafted" the foundation's articles of incorporation and this, apparently, was part of the IRS's bag of information when in April of 1969 it gave notice of its intention to revoke the foundation's tax exemption. The notice kicked off a proceeding that lasted for two years before the Treasury Department finally dropped its complaints and charges.

At last the board of directors met at Santa Barbara, California, on May 21. Douglas, citing the expected increase in "the workload," submitted his resignation as chief executive officer and as a director. With the customary expressions of regret, the resignation was accepted. A new top director was chosen. The embattled finance committee was dissolved. Its purpose, to protect Douglas from the effects of controversial investment decisions, had never been served, but now there was no need to try.

Justice Douglas was never impeached, but he was maimed. He was partially crippled in his Supreme Court work by accusations that, however motivated, literally required a congressional investigation to disprove. He paid the price of his own independence by making himself vulnerable to political attack. He might have suffered less if, uncharacteristically, he had let the public know of his own hidden concerns which, after all, only paralleled the legitimate worries of eminent counsel and perhaps much of the public. Politically motivated attacks are in themselves unworthy, but who is to say that they serve no social purpose? Could not some of the criticism of Justice Douglas over the years have warned him and others that more serious crises lay ahead? It was foolish and wrong for Douglas to lay waste his powers in this fashion.

3

☆ ☆ ☆

CONFLICTS

An incubus then I thought her,
So I soon threw over that rich attorney's
Elderly, ugly daughter.
The rich attorney my character high
Tried vainly to disparage—

Chorus: No!

Yes!
And now, if you please, I'm ready to try
this Breach of Promise of Marriage!

W. S. Gilbert
TRIAL BY JURY

The resignation of Justice Abe Fortas in May 1969 and the defeat six months later of Clement F. Haynsworth, Jr., as his successor combined in that frantic year to show how much anguish and punishment can be meted out over conduct that is ethically questionable but falls far, far short of outright corruption. Corruption is happily a rare bird in the federal judicial system. Compensation and tenure help to make it so; there are other factors, such as caste, class, and the secrecy of the decision-making process, that help also to make it appear so. No doubt there is more skulduggery behind the scenes than the public ever knows about. But even allowing generously for undiscovered judicial corruption, the federal bench scores well in comparison with other branches of state and federal government. Appropriately, therefore, higher standards are set for judges. The public expects and tolerates some aloofness on their part and looks for loftier behavior in return. Nearly a hundred men had been appointed to the Supreme Court before one, Abe Fortas, resigned under fire. Significantly, when he quit the Court, there was no concrete evidence of illegal conduct; appearances were enough to drive him from the bench.

Perhaps because the federal bench really does have an unusually high proportion of law-abiding citizens, or perhaps because of the difficulty of proving misconduct, outright criminal behavior has been less of a concern over the years than unethical behavior. Of the eight jurists who have been impeached, four were convicted and removed from office; but only one of them, according to a survey by Joseph Borkin, was charged directly with corrupt activity. No federal jurist has ever been both removed from office by the impeachment process and criminally prosecuted as well, although the Constitution makes clear that removal does not bar prosecution. Only four times in American history has a sitting federal judge been indicted; the fourth, Otto J. Kerner of the Seventh U.S. Circuit Court of Appeals, was indicted in late 1971 and convicted in 1973 for conduct while he was governor of Illinois.

Perhaps general prosperity contributes to this state of affairs. The problems of a man who is financially secure but is momentarily experiencing a "liquidity problem"—being a little short of the loose cash needed to make a timely investment or pay a bill—are not the same as the problems of a man who is going broke or has secretly gone broke. "To a certain extent," Borkin wrote in *The Corrupt Judge*,

economic conditions play a part in the sorry spectacle of corruption. In fact, the greatest incidence of corrupt judges, lawyers, businessmen, and fixers makes its appearance as part of the debris of a business depression. The frequency of corruption, the disfavor of lawyers with the public, and moral standards of some business interests all seem to have a definite correlation with the business cycle.

Borkin's narratives of three federal judges who went seriously wrong in the 1930s and 1940s—Judge Martin T. Manton of the Second U.S. Circuit Court of Appeals, Judge J. Warren Davis of the Third Circuit, and Judge Albert W. Johnson of the U.S. District Court for the Middle District of Pennsylvania—have among their common themes the fact that bad aromas emanated from their judicial work even before they were exposed as corrupt. The odor was noticeable at times only in judicial circles, at other times to the local press, at still other times to visiting federal prosecutors. Chief Justice Taft so doubted the integrity of the talented Manton that he used his influence to head off a feared appointment to the Supreme Court.

In the view of many judicial and bar leaders, compensation for jurists is currently and chronically inadequate. These experts focus on the difficulty of attracting able lawyers to the bench when many of them earn multiples of the federal salary in private practice. Curiously, judicial salaries have been held down of late, like those of other federal officials, under a reform measure that was designed to keep judges' compensation apace with the cost of living and the salaries of cabinet members and congressmen. The plan has been to have salaries set by an independent commission whose recommended increases go into effect automatically unless Congress affirmatively intervenes. Unfortunately for the judges, the system does not give the congressmen the courage—or the gall, depending on viewpoint— to let their own raises take effect, and this in turn leaves the judicial increases in the same limbo. It is probably wise for the judiciary to leave its wagon hitched to the congressional star, for it is then more difficult for Congress to deny judicial raises merely out of pique over particular decisions. The Constitution protects federal judges from salary cuts but it does not require Congress to enact cost-of-living increases. The salary outlook, then, is a pay level for justices and judges that does not match what some of them could make in the marketplace but that amounts to prosperity for most laymen. Today, particularly because compensation is widely considered reasonably ample for most of the federal judges, even a mild suggestion of conflict of interest suffices to arouse public anger and usually some sort of corrective action.

But prosperity does not dispel ethical problems. A judge with surplus capital has the problem of deciding where to invest it to maximize income and minimize taxes. Increasingly he may find that where he invests may also be where others are investing and also where the litigation is. There is a resident industry to tempt judges in the South and Southwest—oil—that offers income advantages and tax shelters. In the Washington, D.C., area, where dozens of top jurists live and where big government is the big industry, investment in real estate is a promising field for extra capital. President Nixon, thinking he was avoiding any challenge to his personal propriety in financial matters, divested himself of stock when he entered the White House and became heavily involved in real estate. In Detroit the industry is automobiles, and, surprisingly, there are judges in Michigan who are so confident of their own rectitude that they do not resist the temptation to buy and keep automobile stocks. Of such stuff are conflict-of-interest problems made in good times today.

Good times or bad, jurists have looked to the future when their income will be down or when they will have needy widows. Justice Douglas's moonlighting in part helped him save for a pension annuity, and Justice Fortas, as we shall see, provided for his estate in his arrangements with a private family foundation.

Ironically, the judicial conduct that ignited an ethical crisis in the late 1960s was pale compared with the venality of the corrupt judges of the 1930s. The times differed, of course, not least in the level of popular expectations of morality in public officials. The judiciary no less than other governmental branches felt the new pressures of participatory democracy as new groups of people, having made their presence felt in the executive and legislative branches, began hoping to share the experience of making the law "work for them." A "law explosion" had forced judges to hear the claims of minorities. Antipoverty lawyers subsidized by Congress, environmentalists spurred by courtroom victories and new laws, consumer advocates, and others added to the variety of persons bringing their interests and their ethical concerns to bear on the legal system. Not to be outdone by the newly aroused poor, the middle class joined in. Labor unions began negotiating for legal insurance in their employment contracts.

Politics, of course, fueled the debate, which might have been too theoretical or abstract without interested and ambitious politicians to press the argument. Among the major political factors that conditioned the controversies over Fortas and Haynsworth, which this chapter surveys, perhaps the most important was President Nixon's push for a reconstituted Supreme Court.

A word may be needed to place politics in its proper context. To many on both sides of the Fortas and Haynsworth controversies, everything was political. The attitude that the fights were principally matters of power and prerogative was especially prevalent within the Nixon administration, whose strategists seemed at times slow to recognize meritorious ethical questions as anything but political weaponry and were thus hindered in their ability to cope with accusations against their candidate as they emerged. Undoubtedly, for many administration opponents such questions as ethics were "covers" that they found convenient for political use. In such an arena, none of the contestants can be expected to agree over how much principle and how much cynicism is involved. But throughout the turmoil the most politically cynical and the purest moralist would have had to agree on two things: one, politics *was* involved; and two, at the same time there was truly a crisis of public confidence in the judiciary, with the consequence that ethics was an issue with vitality of its own.

It would therefore be diverting to explore more fully the political aspects of the period—too diverting for the purposes of this book—just as it would be unrealistic to ignore them. In a sense the ethical issues rained down on Democrats and Republicans, liberals and conservatives alike. Benefits and penalties were distributed with indifference to politics or persons. Fortas's ethical difficulties presented President Nixon with windfall opportunities to fill two vacancies, Fortas's own and the seat he would have occupied if confirmed as chief justice. Yet similar ethical considerations played an important role in denying Nixon the fruits of the windfall for a full year, the longest period in history in which a seat on the Court had been vacant. The force of the ethical idea can hardly be denied when, by common understanding, in the close battle over Haynsworth, ethics provided the margin of his defeat. With this appreciation of some of the forces at work, we turn to the climactic ethical episodes of the troubled period: the ouster of Fortas, the Haynsworth battle, and finally the Blackmun confirmation.

☆

The revelations about Fortas's financial relationship with convicted financier Louis Wolfson came as a shock, though not a total shock. To a degree, the way had been prepared for the Wolfson disclosures by the previous summer's controversy over his $15,000 fee for teaching seminars at American University, a stipend arranged by a former law partner with generous help from firm clients. In addition to tarnishing Fortas's liberal image, the seminar fee served to heighten the impression of a jurist whose generous spirit in human rights cases was balanced by a sharp awareness of and an appetite for the fast-moving business practices of the "real world." From the beginning of his Court service Fortas berated his colleagues for lack of business realism. "I do not think all mergers are bad," he declared, implying that the majority was impelled by something other than the antitrust laws to strike down most corporate consolidations. In 1967 when Douglas and Brennan were demanding a more searching inquiry into the Penn Central rail merger, Fortas was leading the dissenters with the cry: "The courts may be the principal guardians of the liberties of the people. They are not the chief administrators of its economic destiny."

This is not to say that all of Fortas's work as a justice gave rise to an ethical question. Instead, some of it merely reminded lawyers and Washingtonians of a certain ambivalence. His wife's refusal to curb her tax practice caused considerable, though suppressed, alarm in the legal community. Clearly enough the Arnold & Porter firm would gain nothing in direct tax law decisions, but it was inconceivable that any tax issue sufficiently important for the Supreme Court to consider would fail to affect any among Carolyn Agger's impressive array of clients. Sharp and caustic questioning from the bench, which came easily to the combative former advocate, was often suspect among tax lawyers when that questioning was in tax cases. Their unease was not a matter of hard proof; it was a matter of appearances.

All this was prologue to May 4, 1969, when *Life* magazine released the news that Fortas, while a justice in 1966, had accepted and months later returned a $20,000 fee from Louis Wolfson, who at the time of the story's release had just gone to prison for illegal stock dealing. Investigative reporter William Lambert did not claim to have evidence that Fortas ever tried to fix a case for Wolfson, nor could he prove that Fortas ever sought to intervene for him with the Securities and Exchange Commission, where Wolfson's troubles began, or the Justice Department, which obtained separate indictments against him in September and October of 1966. Instead the story, which called the matter "A Question of Ethics," grounded its heaviest criticism on appearances. Wolfson and others had been dropping Fortas's name along with suggestions that the financier could extricate himself from his predicament by the use of influence. Suspiciously, the money had been paid in January and not returned until December, after the indictments. The article gave Fortas's side of the story—or as much of it as Fortas had been willing to divulge—including the justice's wish to help promote the charitable and civil rights causes espoused by Wolfson's foundation. But critically, Lambert pointed out that the $20,000 fee seemed "generous in the extreme" when compared with the foundation's total charitable outlay that year of $77,680. Much more information was called for on the kind of services Justice Fortas could render for this kind of money. Given Wolfson's reputation and the aura of wheeling and dealing previously generated by the American University fee, the unknown facts loomed larger than the known ones. Clearly, Fortas had much explaining to do.

Hindsight has caused some to wonder whether Fortas could have ridden out the storm by remaining silent, especially in view of the burden of proof placed on anyone inclined to prosecute or remove him from office. Such speculation often fails to recall the temper of the moment and the cascading demands for information. Unlike the fight of the previous autumn when Fortas had had the insuperable burden of mustering the confidence of

two-thirds of the Senate to bring the nomination for chief justice
to a vote, this time Fortas held title to the office in question and it
would be up to others to take it away from him. But the bare
claim of title was hardly enough for Fortas or any other member
of the highest court. The office had to be held legitimately. Thus
the ball was in Fortas's court even if no further damning facts
came to light—which they did.

Against this yardstick, the justice's reply was woefully inadequate. He denied having accepted "any fee or emolument" from
Wolfson. He said a fee was "tendered" but later returned with
thanks when he concluded that "I could not undertake the
assignment." No amount was specified nor were any dates given,
raising suspicions that perhaps more money and more damaging
facts were yet to be uncovered. Fortas denied communicating
with any official about Wolfson's SEC or criminal problems,
denied giving Wolfson any legal advice, and noted that he had
disqualified himself when Wolfson's case had reached the
Supreme Court.

The ensuing eleven days were punctuated with demands for a
more satisfactory statement, for his resignation, or for his
impeachment. Senators introduced legislation calling for public
disclosure of outside income by judges and justices. One bill,
offered by Senator Robert P. Griffin, the Michigan Republican
who had spearheaded the drive to block Fortas's elevation the
previous year, together with Senator Robert H. Taft, Jr., of Ohio,
ironically would not have caught the Wolfson fee, since Fortas
had returned it in the same tax year and thus had no reason to
report it as "income." The legislation went nowhere, but Fortas
critics advanced on other fronts. As Griffin and Taft made their
move, Attorney General John N. Mitchell was reported to have
held a secret meeting with Chief Justice Warren, who now was
within a month of final retirement.

Fortas gamely undertook to meet his speaking engagements
which had been made previously by a booking agent. At
Northeastern University in Boston he delivered a fairly set
speech on the generation gap and opened himself up to student
cross-examination—provided the audience did not ask about his
current predicament. No question was too tough, be it whether

the Court was "coddling criminals," whether America was turning its back on black citizens, whether Lyndon Johnson's establishment was responsible for the horrible Vietnam war—as long as the subject matter was confined to that of his address. Meekly, the supposedly rugged audience of thirteen hundred students, including a full complement of militant-looking anti-administration, antiwar demonstrators, obeyed the Fortas injunction. Whether or not they were disturbed about judicial ethics, the students vented their feelings only about the war. After resounding ovations Fortas darted from the auditorium into a waiting sedan.

Two days later he repeated the performance at a theater in Richmond, Virginia, with the same ground rules and the same compliance by a large audience. One man called out, "Honest Abe!" but Fortas probably did not hear it. He told the audience that today's young people had strong justification for feeling that society was "so shoddy, so corrupt, so shabby that it no longer deserves obedience." Then he went on to warn against violent protests that would only beget more violence.

On the following Monday, Chief Justice Warren confirmed that he and Mitchell had met. Mitchell issued a statement that he had passed "certain information" to Warren, a statement that seemed to portend further previously undisclosed and presumably more damaging information about Fortas. Although this mode of disclosure smacked of tactics designed to bluff Fortas off the Court, Mitchell undoubtedly did convey important information to Chief Justice Warren. By the time of their meeting, as Robert Shogan reconstructed events in his book *A Question of Judgment*, Mitchell knew that the Fortas-Wolfson arrangement was more than a one-time affair but in fact entailed a lifetime payment of $20,000 a year with the payment continuing to the justice's widow. Mitchell also knew that Wolfson had told federal agents that Fortas had discussed legal matters with him. Wolfson, by now a convicted felon, was not the world's most credible witness; but the damage to be done by his version of the story was unmistakable.

Fortas kept a speaking engagement in his native Memphis and, upon his return, conferred at his Georgetown home with

Justice Douglas, who had returned from a South American trip burdened with troubles of his own (referred to in the previous chapter) and who perhaps needed to confer with Mrs. Fortas about the Parvin Foundation's difficulties. On Tuesday evening, however, Fortas failed to appear at a scheduled dinner meeting of the federal judges of New England at Portsmouth, New Hampshire. It was the Judicial Conference of the First Circuit, and Fortas's duties included supervision of First Circuit business in the Supreme Court; but the embattled justice sent a law clerk with a speech on court backlogs, and speculation increased that his days on the Court were numbered.

Throughout Wednesday, May 14, concerned administration officials, still hoping for a resignation, labored with difficulty along with ranking members of Congress to prevent the filing of impeachment petitions and other lid-blowing documents. Late in the afternoon, while President Nixon was preparing to occupy center stage with a televised address on Vietnam, a letter arrived at the White House from Fortas, tendering his resignation. A second, longer letter of explanation was sent to the chief justice.

This explanation was hardly more satisfying than the statement issued eleven days earlier, but it did furnish new details. The $20,000, previously characterized as a "tendered" fee for an "assignment," was indeed the first installment under a lifetime annual payment arrangement that had been deemed preferable to "variable compensation"—both higher and lower—from time to time for work done. The "continuing services" on "a long-term basis" involved the expansion of the family foundation into new areas of social concern, a point Fortas may have made to answer the charge that the compensation seemed disproportionate to the foundation's activities. As if to answer any charge that he had given legal advice, Fortas acknowledged that he, like many other friends of the financier, had received unsolicited material about Wolfson's plight, but he emphatically denied interceding for him in any legal matter. In addition to the previously cited reason of the Supreme Court's work load, Fortas said he quit the foundation project because he had learned (he did not say how) that the SEC case against Wolfson had been advanced into the criminal realm. Once more swearing, "There has been no wrongdoing on my part," Fortas said his only desire was to relieve the Court's suffering. The document failed to answer many more questions, not the least being why Fortas had committed such an indiscretion and whether he had needed the money.

Despite its incompleteness, the Fortas letter was considered sufficiently informative by the American Bar Association's Committee on Professional Ethics to warrant the conclusion, announced within a week, that the former justice had acted "clearly contrary to the Canons of Judicial Ethics, even if he did not and never intended to intercede or take part in any legal, administrative or judicial matters affecting Mr. Wolfson." That quotation constituted the committee's entire judgment on the Fortas case. No discussion of the facts, no description of where Fortas crossed the line between propriety and impropriety, no specificity of any sort embellished the brief committee report, other than the recitation of eight of the canons drawn up in 1924, most of which intoned somewhere in their texts that the "appearance" of propriety must be safeguarded as well as propriety itself.

The committee, which was acting in response to demands for a judgment by Senator John J. Williams, Republican of Delaware, was of course correct as far as it went; Fortas *had* violated the cited canons. Curiously, however, the committee report seemed to arouse more dissatisfaction with the canons than it did over the committee's performance. But the trouble did not lie with the canons, quaint as their language and lofty as their principles might have been. The trouble lay with the committee's failure to use the facts as a vehicle for giving meaning to the generalities of the canons. Assuming that the ABA committee had a duty to answer Senator Williams's inquiry—a question that was much debated within the organized bar itself—it then became the committee's task to apply the canons' principles to the specific facts before it.

Much of the admitted vagueness of the "appearance of justice" standard could be cured if the judges of ethics would specify in their opinions just what it is about a judge's questioned conduct that looks bad. Each opinion might then give added content to

the standard. In the Fortas case, for example, the ABA committee might easily have declared that long-term contracts for
outside compensation are unseemly because a Supreme Court
justice should know in advance that he could never have time to
do $20,000 worth of work in a year even for the worthiest of
causes. Or the committee could have said that even a legitimate
arrangement becomes tainted once the benefactor brings his
legal problems to the attention of a judicial officer of Fortas's
rank. Or the committee could have stated that disqualifying
oneself in any Wolfson-type case is not a cure for every ethical
problem. Or it might have explained, or at least articulated, its
implicit decision that "appearances" are violated even when
arrangements are secret. Clearly, judges must be made aware, if
they do not know, that the test is, and has to be, "How would it
look if made public?"

A word about the role of the Justice Department is in order in
view of the widespread belief that its pursuit of Justice Fortas
was politically motivated. Unquestionably, Attorney General
Mitchell and others in the Nixon administration relished the
chance to exploit Fortas's embarrassment. At the same time,
however, it seems clear that many of these officials sincerely
believed that Fortas was guilty of impropriety and were genu-
inely surprised when days passed without his resignation. Furthermore, it was perfectly proper for Mitchell to call upon the
chief justice if he had relevant information. The Justice Department is required to be lawyerlike and discreet in handling such
matters, but neither executive officials nor private citizens have
any obligation to act so judiciously that they take it upon
themselves to withhold information from the courts. Finally, even
if the Nixon administration was malicious, the hazard of
disclosures animated by malice has its healthy aspects. Judges
and justices ordinarily have an absolute shield against this kind
of attack: they can avoid the appearance of impropriety.

☆

By the time Clement F. Haynsworth, Jr., was nominated in
August 1969 to succeed Fortas, the Senate and public had been
conditioned for ethical strife. Swiftly after Fortas's resignation,

Warren E. Burger was nominated and confirmed for the vacancy created by Earl Warren's retirement. Before leaving, Warren staged a home-stretch drive to clean the judiciary's own house. The ABA launched its study and overhaul of the bar's own code of ethics for judges, and the rules were in flux. The setting of the Haynsworth confirmation of that autumn was ideal for battle over ethics if the interested parties were so inclined—and they were. The raw material for the controversy was unearthed chiefly by a coalition of civil rights and labor interests who with their lawyers were anxious to halt the execution of the Nixon administration's "Southern Strategy."

The administration took three months to settle on a replacement for Fortas and actually to place his name in nomination. There seemed to be no necessity for speed and plenty of time to let the confirmation process run its course before the opening of the Court's new term in October. Burger's nomination had sailed through in three weeks' time. These were months during which President Nixon was preoccupied with such matters as a trip to Asia and Romania. They were also months of rapidly increasing concern among civil rights advocates that the political strategy of the 1968 campaign was gaining its foothold in administration policy. The president was proposing a slowdown of school desegregation and he seemed to be keeping his pledge to appoint jurists who would do their part to implement that slowdown. Liberal young lawyers within the Justice Department's Civil Rights Division seethed at what they considered sellouts by their politically minded superiors, and their dissatisfaction spilled over into the open revolt of unauthorized protest meetings.

Throughout these months, Clement Haynsworth was widely considered the front-runner for the Supreme Court vacancy. The delay in nominating him provided time for civil rights groups to grumble about Haynsworth's votes in the racial discrimination cases that had come before the Fourth U.S. Circuit Court of Appeals, time to ponder whether the nominee's philosophy could be used against him, and time for organized labor to consider whether its bitterness over some of Haynsworth's decisions should mature into a campaign to block his confirmation.

In the few days before the nomination, labor leaders com-

plained quietly, then publicly, that Haynsworth had committed
a breach of ethics while sitting in judgment of one of organized
labor's most significant court cases. The case was the Fourth
Circuit's 1963 decision in favor of the Deering Milliken textile
conglomerate and against the Textile Workers Union of America
(AFL-CIO). Haynsworth had cast a deciding vote in the
appellate court's three to two ruling that a Deering subsidiary,
Darlington Mills, had a right to go out of business rather than
deal with a union attempting to organize the workers in the
North Carolina plant. Less than two years later the Supreme
Court reversed the decision. The Court agreed that Deering, the
parent company, had a right to go out of business altogether but
said it would be a violation of labor law for Deering to drop *part*
of its business, its Darlington subsidiary, to chill unionism. The
case was sent back to give the union and the National Labor
Relations Board a chance to develop evidence on the issue that
now was more carefully defined.

The initial ethical charge against Haynsworth was that, while
a judge in the Deering-Darlington case, he owned stock in a
concern called Carolina Vend-A-Matic, which installed and
serviced vending machines in Deering plants to the tune of about
$50,000 worth of business annually and doubled that volume
during the time of the litigation. The charge, then, was that
Haynsworth had had an undisclosed financial interest that
required his disqualification, but he sat in the case anyway to the
great prejudice of one of the parties. It was an accusation of
judicial conflict of interest. A far more serious charge, bribery,
had been suggested and refuted in 1963, and Haynsworth's
supporters quarreled with his detractors over whether the ethical
question had been raised and resolved along with the criminal
question in that year. The gravamen of the bribery charge was
that the textile manufacturer had thrown business to Vend-A-
Matic as a quid pro quo for his favorable vote. Attorney General
Robert F. Kennedy had the matter investigated at the time and
had put in writing that he had "complete confidence in Judge
Haynsworth," which the Nixon Justice Department took for total
absolution ethically as well as criminally—a judgment that may

have reflected Mr. Nixon's and Attorney General Mitchell's unawareness of the latent potential of the ethical issue.

Although evidence both for and against Haynsworth was emerging in tiny daily increments, it seemed at the outset that nothing could stand in the way of confirmation for long. Three more weeks passed before the scheduled opening of Senate hearings, and this stretched into a fourth because of the death of Senate Republican leader Everett M. Dirksen of Illinois. The passing of Dirksen, a supporter, was one of the many events whose significance for the Haynsworth fight could be appreciated only after the battle was over.

The Justice Department and Haynsworth's Senate backers advanced the argument that the nominee was not disqualified from the case because his stock ownership was not in a party to the lawsuit—hence he had no direct financial interest in the outcome of the *case*—but was instead a third-party, remote interest at most. Under doctrines adopted by judges over the years, Haynsworth not only had no duty to abstain from taking part in the case, he had a "duty to sit" and do his part as a functioning member of a multijudge court.

The doctrine that a judge has a "duty to sit" unless he is clearly disqualified was developed over the decades in several federal courts by judges who deemed it their obligation to preside over cases where the issue of disqualification was unclear. Opposed to the "duty" doctrine is the school of thought that marginal cases provoke some unseemly situations in which a judge would do more for public confidence in the judiciary by not sitting. Federal judges in several areas of the country interpreted the congressional disqualification law to embody a "duty to sit," while the ABA Canons of Judicial Ethics counseled greater use of disqualification to avoid the "appearance" of impropriety. In the view of some, the duty doctrine is an important antidote for the notorious tendency of some judges to recuse themselves for little or no cause and thus avoid hard or complicated cases.

The basic federal law on disqualification dated from 1911 and had been amended in 1948 to include in its coverage Supreme

Court justices as well as lower federal judges. It read, "Any justice or judge of the United States shall disqualify himself in any case in which he has a substantial interest, has been of counsel, is or has been a material witness, or is so related to or connected with any party or his attorney as to render it improper, in his opinion, for him to sit on the trial, or appeal, or other proceeding therein." Quite naturally, Haynsworth supporters eventually took the view that the statute must be understood in the light of the "duty to sit" doctrine that judges had engrafted upon it, while opponents took the position that the ethical consideration of the "appearance" of impartiality should have governed Judge Haynsworth's interpretation of his duties under the law.

The "duty to sit" argument was advanced by Assistant Attorney General William H. Rehnquist in a legal memorandum adopted by the nominee's supporters in the Senate. As Rehnquist was to admit when his turn came to undergo confirmation hearings for the High Court, both he and his lawyer colleagues overlooked the latest Supreme Court pronouncement on the subject, a decision rendered in November 1968 in a case called *Commonwealth Coatings Corp.* v. *Continental Casualty Co.* Indeed, a large segment of the legal profession probably missed the significance of the case at first, since it was the result of a dispute in the relatively specialized legal field of contract arbitration. The losing party in an arbitration proceeding was contesting the fairness of the arbitrator's award to his opponent. Despite the narrowness of the question if one looked only at the surface of things, the Supreme Court's six to three majority, in an opinion by Justice Hugo L. Black, deemed it a question of what "strict morality and fairness" required in any adjudicatory proceeding. "At issue in this case," said Black, "is the question whether elementary requirements of impartiality taken for granted in every judicial proceeding are suspended when the parties agree to resolve a dispute through arbitration." The answer in this case: Citing a rule of arbitration and canon 33 of the American Bar Association's judicial ethics and reading them together, it was clear that tribunals who have the right to try cases "not only must be unbiased but also must avoid even the appearance of bias." As a result, there was a duty on the part of the arbitrator to disclose to one side a close business connection he had had with the opposing party, and failure to do so would authorize a court to set aside the award under the federal arbitration law as an award "procured by . . . undue means" or "where there was evident partiality . . . in the arbitrators"—this despite the total absence of any claim of *actual* bias on the arbitrator's part. Justice Fortas, in one of his last recorded dissents, was joined by Justices Harlan and Potter Stewart in the minority opinion. To them, evidence of an undisclosed business relationship could be used to show actual bias, but only proven bias—not apparent bias—should disqualify the arbitrator. The dissenters feared that "insistence upon set formulae and rules" would hamstring the "essentially consensual and practical process of settling contract disputes without formal litigation." Perhaps most significantly, the dissenters made no objection to the majority's references to judicial ethical standards. Their objection was precisely that the Court was imposing stricter rules that previously had been "applicable to judges" only.

Failure to cite the Supreme Court's latest pronouncement on ethics, though an inadvertence, was not one of those technical omissions of concern only to hairsplitting lawyers. It was a major deficiency from which, on the legal side of the controversy, the administration never completely recovered. One reason for this was that failure to cite the case meant failure to address it directly with arguments attempting to minimize its significance or relevance. It was not the kind of legal precedent that could be addressed indirectly or, as some late-filed memoranda sought to do, in an inserted footnote. Even without this embarrassing handicap it is doubtful whether a convincing argument was available to overcome the significance of this case. Although its legal holding was pinned to the federal arbitration laws, it spoke in broad terms commonly associated with due process of law. When Justice Black sought analogies to explain the ruling, he relied on *Tumey* v. *Ohio*, the 1927 decision discussed in the opening pages of this book which stated that the justice of the peace could not, under the U.S. Constitution, decide a case if he had the "slightest pecuniary interest" in its outcome; part of that judge's earnings were from court fees collected from convicted defendants. The most devastating feature of the *Commonwealth Coatings* decision for Haynsworth's supporters was the way it *assumed* the need for disclosure and totally negated any "duty to sit" in the absence of such disclosure.

As noted in chapter 1 in connection with the 1968 confirmation fight over Abe Fortas, the Senate Judiciary Committee can be a rough place for a High Court nominee if circumstances combine against him. The committee members did not show Haynsworth the discourtesy that had been shown Fortas, but opponents were unquestionably searching for the nominee's weakness when he appeared as his own opening witness.

An important element in the Haynsworth hearings was the Judiciary Committee's practice, which had become commonplace by 1969, of requiring generous financial disclosure by nominees. Often in the past, potential opponents would have had a more difficult time justifying demands for listings of personal investments, debts, and other items of income and net worth. Particularly after Fortas, however, a senator's inquiry could be made without necessarily impugning the integrity of the nominee, amply justified as it was by the need to carry out conscientiously the Senate's duty of advising and consenting. The nominee, for his part, could only comply with the disclosure request, even if he were not so inclined, expressing all the while his earnest desire to be completely candid with the Senate. The charges of organized labor could be investigated by senators who, though inclined to oppose the nominee, could probe deeply and at length before it became necessary to take a position on the merits of the case. Senator Birch Bayh of Indiana, who led the opposing bloc of northern Democrats, was able to carry on his investigation and cross-examination of Haynsworth under the banner of an inquiry into what the ethical standards for the judiciary should be in the 1970s.

Although it was charged that Haynsworth's political opposition was motivated in part by a desire to get "revenge" for Abe Fortas, evidence of this was virtually impossible to detect, particularly in the sense of personal revenge. Fortas had engendered little personal loyalty but had rather become a burden to politicians of similar philosophical persuasion.

Before Haynsworth could utter a word, his financial matters were made a part of the committee record along with testimonials and memoranda pro and con. His principal Senate sponsor, Ernest H. Hollings, Democrat of South Carolina, lamented that weeks of investigation by "special interests" made possible by delay had meant that when the president finally submitted the nomination, "there was an eerie feeling that perhaps he had been indicted rather than appointed."

Indeed, little time was devoted to praise. And while the political and ethical landscape had changed, Haynsworth, cross-examined at length over several days, emphatically stated that to him at least the ethical situation in 1963 was the same as in 1969—that is, neither then nor later did it occur to him that any proprieties had been slighted. He had no consciousness of any business relation between Vend-A-Matic and any Deering Milliken subsidiary and he saw no impropriety in continuing to hold $24,000 worth of stock in another textile giant, J. P. Stevens Co. The judge was supported by John P. Frank, a Phoenix attorney who was a student of the Court and a prolific writer on major legal subjects. Frank's 1947 *Yale Law Journal* article about judicial disqualification appeared to qualify him amply to give an expert opinion on that subject, which had few experts. Chairman Lawrence E. Walsh of the American Bar Association's Judiciary Committee defended the nominee on ethics and across the board. Labor witnesses, led by AFL-CIO president George Meany, attacked the judge as antilabor, anti–civil rights, and unethical. Senator Sam J. Ervin, Jr., of North Carolina, who had taken part in the Supreme Court's oral argument in the Darlington case, went to great lengths to defend Haynsworth only to have Meany question the senator's own objectivity in light of his textile constituency and his refusal to say how much the industry paid him to argue its case. Questioning Ervin's ethics, said the senator, "is the funniest thing I ever heard since Bud Fisher began drawing Jeff and Mutt." Another Haynsworth defender, attorney John Bolt Culbertson of Greenville, told the

committee, "You do not do business and make a living in
Greenville, South Carolina, unless some way you are connected
with the textile trade."

As a week of hearings drew to a close, opponents had amassed
a respectable though hardly airtight case against Haynsworth's
ethics. Strong opinions on both sides did not resolve the
Darlington issue. For all the magnitude of the case in the eyes of
the participants, the ethical issue could be dismissed on rather
technical grounds if one chose to do so: whatever the judge's
interest, it was not a direct financial stake in the manufacturer.

Then came an odd and perhaps decisive development. Over
the weekend, the Justice Department disclosed what both friends
and foes in the Senate were already discovering, that Haynsworth had sat in a case and simultaneously owned $16,000 worth
of stock in one of the litigants. It was possible to argue, as
Assistant Attorney General Rehnquist promptly did, that the
judge could not hope to gain financially from the decision he
helped render in favor of the Brunswick Corporation, the
nation's largest supplier of bowling alley and pinsetting equipment; but it was not possible to argue that the judge had not
violated the federal disqualification statute, which commanded
that "any justice or judge of the United States shall disqualify
himself in any case in which he has a substantial interest."
However the law was interpreted, it could not be read as
dismissing $16,000 worth of ownership in a company as an
insubstantial interest in that company's case.

Haynsworth and two other appellate judges were assigned in
October 1967 to hear the company's appeal from an adverse
decision in a lower court over Brunswick's right to repossess
bowling equipment from a failing bowling alley operator. It was
a contest with the operator's landlord and, as a case that comes
into federal court because the parties are from different states,
the outcome turned on a relatively arcane point of South
Carolina law, which governed the case. The three judges had no
difficulty deciding the case in Brunswick's favor after hearing the
oral argument in November, and the opinion writing was
assigned to Judge Harrison Winter of Baltimore. At this point
Haynsworth did not own any Brunswick stock.

But in December, acting on his stock adviser's suggestion, the judge purchased a thousand shares of Brunswick, vaguely conscious of the litigation but unaware, he said later, that the decision had not been announced. Seven days after the transaction, Judge Winter's draft opinion was circulated. Judge Haynsworth transmitted a few suggested changes, and in February 1968 the final decision was released. The losing party belatedly petitioned for a rehearing, a move that is rarely successful and was not in this case. The judge, still owning the stock and not disclosing this fact to his brethren, technically continued to participate in the case until the court's last order was issued in August 1968. During that time voluminous correspondence and legal paperwork had accumulated and the judges, individually or collectively, repeatedly labeled as overdue and frivolous some of the contentions of the losing party.

Understandably, the Justice Department contended that the case had been "substantively decided" at the time of the stock purchase. Opponents predictably replied that all judges know that cases are not over until decisions are actually rendered publicly, because the court's internal deliberative processes could produce and occasionally do produce different answers from the initial tentative votes. Less stress was laid on the months consumed in finally issuing a denial of a rehearing, except as that elapsed time bore on the possibility that Haynsworth's awakened consciousness of the stock ownership might induce him to notify his colleagues—or at least get rid of the stock.

Suddenly it seemed that a critical mass of evidence on ethics had been gathered from the joining of the unarguable violation, the Brunswick case, with the arguable one, the textile case. But Haynsworth, recalled to the stand, explained that his consciousness was triggered by the circulation of the draft opinion, by which time the case seemed so "easy" that getting out would be a waste of judges' and lawyers' time. He told the committee he was "very sorry" and indicated that he now had a system of checking cases against his portfolio to avoid such occurrences. That seemed to quiet matters, but such men as Senator Williams of Delaware, respected in the Senate for his strict construction of official ethics, was changing his mind, and Senator Griffin was in the process of defecting to the opponents at the very time he was succeeding to the Republican leadership post of Senate minority whip. *The Washington Post*, which had defended Fortas during his 1968 confirmation hearings, editorialized on September 29 that Haynsworth, like Fortas, had acted in a "misguided" fashion but was not disqualified for confirmation. But in the same pages Herblock, the political cartoonist, lampooned the judge as a hapless and disorganized fool astride a vending machine labeled "Vend-A-Justice" and being wheeled up to the Supreme Court by Attorney General Mitchell, President Nixon, Chairman Eastland, and Senator Strom Thurmond of South Carolina. Indeed, there seemed to be no doubt that Haynsworth was disorganized by this time. Bayh made requests, deemed reasonable by Chairman Eastland and the committee, for more detailed financial information, and a final committee vote to clear the nomination for the floor was delayed by Haynsworth's own inability to provide the information promptly. The burden had so shifted to Haynsworth that each day that passed without satisfactory disclosure heightened the embarrassment of his supporters. Even sympathetic senators found themselves unable to make a commitment to Haynsworth, in part because the nominee and his supporters were unable to give assurances that no further conflicts of interest would emerge. The nominee offered to put his holdings beyond his control to avoid future conflict of interest problems, regardless of whether he was confirmed for the Supreme Court; but his elaborating statements indicated that he considered such a step unnecessary except to appease his critics, inasmuch as he remained certain that he had committed no impropriety.

Disarray among Haynsworth's supporters continued well past the surprisingly close ten to seven vote, on October 9, to clear the nomination for floor action. Bayh was accused of reckless exaggeration in his catalog of alleged conflicts of interest, but the senator was able to reply without serious contradiction that failure of the nominee to furnish adequate information had frustrated the task of compiling his bill of particulars. There was some justice in the complaints of exaggeration, but they had a ring of self-pity that did not help the morale of supporters.

Among the dissenters within the committee was Senator Charles McC. Mathias, Republican of Maryland, who pointed to the previously undisclosed fact that the ABA's Judiciary Committee, which had supported the nominee during the hearings, was going to meet again to reconsider Haynsworth. It did meet and reaffirmed its confidence in Haynsworth, but Mathias remained opposed. Senator Williams of Delaware withheld announcement of his intention to vote against Haynsworth as a special courtesy to the White House, but like most of the uncommitted senators he was opposed to confirmation. The floor vote on November 20 was fifty-five to forty-five against confirmation.

Was the ethical judgment on Haynsworth fair? This question divides people years later as deeply as it did during the battle. The answer, as usual, turns significantly on how the ethical issue is framed; but the answer must be sought if only because of the need to ascertain whether the correct ethical standard is being applied for the present and future. The Nixon administration felt deeply that an injustice had been done to its nominee, and this feeling remained firm even among those who conceded that the successor nominee, G. Harrold Carswell, was, as the Senate held, unqualified. Many a middle-of-the-roader and liberal has said in one form or another, in light of the subsequent Carswell nomination, "We were too hard on Haynsworth, we should have settled for Haynsworth." The nominee's own courage in the face of defeat won him deep sympathy from opponents, and his continuing dedication to the law in subsequent years won him still more admirers. But unfortunately or otherwise the evidence compels the conclusion that ethical principles were sufficiently violated to justify denying Haynsworth promotion to the Supreme Court. Promotion, after all, was the question; not whether the judge should be retained on the bench. With the burden properly located on the candidate, in the context of the ethical situation of the moment, Haynsworth was wrong in every significant dimension of the problem.

The Darlington case was not just an important one. It was the major labor case of a decade, a widely advertised test of management and union power that all sides understood might control the entire industrial pattern of the South, where textile

manufacturers had fled in great numbers largely to save money
on wages and where organized labor was asserting the right to
organize. If the Darlington plant could be shut down by a
company that chose this route rather than submit to unionism,
the writing would be on the wall for all to see, the unions and
those who were thinking of joining unions. The stakes for
management, textile and other, were just as high. As the
companies framed it, the issue was whether things had gone so
far in this country that a businessman could not even liquidate
without permission from Big Labor. The question could be posed
and decided on a less extreme basis, and in fact it was by the
Supreme Court. In its decision the highest court acknowledged
the right to go out of business altogether, but not selectively to
defeat legitimate labor organization efforts. To decide fairly
either the ultimate issue of management prerogative that seemed
to be there, or the narrower issue that the Supreme Court
perceived, demanded the utmost in judicial sensitivity, competence, and disinterestedness.

Haynsworth failed to recognize that he was "interested" in the
Darlington case by reason of his stock holdings and his personal
business ventures. Despite the admonition of canon 26 of the
1924 ABA judicial code, he persisted in holding his stock in J. P.
Stevens, in the eyes of labor one of the worst labor criminals in
the South and a company that shared with Darlington a deep
concern with the Darlington result. The canon forbade ownership of stock in companies apt to come before the judge's court in
litigation, and Stevens was famous for the frequency with which
it was in court resisting the National Labor Relations Board and
the unions. Haynsworth justified retention of his Stevens stock on
grounds that as a former counsel (though not labor counsel) to
Stevens in South Carolina, he could never sit in a Stevens case.
The Senate Judiciary Committee's majority agreed with Haynsworth that the canon's purpose was to avoid the necessity of
frequent disqualification and that the judge need not obey the
canon because he was already disqualified. Opponents queried,
with reason, why an extra disqualification relieved the judge of
the burden of compliance. In addition, one must wonder whether
the canon might not have had a broader purpose as well as the

obvious one of limiting disqualifications—that is, to obviate an unseemly situation in which the chief judge of a circuit could invest so heavily in one of the major industries of his state and jurisdiction.

The Judiciary Committee majority report, which means ordinarily the Justice Department's legal brief to the extent that the committee majority agrees with it, minimized every aspect of the Darlington controversy. The skeleton of its argument was simply that whatever Haynsworth's interest may have been in Vend-A-Matic, it was not an interest in Deering Milliken or its Darlington subsidiary, neither of which had vending contracts with Vend-A-Matic.

Putting flesh on the bones, however, yields an analysis that is radically different in tone and substance. First, Haynsworth's interest in Vend-A-Matic was extensive. He was a founder, officer, director, and one-seventh owner at the relevant periods of time. (Opponents from organized labor claimed that even when questions were raised in 1963, Haynsworth disclosed only his officership and directorship, not his ownership.) The judge's stake in the vending company was increasing dramatically in these years, growing from an initial $2,500 outlay to an interest worth $450,000, or about half his personal wealth, when he sold it in 1964. Although he said his duties as director were nominal, he was paid $12,270 in director's fees between 1957 and 1963. The judge said he resigned as vice-president in 1957, but corporation records listed him in that post until 1963. His wife was secretary of the corporation in 1962 and 1963. When the enterprise was struggling, Judge Haynsworth endorsed between $300,000 and $500,000 worth of bank notes to help obtain credit the company could not have achieved on its own.

The corporation could be said—and was said—to have done only 3 percent of its business with the Deering Milliken combine and none in the Darlington plant. But put another way, the company doubled to $100,000 its annual business with Deering while the case was in the court of appeals. The vending company did most of its business with more than three dozen textile plants, virtually all of which were nonunion. It was said that vending machines were placed at industrial sites on the basis of competitive bidding, but the corporation also deemed business getting the kind of duty that would justify director's fees, according to company documents. Locally in Greenville, Haynsworth had the reputation of a lawyer who had been instrumental in relocating northern industry in his state.

In addition, one must consider Judge Haynsworth's total lack of apparatus for determining for himself when an ethical question existed. Although he had an active portfolio with frequent purchases and sales, the *Brunswick* case showed that Haynsworth gave no instructions to his broker, who was a longtime friend, as to whether there were any stocks that might well not be recommended. Nor apparently was there even the most rudimentary system with secretary or clerk to match incoming cases with stock in his portfolio. Haynsworth, tragically, never equipped himself to deal with conflicts of interest, apparently because he felt secure in his own sense of rectitude.

Finally, what is one to do with Judge Haynsworth's lack of insight into the entire problem? Except for the admitted lapse in the purchase of Brunswick stock, he was unwilling even to acknowledge that his future policy should be significantly different from the past because of the evolution of judicial ethics. Perhaps by merely uttering a vow to adapt to current standards, Judge Haynsworth would have been Mr. Justice Haynsworth. To his credit, he did not utter any magic words that he did not believe, but it is unfortunate that he did not believe them.

☆

Quite another set of facts came to light when the Senate set about confirming Harry A. Blackmun of the Eighth U. S. Circuit Court of Appeals for the highest court. (The intervening Carswell fight raised little in the way of conflicts of interest, partly because that judge was in debt and owned no stocks.) One could say, and many did say, that Blackmun received kid glove treatment because he was not the victim of regional prejudice. Senator Hollings supported Blackmun's elevation but lamented on the Senate floor that he and Haynsworth were no different on "fundamentals" with regard to ethics. Critics of both nominations expressed the same sentiments. Undoubtedly instructed by the revelations of chaotic methods that contributed to the ruination of the Haynsworth and Carswell nominations, Blackmun and the Justice Department quickly volunteered that the judge had participated in four cases in which he held stock in a corporate party. None of them involved anything close to the public importance of the Darlington labor case. While in the opinion of most observers—and apparently in the opinion of Judge Blackmun himself—he should not have sat in the cases, there were not the multiple reasons for disqualification suggested by the many-faceted *Darlington* case.

Critically different, as Blackmun presented the history of the conflicts to the Senate, was the judge's own attitude: he had reluctantly joined his fellow judges in the practice of sitting in cases of so-called insubstantial stock holdings in a party—with the major proviso that the jurists at least disclose their interests to each other—and he was happy to acknowledge that in any event it was time to adjust to a new, stricter standard. Although any well-coached witness would have been astute enough to acknowledge, as Haynsworth had steadfastly refused to do, that "times have changed," Blackmun's sincerity was unquestioned. His strict attitude toward ethics had been widely known among federal judges and his confirmation testimony was corroborated.

Blackmun owned fifty shares of Ford stock when he joined the Eighth Circuit for his first session in November 1959. Noticing that he had been assigned to hear a case involving a Ford dealership, he raised questions of ethical policy with Chief Judge Harvey Johnsen, and with senior Judge John B. Sanborn, the respected legal mentor for whom he had been law clerk and whose seat Blackmun was assuming on the appellate court, which embraces the states from Minnesota to Arkansas in the country's midsection. Blackmun testified: "Chief Judge Johnsen advised me at the time that my holding of Ford was so small that I should not disrupt the court's calendar by disqualifying. In fact, he gave me a lecture about the integrity of the court and the fact that I as a junior was to act as a judge and not as somebody who is supersensitive to some of these outside influences."

Senator Bayh then surveyed recent developments in ethics, including Justice Black's opinion in the *Commonwealth Coatings* case, and asked whether the disqualification statute should not be interpreted as removing a judge for any stock interest in a party. The nominee replied that whatever he might rule as a member of a court in a specific case, "as applied to me of later years, I hope, and in the future, I most sincerely hope, I would interpret it as you have just described it. . . . For me, I repeat, your description is the applicable standard."

Said Bayh, "I would like to see the country or the Supreme Court or all judges adopt the Blackmun standard."

Though still unreconciled to the defeat of Haynsworth, the Justice Department supported Blackmun in his view of ethical standards, including the judge's decision to recuse himself when another Ford case had come his way a few months earlier in February 1970. Deputy Attorney General Richard G. Kleindienst wrote the Judiciary Committee that

the intervening Senate debate over the confirmation of Judge Haynsworth had focused critical attention on the language of the statute, the provisions of the applicable Canons of Ethics, and the interrelationship between the two. The vote by a majority of the Senate to refuse to advise and consent to the Haynsworth nomination could fairly be deemed an interpretation of the relevant provisions regarding disqualification which suggested a stricter standard than had obtained previously.

As Blackmun told the same Senate committee, "I think, Senator Kennedy, the times have changed. . . . I think the times have changed a great deal in the past 5 years and I would not say for the worse by any means."

4

☆ ☆ ☆

THE VELVET BLACKJACK

"Now, I know, for example, Judge Hand, I think everybody who
has ever practiced in New York knows that he had 25 shares of
Westinghouse stock and he would start off by telling the attorneys that
he had that investment. He would always sit because no one would
want to give [up] Judge Hand's participation in a case because he had
25 shares of Westinghouse stock. But there is a problem there. . . .

Lawrence E. Walsh, testifying for the American
Bar Association at Haynsworth confirmation
hearings, 1969

Many of the conflicts of interest among judges in the
courts of the United States are perpetrated with the cooperation,
active or passive, of lawyers. Active connivance between a lawyer
and judge to purchase a judgment is criminal and since it is not
amenable to prevention or cure by elevating ethical standards, it
will not much concern us here. The passive variety, which often
implicates judge and lawyer in a coercive relationship, is far
more common, far more subtle, and much more difficult to
manage, for it often does not entail purposeful evil but rather
winking at violations of the legal rules. Tolerance of judicial
conflicts of interest can be one of the breeding conditions for
out-and-out corruption. Short of that, it fosters an atmosphere of
permissiveness in which it becomes harder and harder for jurist
and counsel even to recognize the existence of conflicts of interest.

Typically, the problem manifests itself when a judge is assigned to a case in which he has an interest, clear or not so clear, financial or other, in some party or issue involved and when counsel is aware or is made aware of that interest. A judge may, for example, announce in open court that he owns two hundred shares of XYZ stock, appreciating that the case involves XYZ Corporation. Does counsel object? "I'm sure," replies prudent counsel for the party opposing XYZ, "that if anything Your Honor would lean over backwards to be fair to my client, and of course I have complete confidence in Your Honor. We do not object." His opponent, counsel for XYZ, would be the last to object, unless he saw certain reversal ahead in a higher court. So the disqualified judge sits.

What alternatives are open to counsel? He must know his judge and be sure that registering an objection will not put him or his client at a disadvantage in the case before His Honor—and the next case, and the case after that. On paper, each judge is subject to some higher court review, but as a practical matter, the judge who acquires an aversion to certain counsel can destroy the lawyer's effectiveness in countless unreviewable ways. Simple matters such as continuances, the privilege of filing a slightly late brief, such courtesies of the courtroom as a full oral hearing—all these and many more amenities are sometimes unavailable to the attorney who is in disfavor with the court. The dilemma for the lawyer from out of town is no less acute though he may never have to face the same judge again. More likely than not he is able to appear at all only by the court's indulgence and must associate himself with local counsel whose own relationship with the judge could be jeopardized by any excessive zeal on the part of the visiting lawyer. Counsel must of course weigh the advantages and disadvantages of further delay in his case caused by a reassignment to another judge and also the imponderables of who that successor judge might be. Counsel must consider all this very rapidly and respond without hesitation, for the magistrate is there calling for an immediate answer on the suggested or implied waiver of his technical disqualification. The judge need not be imperious in his inquiry, if indeed he states it as an inquiry at all. He may phrase it in the gentlest possible way. Thus it is with reason that John P. Frank, one of the few longtime students of judicial ethics, described the waiver phenomenon as "nothing more than a velvet blackjack."

Essentially, the Velvet Blackjack is a game based on assumed relationships of mutual confidence; it is, in other words, a species of confidence game. In the typical confidence game, the perpetrator engages his victim in a joint venture that requires the brief loan of the victim's treasure; the critical point in the transaction is when the intended victim has to decide—usually quickly, in a fluid situation—whether to surrender his valuables ever so briefly in the interest of acquiring something more valuable. The victim must decide not only whether to repose his trust in the individual, but more humanly wrenching, he must weigh the consequences of betraying apparent distrust and the risks of offending the other party. When the other party is a black-robed judge and the decision falls upon the lawyer, there is an extra dimension of human difficulty: the technical vulnerability of the judge. By putting a waiver question before counsel, he is admitting some vulnerability and asking counsel to concur in his judgment that it is insubstantial. Something more than what the law calls "the presumption of regularity"—the common understanding that duly qualified officials always do right—is invoked. Lawyers could tolerate the Velvet Blackjack if it was wielded, as it was for years, by the revered Judge Learned Hand in the manner described at the head of this chapter. But the ordinary lawyer with the ordinary judge, while he is anything but happy to be governed by such a practice, may have no choice.

The logistical problem of reassigning a case weighs heavily on the courts and their judges as well as counsel, perhaps more heavily than it should. Solicitude is often expressed for the isolated rural judge who has no available substitute within several hundred miles and whose willingness to sit may earn him the gratitude of all parties concerned. One must conclude that the concept and practice of waiver developed informally, inasmuch as the American Bar Association's 1924 ethical canons made no provision for it. The draftsmen would hardly have omitted mention of any widespread practice, had there been one, governing the mode of disqualification and waiver. Some states, for example New York and California, provided for disqualification and waiver in their legal codes; but however the practice grew, it did grow, and one of the consequences was that it helped to mask the criteria for determining whether or not a judge is disqualified. The ABA committee that revised the canons between 1969 and 1972 devised a waiver procedure, modified it, and got the bar to adopt it as part of the updated Code of Judicial Conduct. Legislation introduced by Senator Birch Bayh and passed by the Senate in 1973, opposed the waiver idea on grounds that the judge must not be relieved of responsibility under so dubious a procedure as the waiver with its coercion potential.

As already indicated and as will be illustrated more fully by a few case histories, the problem is not merely technical, though technical rules must be considered to cope with it, because sensitivities and professional careers may depend upon how it is solved. Three or four examples may illuminate the problem. The first, involving a bankruptcy in Tennessee, shows how more than a dozen lawyers can rally to ratify a judge's participation in a case in the face of ethical charges. Bar support for criticized judges is a commendable and even desired quality—required, in fact, by the Canons of Professional Ethics—but the episode shows that the adversary system alone will not necessarily flush out the conflicts of interest. The second case is in similar vein, a bankruptcy action in Oklahoma; but the lurking ethical issues were surfaced by some out-of-state lawyers whose complaints resulted in a reordering of the many lawsuits involved. It shows how deeply lawyers can become entangled in demoralizing ethical contradictions until they are questioned from an outside source. The third and fourth cases illustrate how some of the world's indisputably finest jurists, members of the Fifth U.S. Circuit Court of Appeals, can become mired in financial matters involving two of the circuit's resident industries, oil and gas, to the detriment of important consumer interests, the injury of private individuals, and the embarrassment of all.

☆

The Tennessee bankruptcy controversy first came to national attention on October 20, 1970, when the *Wall Street Journal* published a front-page story under these headlines:

A Question of Ethics
Federal Judge Presides
Over a Case Related
To His Own Fortune

Friend Who Made Him Rich Is
Involved, as Well as Bank
In Which He Holds Shares

But He Sees No Conflicts

The story questioned whether Judge Frank Gray, Jr., of the federal district court in Nashville should have presided, and continued to preside, in a major bankruptcy proceeding involving a company called Whale, Inc. The ethical questions were twofold. First, Judge Gray had prospered enormously from a favor done him while on the bench by a member of the bar, John Jay Hooker, Jr., prominent attorney and erstwhile candidate for political office, whose interests were heavily at stake in the bankruptcy proceedings. In addition, the judge's brother was a vice-president and the judge himself a stockholder of Third National Bank, a major creditor in the case. The article related that Judge Gray, with Hooker's aid, had been allowed to invest $2,000 in a Hooker enterprise later called Minnie Pearl's Chicken System Inc. and still later called Performance Systems Inc. before shares in the venture became generally available to the public. Staff reporter Jim Montgomery calculated that the judge made a profit of at least $100,000 and possibly close to $200,000 when he sold the high-flying stock before it came plummeting down. The judge was one of more than a hundred specially privileged investors.

In bankruptcy and court-supervised corporate reorganization, two factors among others are always quite critical. One is the wide range of discretion conferred by law on the district judge to decide whether a business enterprise, though failing, can be salvaged and whether the salvage attempt should be made. If the business is permitted to try to recover but fails, creditors may be worse off than if bankruptcy had been declared earlier and a division made of whatever assets remained. Such a business judgment is never easy for anyone, but the bankruptcy judge must make it with the knowledge that someone or some interest will undoubtedly be hurt no matter what he does. Creditors competing for their money—by definition, too many creditors for too little money—have divergent interests often according to their place in line. Another enormous grant of power to the judge is the discretion to group and classify creditors, though federal law lays out guidelines as to which kinds of creditors are preferred. Uncle Sam has an enormous interest in any major bankruptcy because of the tax collector's desire to be first in line to collect delinquent taxes. Of course lawyers, as lawyers and as counsel for administrators, like to be first in line also, and the costs of bankruptcy proceedings including attorney's fees are notoriously high. Equally notorious is the well-nigh universal practice of federal judges doling out bankruptcy trusteeships and other assignments as patronage. In its most benign form the patronage is a reward to a conscientious lawyer for taking a long and difficult criminal case representing an impoverished defendant for no fee. More commonly, bankruptcy assignments have the flavor of courthouse cronyism.

Bankruptcy proceedings routinely operate in semidarkness as far as the general public is concerned, but when they do surface they are often accompanied by a slight aura of something having festered. Joseph Borkin found in his study for *The Corrupt Judge* that "more charges of official misconduct have come in the field of bankruptcy than from all the others combined. The handling of receiverships seems to lend itself particularly to abuse by judges and to criticism by the public." Patent litigation, Borkin found, was the second most fruitful source of corruption charges.

Hooker's interests in the Whale bankruptcy were multiple. He and his brother Henry held the second-largest block of the corporation's stock, holding control at times. The brothers were creditors of the company in the amount of $1.5 million and were guarantors of most of the company's $3.5 million debt to Third National. On top of the financial stake, Hooker's reputation was then very much on the line in what proved to be an unsuccessful campaign for the state governorship.

The *Journal* article suggested that at least two of the American Bar Association's 1924 ethical canons were being violated: canon 4 with its admonition that "a judge's official conduct should be free from impropriety and the appearance of impropriety," and canon 32, "A judge should not accept any presents or favors from litigants, or from lawyers practising before him or from others whose interests are likely to be submitted to him for judgment." Publication of the news story was simultaneous with a scheduled hearing in Judge Gray's court. Within a few days, the judge stepped aside, not on account of the Hooker connection but because of his relationship with the bank. In his chambers, the judge told a reporter from United Press International that he had been "misquoted" by the *Journal* and "crucified" by the entire article. A judge from Memphis was specially designated to handle the case.

Two months later, Judge Gray received an application from fourteen lawyers representing nearly that many parties, all asking the judge to resume presiding: "No lawyer in any manner connected with this case has ever questioned, or thought of questioning the ethics of the procedures to which Judge Gray adhered in presiding over the matters involved herein," the petition said. "It did not occur to any such lawyer that there could be, or would be any criticism of Judge Gray." They reminded the judge that he had gone clearly on record that he would not hear any controversy involving Third National, the bank in which he held stock and of which his brother was a vice-president. Even this disqualification would have been cheerfully waived, the lawyers said. The news article, the only source of criticism in the case, "did Judge Gray an injustice," the lawyers told him.

Whether or not the application of the lawyers was adequate to cope with the bank issue, it did not mention at all the *Journal*'s featured complaint: that the judge had been so involved with the

Hookers as to render his participation in the case unseemly from start to finish. The lawyers urged the judge to return to the case now that matters adversely affecting the bank's interest had been raised and resolved; but the judge, rejecting the proffered waiver, this time stayed out of the case. It was unclear why. It could have been that he saw further bank involvement down the road of what would be lengthy litigation. Perhaps the judge took the position that the press controversy, regardless of its merits, sufficed to make his absence from the case advisable. Possibly he perceived merit in the newspaper's point. In any event, the question was somehow ultimately decided by the judge himself and not by consensus of the parties. To that extent, then, something of value was belatedly salvaged, albeit with a ceremonious display of mutual confidence—a mild assault with the Velvet Blackjack.

☆

The second episode occurred in Oklahoma City, which was no stranger to embarrassments of this sort. One might have hoped that the federal court for the Western District of Oklahoma would have been spared the bother of ethical hassles as it rested between bouts with judicial scandals. During the mid-1960s, four justices of the state's supreme court were convicted of such charges as bribery and tax evasion. And since 1965 Judge Stephen S. Chandler of the U.S. District Court had been waging his fight, all the way to Washington and back, to regain his case load from judges who denied his competence.

Before the courts was the massive bankruptcy of Four Seasons Nursing Centers and its far-flung affiliates. Needed was a court entirely free of any suspicion of impropriety, especially because suspicion ran deep among survivors probing the ruins of the Four Seasons enterprise for remaining assets. Four Seasons had been one of the hottest stocks on the market in the developing stages of a vast chain of proposed efficient, franchised health care centers spreading from Oklahoma through the entire country. The venture was touted as one that would thrive on Medicare, but instead it choked on tight money, stock market decline, reversals for many franchise operations, high construction costs, and—

according to disgruntled stockholders who filed multiple lawsuits —mismanagement and fraud.

Indeed, fraud charges were not confined to cheated investors. The Justice Department brought massive criminal charges against officials of the company and a brokerage firm, accusing one officer of personally realizing a $10 million profit from a $200 million swindle. When that Four Seasons officer pleaded guilty, the government urged a long prison sentence for the leader of what it called "the largest criminal stock fraud ever prosecuted."

None of the charges flying in all directions in the many lawsuits, in proceedings involving the Securities and Exchange Commission and a grand jury, will be resolved within the confines of this chapter. The ethical question is not whether the charges were true or false, but how the charges were handled and whether their truth or falsity was demonstrated under conditions that assured justice. In evaluating the fairness of the legal system, we must keep in mind that the accusers and the defenders either believe intensely in the accuracy of what they say or have a deep interest in prevailing whether they believe what they say or not. All the contestants are entitled to fair and impartial treatment of their claims and defenses. The public also deserves assurance that the system is working that way in the matter of a particular bankruptcy, so that they can approach the legal system with confidence when the law is employed for them. With this in mind, and also remembering that millions of dollars and thousands of individuals have direct stakes in the case, we may examine the issues and the interests, and the conflicts, involved.

The presiding judge when the Four Seasons enterprises applied for the protection of the bankruptcy court was Chief Judge Luther Bohannon, whose performance on the bench had not been spectacular but who had mildly surprised his detractors—especially by dint of courage displayed in desegregating the city's public schools—including the American Bar Association's Committee on the Federal Judiciary, which had vigorously opposed his appointment in 1961. ABA leaders had persuaded Attorney General Robert F. Kennedy that Bohannon was unqualified for the trial court, but his brother, President John F.

Kennedy, overruled that judgment. The reason was obvious. Bohannon, long a member of one of Oklahoma City's important firms, was a protégé of Senator Robert W. Kerr, and Kerr at the time was the most powerful man in the Senate. Senatorial courtesy often, though not always, can be used as a lever to force the nomination of a senator's first choice as well as to block a choice the president might prefer; but the courtesy tradition works magically when one is as powerful as Kerr, whose help the president needed so desperately. Kerr nominated, and the Kennedys reluctantly confirmed.

At the outset the judge had the sensitive job of appointing a trustee to manage the Four Seasons properties as an officer of the court responsible to the judge, gathering the business's assets and inventorying them for a financial report that would help him decide what to do. Federal law requires that the trustee be "disinterested." It is not enough that the judge be disinterested; the judge's appointee, who deals with all parties and who cannot realistically be supervised in every detail, must inspire confidence as well. It is common for the petitioning businessmen to suggest trustees, but the judge must make sure that the actual appointment satisfies the law's demands. For this task the judge approved Norman Hirschfield, an Oklahoma City businessman and successful financial analyst. But Hirschfield, it turned out, had previously served as the hired consultant of Four Seasons and, in that capacity, had recommended the very proceedings that were now under way.

Another questionable move was the judge's appointment as cocounsel to the trustee of a young lawyer named Edward Barth. There was nothing wrong with Barth as an individual, for he was an able attorney. But he was at the time a partner in the firm of Barefoot, Moler, Bohannon & Barth. The Bohannon of that firm, according to the inscription on the office door and the firm's listing in the nationally used *Martindale-Hubbell Law Directory*, was Richard L. Bohannon, who was the judge's own son. The same firm's leading partner, Bert Barefoot, had once been the judge's partner in the firm of Barefoot & Bohannon and had long been one of the judge's closest personal and social intimates. Despite his listed partnership and shared office space with Barefoot and despite the even closer affiliation with the judge's son, Barth had been favored previously with a bankruptcy appointment at the hands of the same jurist.

By embarrassing coincidence, Judge Bohannon took charge of the case after it had been initially, by rotation, assigned to a different judge. There had been nothing shady about the transfer, although it added to the strain on appearances and the need to make the proceedings in all other respects impartial.

Yet another strange circumstance attended these proceedings. Both before and after the formal filing, A. P. Murrah, Jr., son of the retired chief judge of the Tenth U.S. Circuit Court of Appeals, performed legal work for Four Seasons. Young Murrah's senior law partner, John C. Andrews, was for some time a director of Four Seasons and a prime figure in the controversy over who was responsible for the enterprise's downfall. Murrah's handling of any legal matter for Four Seasons became especially embarrassing when his partner, Andrews, was named as a defendant in a stockholder's suit charging Four Seasons management with malfeasance to the detriment of the company and its investors. According to lawyers in the community, the resulting problem of apparently conflicting loyalties had greatly troubled young Murrah himself as well as other bar members and he soon withdrew from any role as counsel in Four Seasons matters. Murrah's father, the judge, an ever-present figure in the legal battles of the federal courts thereabouts, was in addition a permanent member of a court that would ultimately have a major role in the litigation, the Judicial Panel on Multi-District Litigation.

These arrangements, while unacceptable, are far from unique in legal communities across the land, especially the "tight" communities where "everybody knows everybody else" and the relevant work for lawyers is performed by individuals who become familiar to each other over time. Many times no one is hurt, but this was not one of those times—certainly not in the view of a small firm of New York lawyers, specialists in the trade of shareholder suits, who were taking Four Seasons and others to court in the Southern District of New York. In the view of these lawyers, the demise of the nursing home empire was in large part the result of illegal and misleading stock dealings and a fraudulent allocation of resources among the various branches of the empire. On this theory, by which the firm of Sands, Geller & Webb hoped to gain large damage awards and correspondingly large legal fees, the site of the offenses and the proper place to try the Four Seasons lawsuits was New York. That was the headquarters of a codefendant stock firm, Walston & Co., and equally significant it was where the firm was most comfortable practicing law and where it could be in control of the lawsuits.

Only this foreign influence intruded upon the settled arrangement of Oklahoma City, where irregularities could be ignored among friends. It was something of a cultural intrusion as well as a legal one, for the New York specialists in what are called derivative suits on behalf of disgruntled shareholders live in a different world from the lawyers of Oklahoma. Debate rages about the social value of specialists in this kind of litigation. Some of them attempt to portray themselves as Robin Hoods, bringing corporate plunderers to justice for "insider" dealings and other dirty tricks played upon the unsuspecting average investor. Some are deemed mischievous stirrers of court-clogging litigation. An in-between view is that this kind of litigator, the strike suit specialist, although motivated more by hope of financial gain than ethical evangelism, performs the valuable function of helping to police the business world, testing or threatening to test corporate decisions and thereby helping to keep them honest. In the Four Seasons situation, there could be no doubt of one thing: the interests of the New York lawyers were decidedly adverse to other interests in Oklahoma, where a species of Velvet Blackjack, a gently coerced agreement to suppress reservations about anything amiss, was holding sway.

When the many interested parties assembled for their first reorganization meeting with the judge on August 23, there was no formal motion calling attention to the apparent irregularities. There had been, however, an article in *The Washington Post* describing these affairs, the substance of which was communicated to the principals through other media.

Ceremonies opened with universal disclaimers of any intent to impugn the integrity of the court, and the lawyers swore their faith in the judge. For his part, the judge said, "I have never run from a fight" and refused to consider replacing trustee Hirschfield. He did accept "with deep regret" the resignation of Barth as trustee cocounsel. Barth said that nothing had been improper but he wanted to avoid controversy. The judge said he had not intended to reward his son's partner, but he had been favorably impressed by the way Barth had performed in his court in a *previous* complex business failure case—a performance by assignment from the judge.

One discordant note, quietly registered in court papers and not audibly in court, came from James D. Fellers, an attorney with a successful Oklahoma City practice who later became president of the American Bar Association, representing foreign creditors of Four Seasons. The creditors were among the many parties suing the failing corporation. They were seeking return of $690,000 of funds belonging to Four Seasons Overseas, a European wing of the once-ambitious venture, which had been used to pay a debt in Oklahoma just one day before the parent company filed court papers under the Bankruptcy Act to stave off creditors pending reorganization. "While the personal integrity or ability of Norman Hirschfield is not questioned," Fellers advised the court, the trustee "cannot adequately represent foreign creditors who have fraud claims against the very firm for which he is the trustee." Nevertheless, after a brief examination of Hirschfield on the witness stand, the judge reaffirmed his assignment.

A month later, the battle for control and location of the lawsuit shifted to a large, gloomy courtroom at Foley Square in Manhattan, where the Judicial Panel on Multi-District Litigation assembled. This unit, created by Congress in the wake of the lawsuits that proliferated after big electric companies and their officers confessed massive price fixing, sits to consolidate multiple lawsuits, to establish ground rules for orderly trials with access to a pool of documentary evidence, and to iron out just such jurisdictional disputes as the many-faceted Four Seasons fight.

Since its creation in 1968, the panel has been manned by some of the ablest and most experienced judges drawn from federal districts all across the country. Judge Murrah, who disqualified himself when the *Four Seasons* case came before the panel, was the presiding officer. Customarily the technical problems facing the panel were knotty enough, but attorney Ira Sands and his associate, Robert Levin, introduced a more subtle and less familiar question: the "tender subject," as they called it, of whether a "fair hearing" could be had in Oklahoma under the circumstances. Other counsel protested the use of "innuendo" in place of solid evidence of impropriety. Reactions on the panel to the ethical complaints ranged from the chilly responses of Judge John Minor Wisdom, articulate veteran of the Fifth U.S. Circuit Court of Appeals, to the receptiveness of Judge Edward Weinfeld of the Southern District of New York, a quiet scholar with a reputation for extreme fastidiousness in ethical matters. Judge Stanley Weigel of the Northern District of California wondered aloud why the panel should approach the ethical questions. "I very much question the relevance of that," he said. "Why should this Panel pass judgment on the bar of Oklahoma or even deign to? . . . as far as I'm concerned, this is a waste of time."

The panel was urged by the various parties to locate all the trials in Oklahoma, New York, Ohio (where a Four Seasons loan scandal involving state officials had been a political bombshell), or some neutral corner of the nation. That was September 24, 1970. Eight months after that, on May 26, 1971, the panel delivered a Solomon-like solution. In an opinion by Judge Wisdom, the panel said it had selected Oklahoma as the site—but an outsider for a judge. The appointment was given to Roszel C. Thomsen, the widely admired and recently retired chief judge of the Federal District Court in Baltimore. Oklahoma simply had too many factors in its favor, including the undoubted jurisdiction to handle the basic Bankruptcy Act proceedings, Judge Wisdom said. Needless to add, there was nothing in Judge Wisdom's opinion intimating that any judgments had been passed on the performance to date of the bar or bench of Oklahoma City. Only the stiffest resistance had blunted the force of the Velvet Blackjack, but few could doubt that it would strike again.

☆

The third story perhaps exhibits the Velvet Blackjack situation best. It is a spectacle of one of the nation's most highly respected courts, the Fifth U.S. Circuit Court of Appeals, heavily involved in disqualifying business activity while passing judgment on matters of great economic consequence in the area of judges' business interests and actively soliciting from more than two dozen lawyers a waiver of disqualification. As mortifying for judicial reputations as the episode was, its lessons were incompletely learned.

In civil rights the Fifth Circuit, its membership dominated by appointees of President Eisenhower, stood for many years as a tower of strength against Deep South resistance to the law of racial justice. But the court's impressive reputation sprang also from the remarkable size and diversity of the commercial cases generated in the circuit, which embraces the federal district courts of Texas, Louisiana, Mississippi, Alabama, Georgia, and Florida—all seacoast states whose economies expanded dramatically after the Second World War, generating business for everyone including lawyers and judges.

The story's roots are deep but its surface aspect began on October 6, 1969, when three members of the court of appeals sat to hear oral arguments in the massive Southern Louisiana Gas rate case. The case was of immense significance for everyone concerned about the supply of natural gas in the United States. Involved were the rates set by the Federal Power Commission to govern sales of gas from the nation's second-largest production area to a heavily populated, heavily industrialized, and over-dependent northeastern corridor. Impossible to measure in terms of dollars, the case far transcended the size of homeowner gas bills, though in those terms alone it involved at least $80 million yearly in rate reductions and refunds. Beyond this, an entire United States policy of exploiting and allocating energy resources was on the line, for the viability of the energy industry was linked with the fairness and lawfulness of rates.

One may reasonably question whether judges, even judges of so reputable a court, were up to the demands of such questions; but fortunately for our governmental system, it is not necessary to know the answer. Policy decisions in the first instance are committed by Congress to the discretion and alleged expertise of the FPC, an administrative agency. According to design, the agency has the job of informing itself about the gas industry, its supplies and its demands, and the implications of changes for consumer and producer. Courts, including the Supreme Court, theoretically sit in judgment not of the FPC's assessment of its own evidence, but of whether the agency has followed applicable federal law and obeyed the Constitution in carrying out its duties. In practice, as lawyers know, the model is not always recognizable. On occasion, judges will perceive that the FPC, or any of the other dozens of regulatory bodies, has bungled its job, whereupon the judge will set out to correct matters under the banner of strictly limited judicial review. There is much room for differences of opinion over when and whether a court has overstepped, perhaps in righteous zeal, and invaded the agency's proper territory.

Long before the Louisiana rate hearing, the jurist in the center chair, Chief Judge John R. Brown, had gained a reputation for nearly always being near the line when the FPC was involved. A man of great charm, wit, and intelligence, Judge Brown became a student of the oil and gas industry, an understandable pursuit in view of his pre-judicial career as a Houston lawyer. No shrinking violet on or off the bench, Judge Brown reveled in courtroom combat and frequently tested the mettle of industry and government lawyers sent to his court to persuade him.

Flanking Judge Brown were Warren L. Jones of Jacksonville, Florida, a senior circuit judge and member of the court since 1955, and G. Harrold Carswell of Tallahassee, the newest member of the court of appeals despite a brief and abortive attempt of civil rights lawyers to frustrate his promotion from a federal district judgeship in Florida. Still ahead was the bitter fight over his fitness to be a Supreme Court justice. Just ahead, however, and very much a part of the setting, was a Senate vote on the confirmation of Clement F. Haynsworth, Jr., the nominee whose stock dealings and business interests were threatening to defeat his candidacy. Fresh in the minds of all were the sudden fall of Abe Fortas from the Supreme Court and the last-minute reforms, aimed at elevating ethical standards for federal judges, pushed through by the retiring chief justice, Earl Warren. Also in the offing for all federal judges was the deadline of May 1970 for filing confidential reports of personal investment income and other off-the-bench earnings with the U.S. Judicial Conference under terms of the Warren reform.

Judge Jones opened the proceedings in partial keeping with the spirit of disclosure that was abroad in the land. "I think that perhaps I should advise counsel," he said, "that my wife is the beneficial owner of a few shares of stock in Texaco, Eastman Oil [*sic*] and either Consolidated Edison or Consolidated Natural Gas, I don't know which. If anybody thinks I'm disqualified, why, this should be the time for them to say so."

Discreetly, the assembled lawyers refrained from asking how much stock or in precisely which companies. Judge Jones had passed his first screen test. Judge Brown then asked, "Does anyone have any questions about Judge Jones participating in the hearing and decision? I was going to say the court needed him badly. He's the only one that's read the record." Smiles from counsel. The jovial jurist went on:

> I'll tell you something else, I hope I never read all that record. If you do your job, it will be unnecessary for us to read it. I have some doubt any of you have really done it, although you tell your clients you have and have been paid for it.
>
> We'll proceed. It's a very fascinating case, this whole business. I don't know yet how we won out. I understand that there were 80-some-odd petitions filed within 90 seconds of each other, but I'm going to see that our clocks hereafter are kept in better disorder.

The reference was to the notorious fact that when an agency like the FPC issues a ruling that is reviewable in any of a number of courts of appeals, counsel on all sides engage in an unseemly race against the clock. In most cases the first to file in the court of his choice is the winner. Anyone in oil and gas prefers the Fifth or Tenth circuits; the home court for the "consumer side" is the Court of Appeals for the District of Columbia Circuit, where most federal agencies are located. Lawyers for the Southern Louisiana Gas Co. won the race to the Fifth Circuit one spring day in 1969, chiefly because the official clock in New Orleans lacked a sweep second hand, so the clerk was obliged to assign a filing time less than a minute ahead of competing filings in Washington and Denver, the latter being headquarters for the usually industry-oriented Tenth Circuit. The race to the favorable forum reached perhaps its lowest point of absurdity in a related power commission case in 1972 when consumer interests lost by *two seconds* and were again relegated to the Fifth Circuit.

During the ensuing five hours of oral argument—not an unusual ordeal for voluminous gas rate controversies—Judge Brown showed that he had been too modest in denigrating the extent of his own reading. However, not all the reading was in the record of the case, which under judicial review standards is the basis for court action. As many judges do, he complained that years of FPC attempts to establish rate rules had rendered the record "stale" in terms of the economics of the moment. Although the precise issue was the correctness of the agency action when the action was taken, Judge Brown wished the record could be updated. "Now, isn't that kind of absurd?" he asked. "We know that much. We read the papers."

President Nixon's first appointee to the commission made speeches about the impending or already existing shortage of gas supplies, speeches that pointed to higher permissible rates to encourage industry to search for what supplies there were. He wanted the record enlarged; he told counsel:

All these speeches the commissioners are making across the land, incidentally, the court wants the commission to file in the record here copies of all the speeches made in the last six months or nine months by the members of the commission on this question of reserves and the explosive demands of gas apparently not satisfied [indicating higher prices]. I read Foster Reports. Somebody started sending it to me years ago when I got into this business. . . .

It might be noted that there are occasions when a federal regulatory agency takes so long to gather evidence and decide a major case that the record is indeed hopelessly out of date by the time a court reviews it. But when Judge Brown called for the speeches by FPC members he was calling for more opinion, not evidence, and opinion, besides, that would buttress the judge's own view of the energy problem. He was not remanding the case to the FPC for more evidence but instead was seeking more material extraneous to that record. It may seem a bit technical to require courts to act on the basis of a stale record, but in most cases the parties are entitled to judicial review of evidence actually gathered. Judge Brown wanted a second bite of the apple for one side of the dispute, in this instance the gas producers.

When at last the oral session ended, lawyers trudged back to their offices or bureaus, some wondering what the disclosure episode had been all about. They then awaited an announcement about a proposed preliminary injunction sought by industry to block the rate reductions pending the final outcome, and, of course, they awaited the outcome itself.

The next communication from the court was a stunner, and it came within a week. Over the clerk's signature, the letters read:

In addition to the statement made by Judge Jones from the bench concerning stock ownership in which Mrs. Jones had a beneficial interest, the members of the court have checked their respective portfolios and enclose as exhibits the details with respect to other stock holdings of companies which might have some immediate relation to the production, sale, transmission or distribution of natural gas.

When multiplied by the day's stock prices, Judge Brown's portfolio included about $100,000 in oil and gas. About half was personally held and the rest was held in trust for two families. There was $35,000 in Gulf Oil, Tenneco, and Houston Natural Gas alone—all parties to the pending rate case. Judge Brown had said nothing of this when Judge Jones had made his announcement.

As for Judge Jones, his listing consisted of two trusteeships valued at about $500,000 in oil and gas. Trusteeships, in which one manages a portfolio in the interest of another person, are distinguishable from personal holdings, but the distinction is a fine one at best when it comes to potential conflict of interest, since the trustee's duty is to protect the value of the trust. The personal holding entails a similar, though perhaps more selfish, interest in the value of the stock.

There was no listing for Judge Carswell, whose total lack of stock holdings was to become one of his prime assets months later when the Nixon administration was searching for someone to elevate to the Supreme Court.

The letter went on:

If any party desires to raise any question about the disqualification of either Chief Judge Brown or Judge Jones by reason of these stock ownerships, the court requests that this be communicated to the court without delay. In the absence of any information to the contrary, the court will assume that no one has any objection.

Comments, if any, were due by October 21. Under the clerk's signature were two more lines: "P.S. Also enclosed is a copy of a stay order this day entered by the court." That was the order postponing $1.5 million weekly in rate reductions.

Counsel were amazed. Probably the amazement ran highest among counsel for the FPC and the lawyers aligned on the "consumer" side of the case. It was at least technically possible for the oil and gas companies, and through them their lawyers, to know how much a given judge owned in company stock. There was sentiment on all sides, however, that the judges had placed a great onus on the bar. Should Their Honors be told that their own figures disqualified them? Merits aside, would it be in the interest of their clients to file such a pleading, whether or not it succeeded in striking the judges from the case? Did counsel want to go through another long hearing before new judges, and did their clients relish the expensive prospect and the further delay? Some lawyers set about resolving their dilemma by preparing memoranda saying that while Their Honors' good faith and objectivity were not in question, the law looks also to the appearance of objectivity, their clients might not fully under-stand the judicial capacity for putting extraneous influences to one side, and in any event counsel felt unable to waive the rights of clients. Some of the memoranda were actually put in the mail, and the judges had reason to expect some filings from the most courageous lawyers.

Within four days the court itself relieved counsel of their dilemma. Four days ahead of the October 21 deadline, this communication was dictated to counsel by telephone from New Orleans: "The judges of the panel to which this case was assigned are not disqualified by prejudice. Neither are they disqualified by interest, whether individual, fiduciary or otherwise. *Kinnear-Weed Co.* v. *Humble Oil Co.*, 403 F.2d 437."

This was a citation of a decision delivered by Judge Brown a year earlier of which more will be said in the pages that follow. It is sufficient for the moment to note that lawyers understood this to mean that the court was following its own precedent, which was that mere stock ownership in a vast commercial enterprise does not disqualify a judge. The rationale for this was that his holdings, when measured against all the stock issued by the giant concern, could not appreciably be affected by the outcome of the case. The statement continued:

Although we find no basis for disqualification of any judge, the court concludes that it is desirable that any questioning of the qualification of any of the judges be resolved by submission of this case to this panel being vacated and the case being reassigned for argument and determination at an expedited date before an entirely new panel of the judges of this court.

In other words, without waiting for the lawyers, the judges had decided the matter in their own favor but were stepping aside out of an abundance of precaution. Their order continued:

As of this date, the clerk's office advises this panel that no responses have been received from counsel. The court directs the clerk to return unfiled and unnoted any responses which may subsequently be received from counsel in this regard without reference of same to any judges of this court.

In other words, the judges wanted to hear no more about the matter.

So another panel of judges was mustered, a decision was rendered, petitions were filed to the Supreme Court, and while the case was awaiting some action there, the parties all got together and settled the case. As with any settlement there was widespread dissatisfaction but some solace was derived from the fact that yet another court would not be obliged to grapple with the nettled controversy. Nothing was lost except time, energy, and the image of justice—the very stuff of the judicial process.

☆

Yet that was not all, for the court of appeals had not said its last word on *Kinnear-Weed Co.* v. *Humble Oil Co.*, the case the court cited to justify its handling of the gas rate litigation. The Fifth Circuit's handling of the case, which nagged at the judicial system for eighteen years before it ended, showed how little chastened the judges had been by their embarrassment of oil riches. Before the case was over the Fifth Circuit held, in one of several decisions along the way, that a judge was not disqualified from presiding over major oil industry litigation—specifically a suit for millions by a man who claimed to be the inventor of one of the industry's most widely used oil drill bits—despite these facts:

· The trial judge's wife owned $9,000 worth of stock in Humble Oil Co., the principal defendant in the lawsuit.

· The trial judge and his wife leased thousands of acres of Texas land to Humble and other oil companies.

· The trial judge was one-fourth owner, secretary, and general counsel of a company that repaired drilling equipment in the Texas oil fields and whose best customer was Humble.

· Many of the pertinent disqualifying facts about the trial judge, Lamar Cecil of Beaumont, were easily available to the oil industry defendants but became known to the plaintiff, Clarence W. Kinnear, only after the judge's death when probate proceedings disclosed his business holdings.

· The jurists who let this happen were the same Fifth Circuit judges whose oil holdings had so embarrassed them in the Southern Louisiana rate case. Only one member of the court, Judge Elbert P. Tuttle, expressed much sympathy for Kinnear's right to a disinterested trial judge, and he ultimately disqualified himself on grounds that never would have occurred to most of his brethren. Judge Tuttle realized in the course of the litigation that he stood to inherit oil stock from his parents' estate, so because of an economic interest, and despite the fact that the interest was of a type favorable to the oil industry, he recused himself, to Kinnear's detriment.

Clarence Kinnear, who claimed to have revolutionized oil drilling, ended up as an infamous footnote in the annals of judicial ethics. Unlike the other parties in the cases described in this chapter, Kinnear was not afraid to challenge the system. But because the legal system has developed its own "clubbiness" and camaraderie, its insiders often fail to make the necessary points about ethics. And outsiders, when they make them, too often fail, period. The phenomenon of the Velvet Blackjack was specifically and consciously faced by those who wrote the new ethical standards in the wake of these and other scandals. Their failure to correct the problem will be discussed later.

5

☆ ☆ ☆

LIONS ON THE THRONE

"God send me never to live under the law of Conveniency or Discretion. Should the Soldier and the Justice Sit upon one Bench, the trumpet will not let the crier speak in Westminster Hall."

Sir Edward Coke

Many knowledgeable persons consider that for all the might and majesty of the United States Supreme Court the real power lies near the base of the judicial pyramid. That is where the nearly four hundred district judges conduct the trials, issue the injunctions, and impose the criminal sentences. On paper, judges at the trial level in ninety-four federal districts are subject to reversal by two layers of higher courts. Each district is within one of eleven circuits, and a judgment upheld by a circuit court of appeals is still subject to review by the Supreme Court. But in practice, the higher courts cannot supervise the trial courts too closely for if they do the system will break down with more reversals and retrials than we have now.

The Supreme Court can correct some lower court judges, but it does not sit for that purpose. Hundreds of judgments the justices might consider incorrect go uncorrected because the Supreme Court's function is to hear only the most important and compelling cases. Ordinarily the trial judges enjoy vast discretion under rules that give them the benefit of a doubt because of their position on the judicial firing line.

Unfortunately, the system has produced many trial judges who lack the temperament necessary to match their power. Many are tyrannical, heavy-handed, and abusive toward the lawyers and litigants who appear in their courts. Higher court review, even when carefully and selectively exercised, often has no effect on such judges. Ambition for higher judicial office may curb some trial judges' conduct but even that stimulus has diminishing effect with advancing age. The Constitution provides life tenure and a guaranteed level of income to safeguard judges' independence, but in some these enhance arbitrariness as well. Obedient bailiffs and clerks confirm a judge's impression that he is to be respected, and the community rewards him with honorific dinners and honorary charitable functions. Gifted and learned men also grace the bench in large numbers, but the boisterous, cantankerous judge often steals the headlines.

One respected defense attorney, Professor Herman Schwartz of the State University of New York at Buffalo, viewing the scene in many state courts, has this perspective:

Glaring down from their elevated perches, insulting, abrupt, rude, sarcastic, patronizing, intimidating, vindictive, insisting on not merely respect but almost abject servility—such judges are frequently encountered in American trial courts, particularly in the lowest criminal and juvenile courts which account for most of our criminal business. Indeed, the lower the court, the worse the behavior.

The greater visibility of the higher courts may account for better behavior there. A still more likely explanation is that in a court of appeals, a judge sits and votes and works collegially with others. He is not alone at the focal point of the courtroom but is only one among several judges of equal rank, all of whom must learn to share the available time and the spotlight.

What controls are available to protect the consumers of the judicial system from petty or great judicial tyranny? As with the other forms of misbehavior discussed in this book, there is danger that excessive controls would make inroads on the judges' independence, something the Constitution forbids and good sense resists. Nevertheless, some recourse is appropriate and more of the available corrective measures should be applied.

Public criticism, for example, is not totally unavailing as an antidote for the disruptive judge. Although many thoughtful persons deplore uninformed criticism of judicial decisions—and indeed a high percentage of censure proves to be uninformed—judges are fair game for reasoned criticism of disruptive and abusive behavior. A judge who disrupts his own courtroom sheds both the attributes and some of the respect due his office.

Skillful judicial administration is another method of preventing future abuses, the chief instrument being a case load control system that manages, with tact, to steer the difficult cases away from the difficult judges. There is admittedly a corresponding danger that the management function may devolve upon judges who are themselves difficult, since in the federal system it is seniority, not demonstrated administrative competence, that determines who the managers are. Nevertheless, it is possible to teach better techniques even to inefficient administrators, and if the late 1960s taught one lesson, it was that the judicial system could no longer pretend to get by with the expedient of assigning the difficult cases to the judges who by seniority or otherwise found themselves with the most time on their hands.

One application of management technique occurred in the aftermath of the Chicago conspiracy trial over which Judge Julius J. Hoffman presided. Public opinion divided sharply over the rights and wrongs of the five-month trial, but while a sizable majority of the public seemed to favor the judge, many leading jurists were deeply disturbed over his conduct. Many who felt this way suppressed their views for fear they would vindicate the conduct of William Kunstler and the defense team, thereby giving encouragement to abuses by disruptive defendants and their lawyers. Thus when an attempt to cure some of the evils of the Chicago trial was made by the United States Judicial Conference, which sets the administrative policies for the federal courts, it was done quite furtively. The conference declared in October 1971 that cases of special difficulty require and should receive special administrative handling by the chief judges of lower courts. This truism had been widely ignored in the district courts, where judges often insisted publicly that they observed strict rotation on the premise that the judges were interchangeable and equally competent. Of course the rule change left open the perennial question of which judge is fit to judge the other judges, but the step was a salutary one.

It was unfortunate that the conference's action was camouflaged in an announcement that indicated it to be only an efficiency measure. The conference discreetly avoided criticizing a sitting jurist, but it also deprived the public of valuable professional judgment about Judge Hoffman's behavior.

The judges have been much more forthcoming with public criticism of defendants and lawyers, particularly defense counsel. Chief Justice Warren E. Burger did not originate the criticism of lawyers, but beginning in 1970 he assumed the role as the leading spokesman of judicial disapproval. The following year he complained to the American Law Institute that "at the drop of a hat—or less—we find adrenalin-fueled lawyers cry out that theirs is a 'political trial.' This seems to mean in today's context—at least to some—that rules of evidence, canons of ethics and codes of professional conduct—the necessity for civility—all become irrelevant." Burger did not omit mention of the need for good behavior by judges, but he made no effort to apply such terms as "adrenalin-fueled" to them.

In response to a series of controversial trials and the rhetoric about them, the respected Association of the Bar of the City of New York created the Special Committee on Courtroom Conduct to examine the problem. Late in 1973, after a three-year study, the committee issued a massive report and analysis with the conclusion, "Don't panic." Said chairman Burke Marshall, deputy dean of Yale Law School and former assistant attorney general:

In speeches, reports, panels, judicial conferences, and other forums, the bar as a whole acted as if the courts of this country had suddenly been taken over by an organized group of radical lawyers interested only in destroying the system that was protecting their clients. This panic did great and lasting damage to the public perception of the processes of the laws, for it exaggerated far out of proportion the problems that had occurred in a few courtrooms, particularly Judge Hoffman's in Chicago. Further, it confused zeal in the defense of clients with revolution, and thus moved in the direction, with threats of disbarment, of intimidating defense counsel.

Marshall said the system was actually working quite well. "It is more in danger from interference with counsel fighting for justice for their clients than from whatever disruption—and it is not on the whole very great—is caused by their efforts."

As the New York bar study showed, there have always been "disorderly trials" in the United States and abroad, but the modern concept of the problem dates from the World War II sedition trial of thirty pro-Nazi groups and propagandists and the postwar Smith Act trial of eleven top officials of the Communist party. In the 1944 trial of the German-Americans, the defendants and their lawyers used tactics of courtroom disruption, shouting, and dilatory maneuvers in beating back the prosecution; the proceedings ended in a mistrial when the presiding judge, Edward C. Eicher, died of a heart attack. The defendants might have prevailed without such disorders, since the main reason for not retrying them was that under intervening Supreme Court rulings their conduct did not violate existing law.

History's judgment is mixed concerning the Smith Act trial of Eugene Dennis and ten others in 1949. While few have disputed that the defense team was guilty of unethical, obstructive, and abusive tactics, there is divided opinion on whether Judge Harold R. Medina properly handled the situation and indeed whether the judge did not join in the fray. The Supreme Court eventually upheld contempt convictions and prison sentences of up to six months for defense counsel by a five to three vote, the majority limiting its review to the legal question of the trial judge's power to conduct summary contempt proceedings without a jury at the close of the trial. The dissenters argued that this was an unjustified extension of the judicial contempt power. Subsequent decisions have caused lawyers to question whether the contempt power is still as sweeping as the Court declared in 1952. Important rulings have been made requiring judges who become embroiled with the defense to shift the contempt proceedings to another judge, and the power to try such cases without a jury has been significantly trimmed. The New York bar committee recommended in 1973 that the power to punish defendants and lawyers on the spot be eliminated altogether in favor of procedures with more safeguards.

Many judges shared vicariously in Judge Medina's apparent
tribulations, and it was not uncommon for judges to recall the
Smith Act trial whenever an attorney was particularly argumen-
tative. The 1968 trial of Dr. Benjamin Spock and four others for
conspiracy to obstruct the Vietnam military draft was conducted
with the memory of Judge Medina never far from the consciousness of the eighty-five-year-old presiding jurist, Francis J. W.
Ford. At one bench conference Judge Ford warned defense
counsel, "This will not be another Dennis case," a most
inappropriate comparison for a group of extremely civil attorneys.

One of the difficulties at the Spock trial was the need for
defense counsel to make specific objections at each instance of
bias displayed by Judge Ford. At one point in the trial the judge
volunteered the observation that "it's obvious" many Americans
disagreed with Dr. Spock. "The Court can take judicial notice of
that," he said. But when a defense attorney observed that many
sympathized with the defendant, the judge ordered, "Strike it
out." He prodded the defense to "get on" and "go forward"
seventeen times during one ninety-minute examination of a
witness but not once during the prosecution's three hours of
cross-examination. Even when the judge admonished the jury to
keep an open mind as the trial progressed, he referred to "the
conspiracy" or "this conspiracy," the existence or nonexistence of
which the jury was to determine.

Judge Ford's poor hearing contributed to one episode that
showed how jumpy a trial judge could become. A handful of
spectators clapped when the judge ruled in favor of the defense, a
gesture of approval that was improper but brief. "Stop these
demonstrations," the judge roared in front of the jury as he
cleared the courtroom of spectators. The word "demonstrations"
was central to the trial's issue, which was whether the five
codefendants had acted impermissibly in demonstrating their
hatred of the war. Judge Ford dismissed many of the defense
objections to his remarks from the bench, saying that he had
operated well within the right of a federal judge to comment on
the evidence.

Some of the jumpiness of judges was caused by forces that were making the entire nation nervous and had special implications for anyone connected with the system of criminal justice. Even mostly peaceful demonstrations, such as the 1967 Pentagon march that was involved in the Spock prosecution, could put great stress on the system through sheer numbers of defendants to be "processed" and judged. The urban riots and the assassinations of Robert F. Kennedy and the Reverend Martin Luther King, Jr., produced still more anxiety. Many judges feared for their physical safety—with reason, as the tragic killing of Superior Court judge Harold J. Haley in Marin County, California, proved in 1970.

As if the politics of the Vietnam war were not enough to aggravate the situation, the politics of the 1968 election and of Mayor Richard J. Daley's Chicago rubbed nerves raw. In his closing days as attorney general, Ramsey Clark refused to prosecute David Dellinger, Abbie Hoffman, Jerry Rubin, Rennie Davis, Tom Hayden, and the rest of what became the original "Chicago Eight" because he did not consider that they had broken the federal law against crossing state lines to provoke riots. But Chief Judge William J. Campbell of the U.S. District Court in Chicago kept it alive, Clark said later. Clark considered Judge Campbell's interest excessive. The judge simply would not permit the indictment of any policeman on a brutality charge without a compensating indictment against the demonstrators. A stalemate resulted. The situation was left for the incoming Nixon administration with predictable results in view of the Nixon "tough on crime" posture. Eight policemen and eight demonstrators were indicted in the spring of 1969. The charges were symmetrical, the major exception being that the civilians were accused of conspiracy while the policemen were ordered to stand trial one or two at a time on charges of individual, uncoordinated violence.

The indictments set the stage for the uproarious Chicago conspiracy trial of 1969–70. The number of defendants itself was a symptom of the disorder. The New York bar association study found that most celebrated unruly trials involved many defendants, the 1970–71 trial of twenty-one Black Panthers in New York City being the most conspicuous.

Judge Hoffman was later reversed on virtually every point of major controversy that arose during the trial and became an issue on appeal, the court of appeals ruling that the accused had been denied a fair trial and that the long contempt sentences against defendants and their lawyers were unwarranted. Only on the constitutionality of the underlying interstate rioting statute was Judge Hoffman upheld on a two to one split of the appellate panel. Nevertheless, public opinion appeared to favor the judge, who was cast by many in the martyr's role and likened to the beleaguered Judge Medina.

How, then, is one to apportion the blame for the five tempestuous months of trial with the trading of insults, clenching of fists, and gagging of a defendant? In Judge Medina's case, a strong argument could be made that although he erred in becoming engaged in verbal dueling with counsel—at one point calling one lawyer a liar—at least there the judge's involvement was slight at first and the gain in intensity could be attributed to the wear and tear of a long trial. In Judge Hoffman's court the clashes began immediately and the presiding judge was thoroughly embroiled from the outset. Judge Hoffman was glad to join the fray and seemed determined to give as much as he got. Even if Judge Hoffman did not "start the fight" himself—and he may have—the trial judge is not excused from blame merely for refraining from striking the first blow.

One of the very first blows to be struck was Judge Hoffman's action—before the trial could get under way—in rounding up four lawyers who had represented some of the defendants in early postindictment matters but who had withdrawn from the case by telegram. The lawyers, Michael Tigar of Los Angeles, Michael P. Kennedy of San Francisco, Dennis Roberts of Oakland, and Gerald B. Lefcourt of New York, were arrested and spent a night in the Chicago federal jail before facing Judge Hoffman on his contempt citation. The judge, inundated with protests from lawyers who considered the action degrading to the profession, then dropped his charges and released the lawyers. "I have no desire to damage the professional careers of young lawyers," said the judge, who insisted, however, that the proper way to withdraw would have been to travel to Chicago and do it in person. That is not ordinarily required of lawyers, and the judge was both wrong and provocative to attempt to require it in this instance.

Almost as arbitrary was Judge Hoffman's insistence that Kunstler, who represented others and had entered a formal one-time appearance for defendant Bobby Seale, must continue to represent the Black Panther leader over his protests. The court of appeals held that Seale, who wanted his own choice of counsel or to represent himself if necessary, was entitled to be asked whether he wanted Kunstler's services.

There were countless other errors that added up to the appellate court's conclusion that "the demeanor of the judge and prosecutor would require reversal if other errors did not," but one of the telltale signs of bias was not technically defined as error; it was the judge's repeated mispronunciation of the name of Leonard Weinglass, one of the defense attorneys. The repetition was too frequent to have been inadvertent. "It is Feinglass," he said at one juncture. "Oh, is it Weinglass? Did I say Feinglass? It is Weinglass." The trial was punctuated with side discussions about names. Attempting to get away from the informal use of first names, the judge said gratuitously, "They should not be referred to in the United States District Court by their—I nearly said Christian names."

Among the many independent grounds for reversal cited by the court of appeals was one that, while ordinarily too common-place for special notice, bore on the issue of the disorderliness of the trial. Months later a magazine writer disclosed that the jury and Judge Hoffman had communicated several times without the knowledge of the defendants. The impropriety of this is so well settled in American courts that ordinarily the only question is whether such communications actually prejudiced the accused in some way, and failure by the prosecution to demonstrate beyond a reasonable doubt that the mistake was harmless results in automatic reversal and a new trial for the accused.

What made the legal point significant was Judge Hoffman's explanation that he kept the communications to himself because he feared the "disruption" that might ensue if he called the jury into open court to discuss the jurors' notes asking for specific items of evidence or announcing that they were approaching deadlock on a verdict. This kind of explanation, which the court of appeals saw through quickly, might bear on the sincerity of Judge Hoffman's entire public posture about courtroom disruption. As the court of appeals pointed out in its reversal of November 1972, Judge Hoffman need not have brought the jury back to the courtroom; instead he could have summoned counsel to advise him on the proper response to each jury note. Alternatively, even if the judge had written an immediate response to each note for the jury, he could have summoned counsel to inform them what he had done. That would have given the lawyers a chance to suggest additional things for the judge to say, and it would have avoided the ridiculous problem of having to reconstruct from memory just what words did pass between jury and judge.

No less excusable, though not amounting to a basis for reversal by the court of appeals, was a fault exhibited by Judge Hoffman that often makes the power of a federal judge well-nigh intolerable: a judge's inability to resist being funny at the expense of anyone who happens to be the brunt of his punch lines. Quite apart from his theatrical inability to remember the correct name of counselor Weinglass, Judge Hoffman repeatedly played the comedian and commentator. At his sentencing, defendant Tom Hayden told the judge that his regret about punishment centered on his desire to have a child. It was a somewhat pathetic observation, perhaps best ignored by the sentencing judge, but Judge Hoffman retorted that "there is where the federal system can do you no good."

W. S. Gilbert in his lyrics for *The Mikado* listed among society's malefactors who might well be underground, and who would never be missed, the Judicial Humorist. Sir Francis Bacon, in an essay quoted at the head of the original Canons of Judicial Ethics, preached that "judges ought to be more learned than witty." They come down to the same thing: judges who, because of their enormous power, have to be laughed at when they attempt humor, can be positively indecent when they impose their comedy on a captive courtroom audience.

Defenders of Judge Hoffman's conduct might say that such

remarks should not be ripped from the context of a trial transcript that ran more than twenty thousand pages. One answer is that some remarks cannot be redeemed by any context; they are bad in themselves. Beyond that, those who are experienced in the nation's courtrooms know that judges are masters of the transcript, not victims of cold stenography. They know what they are saying, are accustomed to having their remarks transcribed, and are often desirous of being reported verbatim. Many judges are in complete control of the transcription process because of the patronage that governs the hiring of stenographers, and some judges have been known to doctor the records. Many a printed trial transcript should be read with the knowledge of the possibility that any alteration may have been made in the judge's favor. Attorneys, too, at times can make effective use of a written record.

Unquestionably there were serious abuses by Kunstler and his colleagues. The trial judge's calumny was no excuse for their insistence on continuing to argue points of law long after the judge had ruled against them. Their approach to the Chicago trial was aggressive, some might say diversionary, aimed at putting the justice system on trial rather than the accused. It was known that the Chicago defense team looked critically at the lawyers who defended at the Spock trial and decided that they would not emulate their pallid style. If the trial was to be theater, the Chicago defendants would occupy center stage and direct most of the drama. Although the black Bobby Seale was an incongruous member of the "conspiracy" to begin with, and though, whatever his alleged misdeeds elsewhere, he was much put upon by being made a Chicago defendant in light of the most marginal evidence against him, it was in no way proper for the defense to stage a party, complete with a cake, for a courtroom celebration of Seale's thirty-fourth birthday. In spite of the defense's errors, however, an injustice was done to them at the Chicago trial. The corrective actions by the court of appeals could only relieve the pressure on the defendants; they could not repair the damage done to the judicial system itself.

If the judiciary played an ignoble part in the creation of this fiasco by stimulating the indictment and permitting a Judge

Hoffman to preside at the trial, it must be said that the ultimate judgment of the courts themselves allocating blame was quite respectable. It came at the hands of a highly qualified visiting judge, Edward T. Gignoux of Maine, who tried the remnants of the contempt charges after the initial convictions for rioting and contempt had been set aside and reduced in seriousness by a series of dismissals by prosecutors and judges.

Sitting by special assignment from Chief Justice Burger, Judge Gignoux conducted a nonjury trial of the contempt issues that was as quiet and orderly as the 1969–70 trial had been tumultuous. When the trial was over the judge found Kunstler and three of the defendants—Dellinger, Rubin, and Abbie Hoffman—guilty of a total of 13 counts, as compared with the 175 counts Judge Hoffman had leveled against all the accused. Gignoux's verdict was a balanced one, but it was by no means a weaseling compromise designed to diffuse dissatisfaction. Judge Gignoux, himself prominent among the most influential of federal judges, showed no fear of offending the judicial brotherhood as he explained that Judge Hoffman's contentious conduct was a factor in dismissing many of the charges. Yet he refused to condone Dellinger's use of a "barnyard epithet" in one courtroom outburst; nor Abbie Hoffman's telling Judge Hoffman, "You are the only obscenity in this courtroom"; nor Rubin's likening the judge's conduct to "the gestapo" and calling him "the laughingstock of the world." As for Kunstler, Judge Gignoux cited "diatribes" at the trial judge, "vicious action" that flagrantly delayed and obstructed the trial, and Kunstler's persistence, not in pressing his case but in continuing to make the same arguments after a point had been made and rejected, for special denunciation. "Lawyers are permitted to be persistent, vociferous, contentious and imposing—even to the point of being obnoxious," said Judge Gignoux, but Kunstler's behavior "exceeds the bounds of trial advocacy."

Judge Gignoux executed his final judgment brilliantly. On December 6, 1973, two days after delivering his contempt verdicts, he pronounced sentence—which was no imprisonment at all. He declared that the accused had been adequately punished by the contempt judgments and the time already served by Dellinger, Hoffman, and Rubin: two weeks in prison when the trial judge refused to grant them a posttrial appeal bond. And even though Kunstler had served no time in confinement, there would be no purpose in sentencing him "other than the impermissible purpose of vindictiveness." Although Judge Hoffman's own conduct did not constitute a legal excuse, nevertheless in fixing punishment Judge Gignoux said he must "consider the extent to which the conduct of the trial judge and the prosecuting attorneys" had provoked any of the misbehavior. Except for the time Abbie Hoffman and Rubin demonstrated in court by wearing judicial robes and trampling upon them, Judge Gignoux said the contumacious conduct "can in each instance reasonably be said to have been in response, albeit as the court has found, in excessive response, to peremptory action from the judge."

In its totality, Judge Gignoux's judgment was an eloquent commentary on the whole sorry affair: it was never anything to get so riled up about, none of it ever should have happened, but unfortunately some things did happen that could not be ignored. One had the feeling that with a jurist like Gignoux in command, nothing like the Chicago escapade would have happened. Even the defense found itself able to praise this jurist. Judge Hoffman, burned by the implied and explicit condemnation of his handiwork, called the press room shortly after the non-sentencing to volunteer to newsmen that he had no comment. Kunstler braced for a defense of his license to practice law.

One of the most notable judges for insisting on regularity by counsel but failing to deliver justice in his courtroom was G. Harrold Carswell, from 1959 through 1969 a judge of the federal district court at Tallahassee, Florida, briefly a member of the Fifth U.S. Circuit Court of Appeals, more briefly still a 1970 nominee for the Supreme Court, later a candidate for a GOP Senate nomination, and finally a part-time referee in bankruptcy in his former district court.

Carswell was so lacking in qualifications for the High Court that Senator Roman L. Hruska, Republican of Nebraska, felt obliged to defend him as emblematic of the underrepresented "mediocre" in American society, and the Senate, often appropriately shy of finding any nominee unqualified, actually conducted much of the debate over Carswell on the subject of his professional shortcomings. The nominee's rude courtroom behavior toward civil rights lawyers no less than his imperious rulings against them stirred bitter opposition and produced his defeat. Racially biased off-the-bench activity, in the form of converting a public golf course to an ostensibly "private" all-white country club also contributed heavily to Carswell's fate.

Appearance and reality were indivisible when it came to some federal judges in the Deep South during the civil rights movement's upsurge in the 1960s. For blacks seeking elementary rights of citizenship, the vote, equal access to public accommodations, or whatever the segregated society was denying them, a trip to court to obtain "justice" often meant the infliction of still more insults from the justice system itself: segregated seating, condescending talk from officials, and short shrift from the judge on the basic complaint. Such a dispenser of injustice was Judge W. Harold Cox of the Southern District of Mississippi. To his failure to enforce the civil rights laws, Judge Cox added racist courtroom statements, referring to blacks as "niggers" and asking during a hearing on attempts by Negroes to register and vote, "Who is telling these people they can get in line and push people around, acting like a bunch of chimpanzees?"

Although the federal judges who are most often branded as tyrannical seem to be predominantly "progovernment" in the eyes of their accusers, Judge Cox surely disproves that rule. In truth, no neat formula of proprosecution, anti–civil rights, or any other set of biases can characterize the judicial tyrant. If a progovernment and proprosecution sentiment appears to predominate, the explanation could be simply the strong role the Justice Department plays as recruiter and sometimes the source of manpower for the federal bench.

From time to time there is a heavy emphasis on the need for trial experience as a prerequisite for appointees to the federal trial courts, with the American Bar Association in its most influential periods laying down a firm requirement in this regard. Federal prosecutors and former federal prosecutors often have an edge in trial experience over otherwise comparable candidates for judgeships, and this may help produce a high proportion of prosecution-oriented judges, both fair and unfair.

But the tyrannical judge often appears more than merely biased toward the prosecution. At times he seems heavily invested in the case, so heavily that he tries to take charge of the case and remove it from the prosecutor's control. Judge Ford was quoted as having told his clerk after a gaffe during the Spock trial to tell the prosecutor to "cut it out, he'll blow this case."

What, then, is one to say of the now-famous jurist who presided over the trial of seven Watergate burglary defendants and, totally dissatisfied with the work of the prosecutors, took over the proceedings and broke the scandal wide open? Perhaps never has a trial judge so conspicuously abandoned the role of impartial umpire as did Chief Judge John J. Sirica in Washington in 1973. He insisted that a criminal trial produce more than a victory between two contesting sides—that it produce, in fact, deeper truths than either side was divulging. Even those who were pleased that the truth did win out were obliged to admit that this was not exactly the American adversary system of justice.

Nor did it seem necessary that a trial judge carry out his self-assigned function in a manner that seemed laden with the risk of reversal. Some of the errors were on an elementary level, such as reading to the jury the transcript of remarks that had not been made in the jury's presence—an error because the conversations of judge and counsel at the bench were prejudicial. One such remark thus communicated to the jury was by counsel for G. Gordon Liddy, alleged ringmaster for the break-in of the Democratic National Committee's Watergate headquarters, that certain testimony threatened to damage his client. Another disruptive incident was Judge Sirica's interruption of counsel to remark: "Of course the jury is going to want to know why the men went in there. Let's get down to the details and find out why they went in there and you have some evidence as to that. This is one of the crucial issues in this case. . . ."

When Judge Sirica told counsel and the world, "I could care less about what happens to this case on appeal" and "I could care less what the Court of Appeals does, if this case ever gets up there," he epitomized the trial judge's jealous pride: the appellate court could say what it wished about the law of the case, but this trial judge is king while the case is in this courtroom. The Watergate proceedings had, in fact, already been interrupted several times by piecemeal appeals when Judge Sirica sounded off in that vein.

Yet it must be remembered that the adversary system had broken down long before the start of the Watergate trial. Officials in the White House, where the ultimate targets of the investigation resided, monitored the FBI's work, moved the acting FBI director, L. Patrick Gray III, like a pawn on a chessboard, arranged to have a witness of such stature and importance to the probe as chief campaign fund raiser Maurice H. Stans excused from a personal appearance before the grand jury, withheld evidence from the duly constituted government investigating agencies, and countenanced the perjury of witness Jeb Magruder at the trial itself. An experienced trial judge, former prosecutor, and former local GOP functionary such as Judge Sirica could hardly have avoided the sensation that something fishy was going on around him and that he was presiding over a farce.

It does not excuse the trial judge's conduct that he gave vent to outrage increasingly felt by the general public, since judges are not afforded the luxury of behaving like members of the public. At the same time, it is not demanded of judges that they sit passively by in all circumstances, even when their passivity has the apparent effect of lending judicial blessing to the proceedings before him. Reviewing courts and historians will scrutinize Judge Sirica's conduct for many years to come and the verdict is certain to be mixed, which certainly seems the appropriate judgment. Sirica and other jurists must be scored individually for their acts—praised for their proud moments and criticized for their mistakes. For the basic motivation that underlay Judge Sirica's handling of Watergate, then, high marks; for specific errors and displays of temper, low grades and a reminder that judges, above all, are bound by standards of courtroom conduct.

6

☆ ☆ ☆

THE JUDGES LOBBY

"In other words, federal judges, in conference assembled, are to
be a legally constituted and publicly financed propaganda organization
on behalf of the federal judiciary of the country."

*Representative Clarence F. Lea, Democrat of
California, 1921, commentary on the bill to
establish the Judicial Conference of the United States*

To the extent that the federal judiciary is governed at
all, it is governed by the chief justice of the United States and a
committee of its oldest and highest-ranking judges. The committee of twenty-five is the Judicial Conference of the United States,
established by Congress in 1922 as a clearinghouse of judicial
administrative matters. Its original purpose was the elimination
of judges' "arrears," a term used by Chief Justice Taft to describe
docket backlogs, through meetings to talk over local and general
administrative problems. Once gathered together, the conference—originally called the Conference of Senior Circuit Judges
—could explore ways to eliminate such evils as widely disparate
sentencing by different judges. The conference never licked the
backlog problem, and fifty years after its creation the sentencing
practices of federal judges were still notoriously diverse and
chaotic. But over the years the conference did manage to acquire
many new tasks; some were performed admirably and others
only begat further problems of judicial administration. Regret-

tably on occasion the conference completely slipped its leash and, despite its purpose of helping the judiciary run itself, quietly reached out to lend a hand to other branches of government, chiefly the Congress that created it.

Utter confusion of roles has frequently been the result when this conference of two-dozen-odd jurists has assembled, as it does each fall and spring. Some of the confusion is built into the system: the jurists gather not to judge, which is their assigned function, but to administer the judiciary system, an executive function, and often to make rules, which partakes of the legislative function. Since this is the group most dedicated to the well-being of the federal judiciary, and since it meets at the Supreme Court a stone's throw from the Senate and House of Representatives, the function of seeking legislation of interest to the group often devolves upon the conference—in other words, the Judicial Conference is frequently transformed into a judicial lobby. Because the judges meet in secret, only their published actions—that is, such actions as the conference chooses to make public—are ordinarily available to tell whether their conduct is regular and wise.

Few Americans are at all aware of the governance of this one-third of the federal government, perhaps because of its minuscule budget—only about $135 million each year to operate the Supreme Court, eleven circuit courts of appeals, and ninety-four federal district courts—in an age when spending power and political power are often equated. The chief justice is the conference chairman by virtue of the 1922 statute. Eleven of the members are the chief judges of the eleven circuits. Eleven more members are district court judges, elected to the conference by the judges of their circuits, who meet at least annually for little judicial conferences of their own. For example, the district judges of the Fifth Circuit (Florida, Georgia, Alabama, Mississippi, Louisiana, and Texas) got together in 1969 and elected G. Harrold Carswell, then a judge of the federal district court in Tallahassee, as their representative in the U.S. conference. When Carswell was elevated to the Fifth Circuit bench later the same year, he was obliged to yield his seat on the conference to another district judge, since the appellate judges were represented by the circuit's chief judge. Rounding out the roster of the national conference are the chief judges of two specialized Washington courts, the U.S. Court of Claims and the U.S. Court of Customs and Patent Appeals.

The eleven appellate members hold their chief judgeships by virtue of seniority in terms of length of service. This heavily weights the conference in age toward the later years of judicial careers. Thus, there are eleven chief judges who serve because of their longevity, eleven district judges who serve because of their popularity or prestige among their fellows, two longevity-selected members of the specialized Washington courts, and the presiding chief justice.

It was only natural that some barbs were hurled at the idea of a judicial conference in the early 1920s. At that historical juncture the federal courts were perceived by liberals, and especially by organized labor, as instruments of what was then the commercial and industrial establishment. Federal judges had carved out constitutional property rights for corporations and had overridden the resistance of Eugene Debs to keep the railroads running interstate. They enforced "yellow dog" labor contracts and enjoined work stoppages attempted by unions trying to organize. They snuffed out the social experiments of the more advanced state governments as infringing the due process rights of business. They discovered individual liberty only when proclaiming the "freedom" of individual workers to bargain with their employers one at a time rather than encumbered by the group action of unions. All this and more, in the perception of the beleaguered Democrats and Progressives, epitomized the federal judiciary by the time of the Harding, Coolidge, and Hoover presidencies; a national conference to aggrandize the jurists was to them a most unwelcome prospect.

Yet even the early critics could not have foreseen that the conference might one day lend its hearty endorsement to proposed federal wiretapping legislation, would take sides in congressional disputes over social welfare legislation, would repudiate a prison reform measure less than twenty-four hours after a U.S. president proposed it, and would in the short span of six months take a dramatic step forward and then two long strides backward in the field of ethical reforms for judges.

The foundations for the judicial lobby were laid at the very outset of the chief justiceship of William Howard Taft, perhaps the busiest of all the chief justices up to his time and an architect, if not an empire builder, of the modern judiciary structure. Just days before assuming his post, Taft wrote to the attorney general, Harry M. Daugherty, suggesting an annual conference "of the Chief Justice, the Senior Circuit Judges and the Attorney General at Washington to consider the prospect for the year and to make all possible provision for it." The conference could make recommendations to the attorney general "as to the need of additional Judicial force and where and of what rank, so that Congress might have the benefit of judgment formed on nothing but the need of service." It would inculcate "a much greater sense of responsibility" upon federal judges "growing out of the knowledge that they were under observation as to the work they were doing and that their arrears were being noted."

Nothing in the separation of powers doctrine commands a hermetic seal between heads of the governmental branches, but the Taft-Daugherty proposal went a bit further than that. It proposed that the attorney general should be a member of the conference, not merely an invited guest. Taft testified for his bill—which itself stirred some complaints on separation of powers grounds—and assured Congress that he did not intend a role for the attorney general in the actual assigning of judges to specific districts, although he did ask that Congress authorize the judges of the conference to wield the assignment power with as many as eighteen roving judges at their disposal. What was needed, Taft testified, was an "executive principle" within the judiciary; the attorney general, with his executive branch resources, could help infuse that principle.

The criticism of Taft's reform proposal was the customary mix of partisanship and principle, the liberal opposition having practical and philosophical roots in the distrust of the federal judiciary of the era. The criticism was bipartisan only in the sense that the Republican opponents included many a "Bull

Moose" Republican who had been among Taft's enemies in presidential politics.

To Senator John K. Shields, Democrat of Tennessee, the conference would elevate Taft to the rank of a "Commander-in-Chief and senior circuit judges to the General Staff and district judges to the men in the ranks." Judges, he said, "should be wholly judges, always judges, and nothing but judges." Some day, he predicted disapprovingly, the judges would have the power to rearrange the federal districts and circuits and to perform other legislative tasks such as fixing the times and places for holding court. Striking at an issue close to the heart of Taft's vision for the judiciary, Shields said the chief justice had offered himself as "the executive head of the judiciary," a title more appropriate for a British lord. "Now the Lord High Chancellor of England is both a judicial and political officer," said Shields. "Are we not somewhat copying after the system in England and creating a political as well as a judicial head of the Federal Judiciary?" Thomas J. Walsh, Democrat of Montana, an archfoe of Taft's, said the conference meant "absolutely nothing on earth except a junket and a dinner." Senator Thaddeus H. Caraway, Democrat of Arkansas, worried about the proposed power, whether vested in the conference or the chief justice, to send in substitute judges. He saw it as a threat—sitting district judges enforce the laws according to the wishes of a central authority or risk having sudden assistance in their duties.

The opposition to what was called a "flying squadron" of judges proved quite widespread, and like the attorney general's proposed conference role, the proposal did not survive the bill's passage. Senators asserted their prerogative of judicial appointment, that notorious leverage with the executive branch that converted the formal power to nominate into a de facto power of the individual senator. The bill did authorize new judges, but they were to be tied to their districts. The judges could be temporarily transferred between districts under the bill, but only after the circuit chief judges had filed certificates of availability and need to justify the transfer. (In later years, it proved ironically, this transfer power came under criticism for facilitating "junkets," as judges fell into the habit of making themselves available for temporary service in districts with more congenial climates than their own.)

Supporters of the bill also had a lot going for them, including the alarming "arrears" in Prohibition cases and prosecution and other litigation growing out of the world war. The suggestion that a better-organized and better-staffed judiciary might rid the jails of thousands of persons accused of Prohibition crimes doubtless fell on sympathetic ears in 1921 and 1922. Final passage was by a lopsided two to one margin.

Time has vindicated both the supporters of the change and its detractors. The principle of management responsibility within the judiciary seemed a sound objective. If properly contained and channeled, the management power was perhaps the only way to operate the judicial system without inviting other branches, carrying threats of their own to judicial independence, to do the job for the judges. Moreover, Congress fundamentally did not even want the management task with its mundane day-to-day details. But the predicted dangers were also undeniable, and it was only a matter of time before some of the dire prophecies were realized.

By the time the Judicial Conference came under attack in Congress, late in the 1960s, for what it had actually done and not just for its potential, there was a new brand of activism in the federal court system. The judicial activists of the Taft school had been friends of corporations, enemies of labor. Liberals saw them as oblivious to the truly pressing problems of the day. The new activism in the two decades after *Brown* v. *Board of Education* was viewed as a prolabor, pro–civil rights, and often antibusiness brand of judicial behavior.

It happened that one of the most critical administrative challenges these judges faced was closely tied to civil rights: What relief could be devised for the overloaded Fifth Circuit? The logic of case loads dictated that the circuit be subdivided, but that would isolate the courts of the region from each other. A liberal judge from Texas would no longer be available to play a role in a troublesome civil rights case from Alabama. Mississippi blacks, who saw their enjoyment of federal rights already imperiled by the Mississippi federal trial judges, might find themselves similarly threatened at the appellate level if the circuit no longer had the balancing influence of judges from Texas or Florida. Civil and commercial lawsuits might also tend to be handled in a too provincial manner without, for example, the flavoring that a Louisiana judge could lend to a case from Georgia. Thus it was that, despite the apparent logic of redrawing the circuit boundaries, the liberals under Chief Justice Earl Warren who dominated the Judicial Conference's key committees drove toward a different solution: add more judges temporarily and resolve to study the case load problem further. And thus it was with a political and social as well as a management perspective that the conference, in the fall of 1964, turned its back temporarily on the realignment of the circuits.

If the conference's quasi-political adventures have had any single bright hour, it might be said to have been the federal jury reform of 1966, 1967, and 1968. The way federal courts choose their juries cannot be said to be purely a judicial problem or purely political, for it partakes of both elements. Judges must administer the jury system, and they have a deep and valid interest in the underlying selection policies; but it is a matter of high public and legislative concern as well. A "blue ribbon" jury of successful professional men may have great collective wisdom, but it would be deemed "stacked" against a woman plaintiff suing for damages over alleged job discrimination. Racial bias is an old curse in jury selection. Discriminatory and unnecessary intelligence tests, discriminatorily and unintelligently administered, can be an effective instrument of racial prejudice. Since jury service is both a privilege and a responsibility of citizenship, Congress has a great stake in setting a policy that maximizes citizen participation. When President Johnson proposed wider citizen service on federal and state juries as part of his 1966 civil rights program, Congress balked initially, and it had the backing of traditionalist-minded federal judges, many of whom were proud of their high-quality, highly literate juries, in doing so.

State jury reform quickly fell by the wayside in a welter of states' rights rhetoric. There was undoubted authority for Congress to legislate in the federal court field, but federal jury reform was thwarted when it was considered as a civil rights matter. Senator Joseph D. Tydings, chairman of the Subcommittee on Improvements in Judicial Machinery, recognized that the problem was judicial as well, and he assumed jurisdiction when the civil rights package was parceled out among the relevant committees. Prodded by Judge Irving R. Kaufman of the Second Circuit and by Stephen J. Pollak, assistant attorney general for civil rights, the Judicial Conference, the executive branch, and finally the Congress all were persuaded to agree on a system of random selection of federal jurors from voter lists and a screening system free of devices that were susceptible to discriminatory application. The reform drive required that powerful and stubborn federal judges be persuaded of the dire need for change. The lines of separation between branches were frequently fuzzed, but the result this time was beneficial. The system worked and produced the Jury Selection and Service Act of 1968.

What makes it permissible, even laudable, for the conference to participate in the jury legislation when other forms of action are criticized? The line will often be hard to draw, even for the most scrupulous and sensitive jurists, but it should be drawn along a scale with court administration at one end and social policy at the other. Matters safely within court administration are suitable for judges' commentary, while matters of social policy are out of bounds. Legislation regulating the jury system, while partaking both of administration and policy, calls for a major input from the judges who will operate the system, for the judges may have much to tell the Congress about the technical and operational aspects of the law. By contrast, a proposal to restore the power of federal courts to issue certain kinds of labor injunction has some implications for court administration, but these are minor compared with the social and economic sweep of such a bill. If there are technical problems for the judiciary in this kind of legislation, the judges may safely share their expertise with the Congress provided they restrict their advice to those technical matters.

To suggest another line between the appropriate and the inappropriate: It would be very much in keeping with the conference's proper role to propose legislation establishing grievance machinery for federal prisoners, since this would greatly simplify the administration of federal court petitions from inmates. But it would be overstepping to ask Congress to limit the habeas corpus rights of federal prisoners. Prison reform measures in general are pertinent to the conference's work, but again it would be overstepping if the conference were to give Congress its view, for or against, the death penalty. These are matters of judgment in many cases, but the line must be drawn where administration leaves off and social policy begins, if that line can be located at all.

A conspicuous example of judicial overstepping was the conference's meddling in pending federal wiretapping legislation. At its September 1967 meeting in Washington, the conference adopted a resolution endorsing the *purposes* of pending wiretapping and electronic "bugging" proposals. The resolution was transmitted to Congress a few days later, putting the federal judiciary on record with the legislature.

The conference action came at a critical juncture in the development of what became the federal Omnibus Crime and Safe Streets Act of 1968 and its controversial title III, authorizing electronic eavesdropping by law enforcement officers under court order. After years of attempts by several attorneys general and such congressional conservatives as Senator John L. McClellan of Arkansas, the campaign for permissive eavesdropping legislation seemed within sight of its goal. The Johnson administration and its attorney general, Ramsey Clark, opposed such measures, but prospects for their own proposal—a bill to outlaw all eavesdropping, official and private, except for so-called national security taps and bugs—was going nowhere. Some confusion had been introduced into the debate over the constitutionality of pro-eavesdropping bills by a Supreme Court decision the previous June that struck down the bugging section of New York State's eavesdropping law. McClellan, after an initial statement condemning the Court for once again "coddling" the criminal element, came to regard the decision as a blueprint for a statute that would be constitutional, so that legislation he had long sponsored could be merely "tightened" by adding the safeguards the High Court had found lacking in the New York law. Others pointed to language in the decision of *Berger* v. *New York* calling for safeguards that no new statute was likely to bestow upon the targets of government surveillance. If the jurists at the top of the hierarchy were to say at this stage that a constitutional law could be drafted, what a boon it might be to the cause of such a proposal, which its supporters were preparing to offer in congressional subcommittees. Never mind that the jurists would not be speaking *ex cathedra* and would not be treating a real live case or controversy that is the bedrock of their jurisdiction; the advisory opinion would be most welcome. But to go further and have these judges, in conference assembled, actually endorse the aims and policy of court-ordered wiretapping, would be support not to be dreamed of.

Yet that is what the conference resolution did. Acting with little or no debate, the conference adopted noddingly a resolution proposed by a committee on criminal law headed by Judge George C. Edwards, Jr., of the Sixth U.S. Circuit Court of Appeals. His liberalism on issues of police interrogation obscured in the minds of many that he had been a rugged police chief in Detroit, where he developed strong feelings about organized crime and the need for wiretapping to combat it.

Edwards's resolution recited that the committee "considered the various bills designed generally to prohibit wiretapping and/or eavesdropping now pending in Congress," including the McClellan bill for wiretapping and the Johnson administration's bill against it. "Of the various bills studied," the resolution went on, "the committee concluded that the purposes of S. 675, introduced by Senator McClellan for himself and Senator Hruska, were most acceptable." Translation: The purposes of legislation to permit wiretapping by court order were superior to the purposes of legislation to ban wiretapping whether by government agents or private individuals. And among those bills permitting court-ordered eavesdropping, the McClellan-Hruska bill was most acceptable. (Curiously, even legal aides to McClellan and Hruska acknowledged that their bill was more vulnerable to constitutional attack, and thus needed more work, than a bill sponsored by Representative William M. McCulloch, Republican of Ohio, and that the McClellan-Hruska bill was a wiretap bill only, whereas the McCulloch bill covered all forms of electronic eavesdropping.)

After thus performing the legislative function of blessing the policy aims of the prowiretap bill, the Edwards resolution ventured an opinion on its constitutionality, a function more in keeping with judges' occupational skills but an equally improper thing for judges to do at this stage of lawmaking. "The committee feels," said the resolution, that the bill "will have to be revised in light of the Supreme Court's opinion in *Berger v. New York*." Translation: The bill is unconstitutional as written. Congress already knew this, but the question of whether it *could* be redrafted to make it constitutional was an open one for some legislators. The committee concluded by recommending "that the bill be approved provided it be amended to comply with the standards of the opinion in *Berger v. New York*."

Not surprisingly, news of the conference action brought jubilation to the protap forces. The Republican Task Force on Crime, which was developing issues for the 1968 national election, promptly introduced its latest draft of the wiretap bill and said it was "supported by the Judicial Conference of the United States." The task force, headed by Representatives Richard H. Poff of Virginia and Robert Taft, Jr., of Ohio, proclaimed the belief

that this is one of the most significant statements that has ever been issued on the subject during the many years that it has been debated. The Conference is a body of unparalleled prestige. It is headed by the Chief Justice of the United States Supreme Court. . . . The Conference report represents the considered judgment of a purely judicial body. The members are in no way spokesmen for law enforcement. Their stated position, volunteered and unsolicited, can only be interpreted in one way. They recognize the need for electronic surveillance in order effectively to fight crime. However, they recognize that law enforcement can be given this vital tool within the limitations of the Constitution. The impact of this report is staggering. As the totally voluntary act of an eminently responsible group, it undoubtedly reflects the deep concern with which its members view the menace of organized crime and the problems of combatting it. It utterly destroys whatever was left of the Administration's position against the court supervised use of electronic surveillance.

Significantly, none of the wiretap supporters in Congress noted any reservations about the propriety of the conference action. That was to come later, when the conference opposed legislation advanced by McClellan. For now, they were happy to receive this unsolicited backing. And unsolicited it was, as Edwards and perhaps the entire Judicial Conference were surprised to learn. It developed that a few years earlier, in 1965, the House Judiciary Committee had asked for an opinion on an antieavesdrop bill and the conference had responded with disapproval. Since then, judges on the conference and their aides had maintained a watch on pending eavesdrop bills, combing the *Congressional Record* and referring these and other ideas to the conference with or without an inquiry from Congress. The conference clearly acted in 1967 without knowing what it was doing: volunteering legislative advice. Apparently there was no one who saw the need to question whether the advice ought to be given even if requested. It was just this kind of advice, however, that Chief Justice Jay refused to give Secretary of State Jefferson in his lecture on the judicial function and the separation of powers. What could the conference legitimately have told Congress about wiretapping? Perhaps whether the judges could physically cope with the expected case load of applications for wiretap warrants or some other lessons from judges' administrative experience. But the line should have been drawn at discussions about the desirability or constitutionality of such legislation.

At its next meeting the conference noted officially in its report to Congress "that some criticism has been raised" about unsolic-ited advice. It resolved that "it is appropriate for the Conference to study legislation affecting the judiciary and that the views of the Conference should be given in advance of consideration of such legislation even though its views have not specifically been sought. The Conference voted to adhere to its present practice." The resolution thus addressed only the question of volunteering advice. It either avoided or decided wrongly the question of whether all legislation "affecting the judiciary" is appropriate for conference comment. It said nothing about possible restraint in venturing opinions about the policy values in pro- or antiwiretap laws or refraining from prejudging their constitutionality. Utterly ignored was the error that compounded all the other errors: that the conference failed even to inform itself as to whether the advice had been solicited before giving it. There may be situations where the propriety of rendering advice is a close question and the fact that Congress seeks the advice is relevant to whether the conference should take action. But to respond intelligently to any supposed congressional need, the conference must of course at least know that it is being asked. Finally, the conference failed completely to resolve not to be so sloppy in its craftsmanship in the future as to confuse completely the bills in question and the separate issues they might raise.

Judges should draw the line short of meddling in social policy even when their intervention would help a worthy cause. If the wiretapping resolution was improper, so also was the action taken by the conference at its fall 1969 meeting on the merits of pending antipoverty legislation.

The antipoverty issue was over the so-called Murphy Amendment to a bill renewing the authorization for the Office of Economic Opportunity and its legal services program. Senator George Murphy of California, whose antipathy toward legal services for the poor rose with each success of program attorneys in the senator's home state, persuaded the Senate to adopt his amendment severely restricting the program. The matter was pending in the House of Representatives, where the amendment was ultimately killed after strenuous efforts by the American Bar Association, a strong supporter of the program, in protest of efforts to interfere with the ability of lawyers to represent their clients adequately. The amendment would have given state governors an item veto over any federally funded legal services program within his state, leaving the state's officials free to kill, selectively, programs that were most effective in taking state officials to court over alleged denial of the rights of the poor. It would have removed the power of the director of the OEO to override a governor's veto. Not without reason, antipoverty workers and many members of the bar considered this to be repressive legislation, a reprisal for the success of neighborhood legal services offices in California and elsewhere in forcing government to obey the law and the Constitution in its treatment of farm laborers, migratory workers, welfare recipients, and the unemployed among others.

Notwithstanding the high emotional and political content of the issue, the conference resolved its disapproval of the Murphy Amendment and proceeded to inform Congress of its views. Most lawyers were quick to agree that a resolution on the subject was hardly the business of the U.S. Judicial Conference. It was social legislation (or antisocial legislation, depending on one's view of it), and despite its legal aspects the amendment was beyond the scope of the conference's charter to disapprove—or to approve.

The conference's action at the same session on a section of what became the Organized Crime Act of 1970 arguably posed a closer question. Many judges said they feared that the bill would create "runaway grand juries" in their courthouses, whereas grand juries should remain as "arms of the court" and subject to judicial control. In its initial draft the bill would have given all grand juries the power to accuse public officials of less than criminal misconduct if they lacked evidence to indict them for a crime. It would have provided for the automatic convening of grand juries, whether or not deemed necessary by the Justice Department, to check on organized crime conditions. The grand jury could extend its own life despite judges' wishes that it disband, and it could complain to Washington if not satisfied with the zeal displayed by the United States attorney's office. Most of these provisions were somewhat modified later in a manner more pleasing to the judges and enacted into law. The motivation for the proposal was the view of some prosecutors in organized crime cases that Mafia investigations were often threatened by the possibility that a presiding district judge would terminate the grand jury prematurely. More than a trace of prosecutorial zeal is reflected in this judgment: it carries a hint that some judges are "soft" on organized crime to the point of downright corruption. Understandably resentful, the judiciary struck back in the conference resolution to go on record opposing the semiautonomous grand jury idea.

Again, the advice was unsolicited. This time, McClellan resented it bitterly, taking the Senate floor to denounce the judges and tell them to stick to judging. On reflection, one may well conclude that neither side had all the better of the argument. The question was a mixed one of social judgment—what should be done that was not being done about organized crime?—and judicial administration and integrity—must the judiciary take this congressional verdict lying down? Whatever the merits, the conference chose the only clearly wrong way to go about expressing itself: a judgment made in secret, with little public display of evidence, followed by an unsolicited communiqué to Congress registering disapproval in a conclusory and abrupt fashion. The entire explanation of the conference action, McClellan noted tartly in the Senate, was that the bill "would drastically alter an important facet of the judicial process."

This time the conference provoked not only the sponsors of the legislation, Murphy as well as McClellan, but an additional and more formidable critic, Senator Sam J. Ervin, Jr., of North Carolina. Ervin's Judiciary Subcommittee on the Separation of Powers had already been studying the problem of judicial independence posed by the celebrated Fortas and Douglas cases, among others, and was amassing a thick volume of material aimed at countering proposals to control life-tenured federal judges. But just as Ervin condemned restrictions on constitutionally protected judges, he placed high value on keeping the judges in what he considered *their* place. The Judicial Conference should stick to housekeeping chores, and judges should decide cases and controversies. He launched a subcommittee investigation into the conference.

"The Judicial Conference is engaged in activities today which were wholly unintended by Congress when it created the conference in 1922," Ervin said shortly before the hearings began. Not doubting that the conference had gone awry, he declared, "The aim of these hearings is to learn precisely how far the Conference and the Councils (of each circuit) have deviated from the congressional purpose."

Chairman Ervin opened the hearings by offering what appeared to him to be a "compelling" suggestion: Why not open the conference to the public and the press? Conference members do not sit in a judicial capacity when they convene twice a year in Washington.

They certainly do not act as judges when they vote to approve or disapprove of pending legislation, or adopt rules of financial disclosure for their colleagues. Why, then, should the conference meet in secret? I believe that when judges act as policymakers and lobbyists, it follows that their discussions should be public. If the Conference supports or opposes a bill, the Congress and the public should have free access to the Conference's debate on that proposal. The Congress should know how carefully the Judicial Conference researches its positions so that it can attach relative weights to them.

If conference members were aware that their remarks would appear in the next morning's newspaper, "they would likely be more cautious in taking positions on matters that do not concern them."

The defense witness for the conference was J. Edward Lumbard, who had been a conference member for ten years by virtue of his position as chief judge of the United States Court of Appeals for the Second Circuit. A more skilled witness could hardly have been chosen. Judge Lumbard, a onetime rackets prosecutor under Thomas E. Dewey, had won the hearts of Ervin, McClellan, and other Senate conservatives with his legal opinions and his congressional testimony on law enforcement subjects. McClellan, who was enraged when the conference offered unsolicited advice on his grand jury bill, had invited Lumbard to testify before his Criminal Laws Subcommittee when he knew that the judge would support the 1967 version of his wiretap bill. When Lumbard appeared and told the senators that wiretapping was "the single most important tool for investigating organized crime," not only did he not stir a protest from either McClellan or Ervin, but the North Carolina constitutionalist asked Judge Lumbard to look at a constitutional amendment on the use of confessions in criminal cases "and if you think there ought to be some changes made in it, I would certainly welcome them."

Chief Judge Lumbard, an advocate of judicial self-restraint on the bench, stoutly defended all but one of the off-the-bench resolutions of the Judicial Conference during his tenure. Specifically defending the grand jury resolution, he declared: "I do submit most respectfully that this is a matter upon which it was appropriate and even desirable that we should express some opinion. Grand juries are the arms of the court. They are instructed by the judges. What they do is under the supervision of judges." Obviously opinions expressed would be "no better than the reasons which we give for our views" and Congress may disregard them. Asked by a subcommittee aide what restrictions there should be on opinion giving in the wiretapping area, Lumbard said judges should refrain from comment on matters that could come before them on the bench, but there was no problem about wiretapping. The issue in court would be limited, he said, to such matters as whether the statute had been complied with in obtaining a particular wiretap order. The judge did not address the question of whether the act's basic constitutionality might come before him or other conference members—a major omission.

"The only time where I have felt that we stepped over the line," said Lumbard, was the disapproval of the legal services Murphy Amendment. Even that could be explained as the careless acquiescence in the last-minute plea by David L. Bazelon, chief judge of the District of Columbia Circuit. Lumbard said he and Chief Justice Burger, who was presiding over his first conference meeting, agreed afterward that steps must be taken to guard against such "precipitate action" in the future. Henceforth any proposal that had not gone through any of the dozen conference committees would not be voted on except with the approval of three-fourths of the membership. Lumbard said the Bazelon proposal was made without notice before the meeting and was brought up only at the last minute as the judges were beginning to leave. Did no member have prior notice? he was asked. "I didn't," Lumbard replied. "I had no prior notice, and we think that is not the proper way for the Conference to conduct its business." Bazelon, appearing as a subcommittee witness the following month, produced a letter he had written to Chief Justice Burger one day before the conference meeting, copies of which were placed in every judge's folder, in which the recommendation was made. Bazelon testified that several judges talked with him about the letter during breaks in the two-day meeting. The contradiction in testimony was never resolved, so it was never made clear how sudden the conference action was. What was established was that the conference considered precipitateness its only sin and had no apology for actions taken after due deliberation.

In the showdown, Ervin was gentle with the Judicial Conference. Most of his inquiry became focused on proposals that he deemed equally threatening to judicial independence, principally legislation offered by Senator Joseph D. Tydings, Democrat of Maryland, to create a commission to take action against nonimpeachable misconduct by federal judges. Unwilling to forswear all recourse to the judicial lobby, Ervin wrote each of the five hundred fifty or so federal trial and appellate judges asking their opinion on the Tydings bill, venturing his judgment that the bill would undermine their independence and would be unconstitutional. Not surprisingly, nearly all of the sixty-eight judges who replied agreed with Ervin, a handful reserving judgment on grounds that an opinion would be premature. The bill died with the Ninety-first Congress and the defeat of Tydings at the polls buried it. Ervin and the Judicial Conference turned to their other affairs. For the conference, those affairs included setting the ethical tone for the federal judiciary.

7

☆ ☆ ☆

EARL WARREN AND WARREN EARL

I advocate a semi-revolution.
The trouble with a total revolution
(Ask any reputable Rosicrucian)
Is that it brings the same class up on top. . . .
Robert Frost, "A Semi-Revolution"

Two very different types of men occupied the position of chief justice of the United States during the ethical crisis of the late 1960s and its aftermath. Outwardly they were strikingly similar—Earl Warren, tall, husky, and robust; and Warren Earl Burger, tall, stocky, energetic. Each man fully looked the part of chief justice, and each in his own way sought to maximize the powers of the occupant of the center chair on the Court. Both men, reared in humble circumstances and self-made, grew out of Republican politics and both owed their judicial careers to timely alliances with the candidacies of Thomas E. Dewey and Dwight D. Eisenhower.

Despite the many obvious similarities—or superficial resemblances—the two chief justices represented quite distinct schools of thought. By coincidence or otherwise, the differences were not confined to judicial philosophy but extended, perhaps in starker contrast, to the realms of ethical philosophy and judicial administration as well. In judicial ethics as in judicial philosophy, Warren was an aggressive, activist leader when he perceived a wrong that needed correcting. Burger did not shrink from demanding certain standards of conduct from lawyers, and he labored to promote an increase of what he termed "civility" in public discourse; but he exercised the utmost restraint when it came to setting ethical norms for the judiciary.

The contrast between the two men in judicial approach—that is, on-the-bench decision making in legal cases and controversies —was of course quite predictable. It was, in fact, the desire of President Nixon that his appointee would symbolize a new turn in the course of Supreme Court history. Mr. Nixon had made abundantly clear during the campaign of 1968 that he considered the Supreme Court a too-permissive, too-liberal institution under Warren and that it needed what he called "strict constructionist" justices. As for the ethical crisis of 1968 and 1969, its primary effect was to ensure that after the resignation of Justice Fortas, the Nixon nominees would not be presidential "cronies" in the mold of Lyndon Johnson's ill-fated nominees, Abe Fortas and Homer Thornberry. In discussing his choice of Burger as chief justice with the press a week after the Fortas resignation, Nixon emphasized that Burger was nothing more than a distant political acquaintance and a jurist whose work he had admired.

The Nixon administration gratefully received the departure of Fortas as a political opportunity, like the scheduled departure of Earl Warren. This is not the place, and it may not yet be the time, to rehash the Nixon successes and (more notably) failures in his bid to transform the Supreme Court politically. But a lot can be said about the performances of Warren and Burger in the field of ethical and moral leadership for the judiciary, for there the distinction showed quickly and clearly. In simplest terms, Warren met the crisis with measures that amounted to a semi-revolution in ethical norms for federal judges; Burger was part of a counterrevolution.

Important consequences flowed from the change in the direction of the judiciary's ethical leadership after Burger replaced Warren in 1969. The net change was something less than a total reversal in the Warren thrust for a significantly higher standard of ethics and accountability for judges and justices. In a sense—the sense of the poet Robert Frost in the passage that heads this chapter—what occurred was the completion of the revolution in such a way that many of the old values landed again on top, right side up, although the sweep of events did leave some lasting changes for the better. This chapter recalls the story of the crisis period and attempts to survey the gains and losses for the integrity, and the appearance of integrity, of the judiciary. It is necessary to begin with an understanding of each chief justice in the context of the challenges that confronted him.

Warren had been in public office for nearly fifty years when, at the close of a term during which he had hoped to be in retirement, the Court he headed was struck twice by lightning: further controversy over Justice Douglas's relationship with the Parvin Foundation and the Fortas resignation. The chief justice's own career as county prosecutor, attorney general, and four times the elected governor of California in addition to his fifteen years on the High Court had been unblemished by financial scandal. He was politically and fiscally "clean," one might say almost unbelievably so. At the age of seventy-eight, in the spring of 1969, Warren exuded good health and had the bearing of a man totally at ease with his conscience. He had never accumulated a fortune, but he had never sought one, and he had managed to raise a family of six children on his public salary.

Earl Warren had an immense capacity for righteous indignation that manifested itself early in his prosecutorial pursuit of hoodlums in his home state of California and later, astride the high bench, when he rained down on government lawyers the famous unanswerable question, "Were you fair?" The fervor of his moral judgments generated what critics have come to condemn as a simplistic desire to right wrongs and "do justice" at times without due regard for the Court's function of interpreting the laws to establish principles that will work for a long time. This criticism was itself not always fair. Critics often failed to notice the tension Warren experienced between his own revulsion of obscenity and his defense of free speech. While protesting that there is a "right of the nation and of the states to maintain a decent society," his view of the Constitution often moved him to sustain the free expression of things simultaneously repugnant to him personally. Maintaining these values simultaneously was anything but a simple matter.

One of Warren's most famous off-the-bench utterances was his November 1962 address to the Louis Marshall Award dinner of the Jewish Theological Seminary in New York, in which he called for training experts in ethics and using them in business and society, the way corporations summon experts in engineering, finance, and law before making key decisions. "In civilized life, Law floats in a sea of Ethics," Warren said.

Each is indispensable to civilization. Without Law, we should be at the mercy of the least scrupulous; without Ethics, Law could not exist. . . . Is it fantastic to suggest that there is an urgent need in our troubled times for the development of the profession of the counselor in ethics, having the same relation to interpersonal conduct, beyond the Law, that the lawyer has to conduct that is subject to review in the courts?

It was one of history's most conspicuous ironies that Warren, who retired happily from the political arena when he became chief justice in 1953, embarked in 1964 on one of the most far-reaching nonjudicial pursuits of any justice, the chairmanship of the commission to investigate the assassination of President Kennedy. He did it, he explained, much against his will and because President Johnson pleaded with him to undertake the job in the national interest, pulling out all the stops including confiding a fear of nuclear holocaust if the world got the notion that a conspiracy had existed. Years later Warren expressed doubt about the premises of Mr. Johnson's urgings. That major nonjudicial chore aside, Warren for the most part held firmly to the work of the Court, which of course brought him attention, praise, and blame in ample measure. his personal integrity and the public bearing that conveyed his qualities of character were major factors in the Court's ability to withstand the often savage public reaction to its most controversial decisions and to retain the goodwill of multitudes when the justices took unpopular action.

Notwithstanding these qualities, Warren saw the ethical tone of the federal judiciary slip under his leadership. In 1963 the

Wall Street Journal disclosed that lower court judges in significant numbers were performing outside work for pay as directors of corporations, banks, and insurance companies. One senior federal judge in New York had earned as much as $212,600 in 1953—a year when a district judge's salary was $15,000—as a director of the Equitable Life Assurance Society. Three of the six members of the Seventh U.S. Circuit Court of Appeals were directors of Chicago banks. One judge saw nothing improper about presiding over a case in which a litigant was represented by a fellow board member, or participating in another in which the bank's counsel was a lawyer for one of the parties. Nor were the judges inhibited from handling cases involving the competitors of their banks. The moonlighting took place against a backdrop of some ethical uncertainty. No federal law directly prohibited it unless the judge went so far as to practice law. The ABA canons, with their injunctions to preserve the appearance of propriety, said eloquently to some, but not to others, that this moonlighting was unethical. The ABA's own ethics committee had condemned membership on boards of profit-making companies in a 1943 opinion based on its interpretation of the canons, but Judge Win G. Knoch of the Seventh Circuit told the *Journal's* reporter, Jerry Landauer, that the ABA opinion smacked of "sermonizing." Far from preaching, the ABA had merely pointed out the high probability that banks, insurance companies, and like businesses were frequently involved in litigation that could come before the judges' courts. And since all banks publicize the names of their board members to some degree, the ABA had said, "this might create the reasonable suspicion that the judge was utilizing the prestige of his office to persuade others to patronize the bank."

Reaction to the article was prompt. The judiciary responded with commendable pep, especially when Senator Estes Kefauver, Democrat of Tennessee and a member of the Judiciary Committee, began exploring legislation to restrict nonjudicial business activities. The Judicial Conference, at its next meeting in September, approved a resolution that headed off the legislation. By its terms, no federal judge or Supreme Court justice "shall serve in the capacity of officer, director or employee of a corporation organized for profit."

Why did the resolution include Supreme Court justices when only the lower federal judiciary had been publicly embarrassed and the Judicial Conference years later was to disclaim any jurisdiction over High Court ethics? Two answers suggest themselves. One is that only a comprehensive resolution would have sufficed to head off the legislation, and the jurisdictional problem was either conveniently ignored or inadvertently forgotten. Another is that the conference simply borrowed language from the pending legislation, which had been broadly based on the power of Congress to legislate such matters for the entire federal judiciary, including the Supreme Court, and the conference draftsmen purposely or inadvertently failed to observe the jurisdictional limitation. As it turned out, Supreme Court members did not run afoul of this resolution; the Douglas and Fortas controversies concerned outside service with nonprofit charitable foundations, which were not covered.

Other moonlighting by justices, however, was becoming a problem for the Court. Several members were so busy with outside speaking engagements—which paid $300, $500, $1,000, and up per appearance—that they required the services of speakers' bureaus, that is, booking agents, who in turn generated more speaking engagements for a commission. "The whole tone of the place could be improved," one former law clerk said at the time.

Warren could have been spared the climax of all the rising controversy if he had been able to retire when he wished. The blocking of Justice Fortas's nomination for chief justice in September left Warren in that post with a new term already begun. His resignation was nevertheless effective at the pleasure of the president, who would soon be his old enemy, Richard M. Nixon. An uncomfortable period loomed in the weeks after the November 1968 election, but when President-elect Nixon learned of the potential embarrassment to Warren and the potential difficulty for the Court in transition, he made a magnanimous public move, announcing that he had asked

Warren to stay on until June. It was during those borrowed months that Fortas so suddenly left the Court.

Only about a month remained in Warren's tenure after Fortas's resignation in mid-May, and Warren used the time for a crash program to clean the judiciary's house. Within days he convened the Judicial Conference's standing committee on court administration for an emergency meeting on ways to curb nonjudicial activities of federal judges and to institute possible financial disclosure rules. The committee's chairman, Judge Robert A. Ainsworth, Jr., of the Fifth U.S. Circuit Court of Appeals, announced a recommendation that Warren call a special meeting of the conference itself; Warren, not surprisingly, complied. Ainsworth's committee worked secretly but swiftly in time to offer its resolution to the conference on June 10.

On that date the conference met with its usual secrecy, the debate insulated from press and public scrutiny by guards at the Supreme Court building. The judges were urged on by Senator Tydings, who appeared before them long enough to point out that Congress was hovering over their deliberations and would fill the void "if the judiciary fails to put its own house in order."

The committee was armed with two sets of resolutions, one banning all judicial moonlighting, the other a fall back proposal tailored more directly to the problem of compensation but nonetheless greatly curbing outside activities. The first plan was quickly scrapped when several conference members attacked it. The maneuver did not forestall bitter debate on the less severe alternative proposal. A number of judges protested the haste and contended that the proposals of Warren's administration committee were aimed at the wrong people, since justices, not judges, had been responsible for the violations. Warren acknowledged this but said he was sure that if the conference took strong action, he could use it to prevail on the members of the Supreme Court to make a similar move voluntarily. Warren won out over a small but vocal minority.

The conference resolved:

1. No more outside compensation for services rendered unless the nonjudicial work is approved by the judicial council of the

judge's circuit—the members of the court of appeals wearing their administrative hats—as not interfering with the judge's bench work. Such pay must be a matter of public record.

2. Starting May 15, 1970, every federal judge must file with the conference a statement of his income, investments, and other assets and his liabilities during the previous calendar year. This would be a confidential report but the conference would reserve the power to make the files public.

3. Ainsworth's committee would start drafting "standards of judicial conduct for federal judges," an ethical code that would have only moral force unless Congress were to adopt it as law. The committee would start drafting legislation along similar lines and disclosure regulations were to be prepared by September.

True to his word, but with little notice to his fellow justices, Warren put ethics on the agenda of the Court's regular Friday conference three days later. The following Monday he disclosed that his drive had faded in the home stretch. In a terse announcement he said he had reported the conference action and had

suggested the propriety of the justices taking a similar action. Some of the justices urged that because we are now approaching the end of the term and because there will be a new Chief Justice and Associate Justice on the Court when it convenes in October that no action on the matter should be taken before that time. After full discussion of the subject, a majority of the justices agreed to this course of action.

Only Justice Thurgood Marshall went down the line publicly with Warren, announcing separately that he would comply voluntarily with the conference rules by filing his own financial accounting confidentially with his Supreme Court brethren.

The depth of Warren's disappointment was plain. Tydings revived his threats of congressional interest, calling the conference action and Court inaction a "dangerous anomaly." The crowning irony, he said, was that the Supreme Court "to many Americans constitutes the federal judiciary." The following Monday, June 20, on his last day as chief justice, Warren was able to announce that three other justices, Brennan, Stewart, and Byron R. White, had joined him in principle.

While a majority of all the justices considered it inappropriate at that time for the Court as an official matter to deal with the outside activities of the individual justices, or with the disclosures of their assets and income, Justices Brennan, Stewart, White and Marshall individually indicated their agreement in principle with the standards of conduct adopted by the Judicial Conference and their intention to act accordingly.

The three justices who were not represented in this statement were Douglas and Hugo L. Black, long known for their views that the Constitution is hostile to controls over federal judges, and John Marshall Harlan, whose fastidiousness in personal ethics was exceeded only by his desire for personal and judicial privacy. No less concerned over privacy, Brennan, long a gregarious justice and frequent outside speaker, had just vowed to forego all nonjudicial activities except his church membership. But any further action by the justices would have to await the deliberations of the newly constituted Court.

This, then, was the "state of the judiciary" when Burger assumed its top position. Warren had rammed through his special plan for drastic and swift reform, but many judges were unhappy for reasons ranging from lofty factors of Constitution and conscience down to considerable personal apprehension at the formidable duties of compliance. Not only was the supervision of other judges nettlesome, but especially onerous was the looming deadline the following May for filing a confidential statement of income, liabilities, and net worth for the *current year*. No judge could afford to complain openly, but they might have been entitled to more sympathy for the lack of a grace period for getting rid of items the judges might not want to report.

As it developed, no public outcry was needed because the private negotiations among judges proved quite sufficient to arrest and then turn back the zealous reform drive. In Burger the disaffected judges found a true "judge's judge." Indeed, when he was introduced by President Nixon on national television on May 21 as the nominee for chief justice, Burger's response was a bouquet to the lower judiciary: "I hope you won't mind if I say that in a sense at least you pay tribute to all of the sitting judges of the federal and state systems in this nomination, men and women who day in and day out perform the difficult tasks of the administration of justice. I hope I can, in a way, share that with all of them tonight. I thank you very, very much, Mr. President."

Burger had scarcely had time to get used to the idea of being chief justice when his first ethical problem confronted him, and the problem was personal. The White House staff, gun-shy over the matter of charitable foundations then so current in the Fortas case, omitted from its press release about Burger the fact that for several years he had been a trustee of the Mayo Foundation of Rochester, Minnesota. There was nothing wrong with having been a Mayo trustee, although of course it was a form of moonlighting that some jurists wanted to forbid along with others; nor had Burger ever made a secret of it. He was, in fact, quite proud of it, as well he might be as a Minnesotan and a self-made professional who had worked his way to one of his home state's most honored private posts. By failing to disclose the connection, the White House had made it seem somewhat mysterious and unworthy, but that was not Burger's only problem. He had not had time to sort out such matters, but he was expecting in any event to quit the foundation, which had reimbursed him for the expense of attending quarterly meetings until 1966, when trustees began receiving a $2,000 annual honorarium. But to resign at this juncture, in Burger's view, might be construed as a concession that there had been something improper about it or that he disapproved such activity for other judges. There was a vast difference between the kind of foundation service Burger had performed and the deal Fortas had had with the Wolfson Family Foundation—a $20,000 annual stipend for life and beyond for "research," an unusually high proportion of the foundation's income, to say nothing of the flavor of the arrangement with a man in increasing trouble with the law. But such distinctions do not lend themselves to easy public explanations, nor are such explanations very congenial to a man about to assume the chief justiceship hoping for a minimum of rancor over the indiscretions of a departed justice. Burger decided to take the public position that only because of the press of his new responsibilities would he relinquish the trusteeship and he so testified at his confirmation hearing.

Since this was an ethical milestone for Burger, it might be well to point out here that a better course was open to him. He could have said, as his friend Harry Blackmun testified two years later, that "the times have changed a great deal in the past 5 years and I would not say for the worse by any means," and that a new ethical norm was perhaps appropriate, however justified he had felt in holding the trusteeship.

But this would not have been Burger's style, nor would it have fit his priorities. Where Warren had favored strict rules with broad effect to cover a broad range of evils without stopping to make separate moral judgments—"one man, one vote" was such a rule; the rigidity of the necessity for "Miranda warnings" in confession cases was another—Burger preferred the case-by-case judgment of matters of degree, with maximum scope left to the discretion of the judge. Where Warren had coped with an emergency situation at the close of his long tenure, Burger was looking forward to the kind of regime he desired for the indefinite future. From this perspective the Warren rules were an encumbrance from which Burger wanted release. Moreover, he deemed the rules an overreaction to the Fortas affair, which he considered in any event to have been overplayed and unfairly portrayed in *The Washington Post* and perhaps other newspapers. He may have considered that the judges, some of whom had boosted his own candidacy for chief justice, were so essential in his longer-range plan of overhauling the judiciary that cooperation in dealing with the ethical rules was best for him and best for the judges.

A revolt was already brewing against the Warren rules with J. Edward Lumbard, chief judge of the Second U.S. Circuit Court of Appeals and a Burger ally of long standing, being a prime mover. Lumbard, a minority member of the U.S. Judicial Conference at the June 10 meeting, led the Second Circuit's own Judicial Conference two days later to pass a resolution calling for suspension of the new rules pending a more relaxed study. Even if Burger had been temperamentally inclined to drive the judiciary in the same direction Warren had pointed it in the ethical realm, Burger's estimate was that in the wake of Warren's departure, no chief justice had the power to do the driving. And finally, Burger did not consider himself suited for the role of ethical leader, as opposed to being administrative chief, of the judiciary. He considered himself highly competent on court management matters and he was motivated to pursue two related main goals: the structuring of an efficient judicial branch and the withdrawal of the judiciary from many arenas of legal and social combat. He did not feel competent to sit in judgment on the six hundred federal judges, and he viewed that as a necessary ingredient to assuming ethical leadership.

Within Burger's own value system, these sets of priorities had a certain internal consistency and a kind of integrity. Certainly it is ordinarily thought to be a modest virtue for a man to abjure some moral hierarchical role for himself. For example, it was appropriate for Burger to disavow any effort to dub him the bar's "spiritual leader" as well as the federal judiciary's top administrator. Such a suggestion was made at a prayer breakfast at the 1970 American Bar Association convention by ABA president Bernard G. Segal. But Burger deftly and promptly declared: "That is a call to which I cannot respond. Many would feel that judges and lawyers are in need of spiritual leadership, but I am not your man." Yet there is a major difficulty with Burger's basic reluctance to assume a more formal "moral" role among judges: very simply, that the mantle of ethical leadership falls upon the chief justice of the United States, especially after the Warren era, whether the occupant of the post chooses to assume it or not.

Burger's concern lest jurists overreact to the Fortas debacle was heightened by the decision of Justice Brennan to renounce all outside activities save only his church. Those activities had been considerable, including numerous speaking engagements and participation in judicial refresher seminars, one of them at New York University in which Burger had been a frequent participant. Brennan's retreat, in apparent realization that moonlighting by justices had simply gone too far, alarmed Burger. Without making direct references to it in public statements, he urged that judges should not convert to a monastic life because their presence on the public scene was good for them and good for the public.

"I have said, and I repeat," he told the ABA's House of Delegates at the 1969 convention in Dallas,

that judges must not withdraw from the world, either the world at large or the world of the law. The one limit judges must acknowledge, however, is that of time and energy and the absolute priority of our judicial duties. Apart from that they should, and I hope they will, involve themselves in the affairs and activities of the life and community about them. [Applause.] Obviously, there are limits apart from time available. That judges must abstain from partisan politics, from controversy over large political questions, goes without saying. But judges can and they should contribute their experience on the boards of colleges and other philanthropic institutions. They have much to give. In turn they draw and gain from that experience and that exposure.

Unable to commit himself to a fixed schedule that permitted regular part-time teaching, he had given single lectures and taken part in seminars and law school moot courts.

No matter how tired and jaded I was when I undertook these tasks, I left each of them refreshed and exhilarated by the contact with the alert and keen minds of the students. I suspect—in fact I more than suspect after six weeks in my new office—that I will be forced to give up all such activities but I want to make it crystal clear, crystal clear—utterly clear—that only the press of my new duties and burdens, burdens which I did not carry as a circuit judge, lead me to this conclusion and this decision.

Burger's point was an appealing one. Who could be against an arrangement for jurist and student to meet in educational surroundings to their mutual intellectual enrichment? Yet the worthy principle surely had its limitations. Judges and justices should not undertake such outside tasks unless they clearly do not interfere with the work of their courts, nor should they be paid unseemly amounts for their services. Undoubtedly the Fortas law seminar at American University was invigorating for both teacher and learner; but just as surely the $15,000 compensation was shockingly high. Conspicuously missing from the Burger speech was any mention of the question of compensation for these public interest, nonjudicial activities. Newsmen seeking clarification were told emphatically, in some cases angrily, that he was not going to elaborate, at least not at that time.

While Burger was engaged in this holding action, the ABA found the moment opportune to start work on revising the old Canons of Judicial Ethics. This move, widely interpreted as a reaction to the Fortas scandal, actually had been on the bar association's drawing boards for five years as a logical follow-up to the revision of the even older Canons of Professional Ethics. The scandal merely made the project more timely and, in the view of some, more urgent, despite the fact that the ABA's ethics committee had been able to pronounce judgment on Fortas under the existing canons.

Two events that occurred as the judges braced for the fall meeting of the Judicial Conference heightened the timeliness of a new look at ethical standards. One was the nomination and confirmation fight over Clement F. Haynsworth, Jr., who had supported the Warren rules in June but whose own alleged conflicts of interest rekindled the debate that had begun with Fortas. The other was the disclosure by the Fifth Circuit judges of their heavy financial involvements in the oil and gas industry. The question became, Would the federal judges have the nerve at such a juncture in history to go back on the rules adopted only the previous June?

They had the nerve. What they needed was a reason for the move. Incredible as it seemed to the outside observer, the cue was a request by the ABA committee that the Judicial Conference suspend further implementation of the Warren rules while the private bar group pursued its study of the new code of judicial conduct. This was accomplished during the week preceding the conference's scheduled meetings on October 31 and November 1. On October 27, Chairman Roger J. Traynor wrote Burger describing the committee's membership, its budding program, and its hope to have a tentative draft of proposed new standards in circulation by the middle of the following year. The code would apply to both state and federal judges. The Traynor letter continued:

There will be obvious advantages if the rules finally developed for federal judges can take into account the work of our committee. It will be fortunate if both the federal and state judiciaries can eventually abide by the same set of basic canons, and if the federal judiciary can avoid the possible clash of Circuit Councils in interpreting what is considered appropriate non-judicial services. To achieve these ends the members of the committee respectfully suggest that the Conference may wish to consider suspending for as long a period as it deems appropriate any further action on all the resolutions adopted in June.

Not surprisingly Burger replied on October 30 that he would inform the conference of the committee's views and that his personal cooperation with the ABA was assured. The stage was set for the resolutions hammered out and released on November 1. The resolution suspending most of the June 10 rules gave two reasons. One was that the ABA study, which would be substantially completed by the summer of 1970, "will permit a more thorough understanding of the subject matter." The other was that the June resolution's regulation of nonjudicial activities had not worked out: "It now appears that since the Judicial Conference provided no guidelines or standards the various judicial councils of the circuits acting without standards or guidelines have not acted uniformly."

In lieu of the "suspended" rules, the conference resolved that Burger could appoint a committee of judges to receive quarterly, confidential reports of outside income for nonjudicial services. In the course of circulating the reporting forms the judges would "be asked for their views on the desirability of financial disclosure for judges," a hint that the May 15, 1970, deadline for financial reporting would also be rescinded. The conference resolved to cooperate with the ABA committee and to submit to Congress legislation spelling out the conference's rule-making power.

In this awkward but decisive fashion, the Warren revolution had been countered or, in the Robert Frost metaphor, completed full circle so that it brought "the same class up on top." The forces of reform had combined to forestall the strong first steps toward reform. Why should the official body of the federal judiciary defer to a committee of the private organization of lawyers? Aside from anxiety on the part of the judges, perhaps the prestige of some of the committee's members could account for the willingness to defer to private lawmaking. Chairman Traynor was the universally respected, even revered, chief justice of California's Supreme Court. Vice-chairman was Whitney North Seymour, Sr., past ABA president. Justice Potter Stewart was a member. Beyond this, it was clear that the committee was telling the conference something it was pleased to hear—the counsel of caution in reform from a recognizable group of legal figures.

Several features of the maneuver were unexplained and their correctness was not self-evident. First, there was not an inevitable clash between the long-range ABA study and the implementation of the Warren emergency rules. Surely there was no sign that the ethical crisis had passed—witness the Haynsworth fight and the Fifth Circuit's morass of oil dealings. The experience to be gained under the Warren rules, even if unacceptably diverse in the view of some judges, could have provided still more data for a comprehensive code of conduct. Nor was diversity or lack of "uniformity" among the circuits a vice, but rather a source of still richer practical experience. No examples were cited of lack of uniform interpretations of "permissible" nonjudicial services, nor had any claim been made that the diversity amounted to unjust disparity. Perhaps the point most in need of explanation was why one code of conduct was considered desirable for both federal and state judiciaries. At that juncture it would have been easier to predict that a single code would not serve both judiciaries, in view of the vast difference between the life tenure, adequate pay, and other safeguards for independence in the federal system on one hand and the largely elective and notoriously low-paying pattern of most state systems on the other. Should not a stricter ethical norm be set for the federal bench? Would there not be danger that a code of conduct appropriate for a justice of the peace would be unacceptably lax when applied to federal judges?

Reaction was disappointment in the small circle of lawyers and politicians who had shown interest in the subject. Senator Robert P. Griffin and Representative Robert A. Taft voiced misgivings and said they hoped the action would give new life for bills they had introduced and shelved five months earlier requiring income disclosure. According to Senator Tydings, the jurists had displayed "a dangerous myopia" concerning the threat to the judiciary's integrity; he summoned conference officials for a grilling before his Subcommittee on Judicial Machinery. The conference's chief witness, Judge Ainsworth, testified that it was too early to tell whether the judiciary had retreated. Tydings replied that he would wait until March to see how he would characterize it. "If action is postponed again in March," he said, it would indicate "that they don't want anything done" to restore confidence in the bench.

In early December a stretch-out of compliance began. Burger announced that he expected the ABA project and the moratorium to last "a year or more," not the eight or nine months contemplated in the November 1 resolution. Meanwhile the existing 1924 vintage ABA code would apply, and any uncertainty could be resolved by a judge's inquiry to a panel of judges appointed by Burger, apparently without Judicial Conference authorization.

One bright spot in the picture was the quality of the judges Burger chose to handle the mechanics of the ethical freeze. As chairman of the ethical review committee he named Elbert P. Tuttle, senior judge of the Fifth Circuit Court of Appeals, widely regarded as one of the nation's most courageous federal judges, who specifically accepted the job on the understanding that Burger be aware that he was considered pretty straitlaced on ethical matters. Burger said he was appointing him for precisely that reason. As chairman of the committee to receive the reports on off-the-bench compensation he appointed Judge Edward A. Tamm of the District of Columbia Circuit, a veteran no-nonsense jurist with just enough of a puritan streak—perhaps related to his eighteen years with the Federal Bureau of Investigation—to augur a strict accounting. Under Tuttle were District Judges William B. Jones of Washington, D.C.; Robert Van Pelt of Lincoln, Nebraska; William J. Jameson of Billings, Montana; Roszel C. Thomsen of Baltimore; and Circuit Judges Frank M. Coffin of Portland, Maine, and Harry A. Blackmun of Rochester, Minnesota, the lifelong friend of Burger's who was fated for elevation to the Supreme Court only a few months later. To serve with Judge Tamm, Burger appointed District Judges Alfred A. Arraj of Denver and Frank M. Johnson, Jr., of Montgomery, Alabama.

As it turned out, the freeze on ethical reform lasted two and a half more years. During that time Burger demonstrated just how different his conduct would be from that of his immediate predecessor.

Not all the contrasts with Warren are invidious to Burger. For example, it would be captious to find fault with most of Burger's obviously sincere drive toward prison reform. If Burger, with his zest for mobilizing forces to attack an objective, had shared Warren's interest in ethics, surely he would have enlisted the organized bar and every federal fund-dispersing agency within his reach, and there would probably now be a national ethical institute as a foil for the National Institutes of Health—or perhaps as a branch of it. Burger put his concern for prison reform into immediate programs from his first public appearances as chief justice. He dragooned top ABA officials into committing resources and recruiting a commission, headed by former Governor Robert J. Hughes of New Jersey, to study action programs. As a justice, his votes did not always show that he heeded the advice of the commission, as when the commission urged wide federal court review of prisoner complaints and Burger voted to curtail it. But it would have been wrong for him to have hewn to a party line on the subject. Still, one reservation must be expressed about the good works that a judge does off the bench: they can become a diversion from doing good works on the bench. A judge may comfort himself in permitting an injustice on the ground that his good works are being performed in the social sphere; but knowing that he is pursuing prison reform in the outside world may fortify a judge's predisposition to deny judicial intervention in a particular case of prison injustice.

With far less justification or propriety than in the prison reform area, Burger launched a program of off-the-bench publicizing in public and lobbying in private to advance the proposition that the federal courts should be relieved of many cases in the consumer protection, environmental, and antipoverty fields. At his first annual "state of the judiciary" speech to the American Bar Association in August 1970, Burger entered the social and political arena in a radically new way. Wearing his hat as top administrator of the federal court system, he called on Congress to stop overloading the courts with legislation that, however worthwhile, imposed an added case load burden on judges. He cited antipoverty legislation particularly as "an example of a sound program developed without adequate planning for its impact on the courts." The $58 million budget of the Office of Economic Opportunity's legal services project, he said, "is almost half of what is allowed for the operation of all the courts in the federal system." The implication, which was not accurate, was that neighborhood legal services attorneys spent their money on little but court-clogging litigation. The fact was that the OEO lawyers had a varied program of individual representation, test cases in which they won significant victories, and the bargaining power that went with their legal successes, and by no means did they attempt or succeed in bogging down the judiciary.

In his speech Burger proposed the creation of yet another federal agency, this one composed of members from all three branches, to review and screen legislation for its impact on the courts. Two years later in San Francisco he said that Congress should require a "court impact statement," akin to the environmental impact statements required of federal agencies before they undertake projects with significance for the quality of life, with every piece of legislation having court litigation consequences. The obvious result of this requirement would be that the new kinds of litigation would need special justification because of their anticipated effects on judicial resources. The thrust of this, counter as it was to some of the major consumer and environmental goals then being pursued, was to invert the principle of the environmental protection laws, putting court efficiency ahead of realistic enforcement of congressionally declared rights, requiring justification for the latter. And for what? Where was the evidence that this sort of litigation was the source of the alleged breakdown of federal court justice machinery? Burger offered none, but conservative members of Congress got the message anyway and cited the chief justice in their successful efforts to bottle up 1970 consumer class-action legislation.

Burger was also active behind the scenes in opposition to the

1972 consumer product safety bill, with its provision giving aggrieved purchasers of unsafe goods new access to the federal courts for suits against manufacturers and merchants. In one of the silliest ventures in lobbying annals, Burger's top aide, Rowland F. Kirks, director of the Administrative Office of United States Courts, accompanied Thomas G. ("Tommy the Cork") Corcoran, a lobbyist for the drug industry and against the legislation, to the office of House Speaker Carl Albert to signal the court impact of the legislation, which had been substantially approved in both the House and Senate and was then on its way to final enactment. When columnist Jack Anderson exposed the visit, quoting Corcoran as saying that "Kirks, acting for the Chief Justice, asked me to take him to the Speaker," Burger's initial response was silence. Eight days later he released a copy of a letter to Albert, thanking the Speaker for telling him in a telephone call that no one had purported to speak on Burger's behalf during the Kirks-Corcoran visit. Since the charge was that Burger had sponsored the mission and this charge was not denied in the letter, Burger had raised fresh questions. Representative John Moss, Democrat of California, a sponsor of the consumer bill, found Burger "highly evasive." Said Moss, "He denied something that was not alleged and did not deny what was alleged." Pressed by reporters, Kirks said the visit to Albert had been Corcoran's idea and that he had acted on his own without Burger's knowledge in calling on Albert. Was it proper to go with Tommy the Cork? "I cannot speak for the Chief Justice in this matter," said Kirks, but his sole purpose was the proper one of trying to inform Congress about the bill's court impact. Neither Burger nor Kirks ever acknowledged the impropriety of accompanying the private lobbyist on this assertedly public interest venture.

Bitter over the efforts to defeat his bill in this fashion, Moss wrote Burger expressing his "shock and disbelief" over the episode. He pointed out that the legislation had undergone extensive and "responsible" review in Congress and continued: "If the information which has now surfaced is true, your action can most charitably be described as naive. But, I would believe a more accurate characterization would be one of arrogant interference in the legislative process." The incident, he concluded, "raises the most basic questions as to your ability to participate objectively in considering any case involving the interest of consumers in the United States."

Representative Bob Eckhardt, Democrat of Texas, took the House floor a few days later to pinpoint his objection to Burger's behavior. He said he had considered Burger's 1970 statements "innocuous" and "innocent truisms" that did not warrant debate but now found them to be

part of a subtle lobbying effort, a tampering in the legislative process that ill becomes a Chief Justice of the United States. I did not consider them to be in 1970, because I had not yet had an opportunity to see how the Chief Justice's statements would be used. I have now. The Chief Justice has also had that opportunity, yet he has repeated them, has continued his tampering with the legislative process. Thus, I have overcome my reluctance to find fault with the Chief Justice.

No longer willing to give Burger "the benefit of the doubt," Eckhardt said that since 1970,

I have found that the consumer class action bill, the product warranty bill, the consumer agency bill and the product safety bill have been assailed by a cleverly intermeshed program of opposition which has included the U.S. Chamber of Commerce, the drug lobby, the District of Columbia antitrust bar, the Justice Department, the Office of the President and the Chief Justice of the United States.

Two months later in the judiciary's newsletter, Burger asserted once more his right to inform Congress about the needs of the judiciary. Compared with Chief Justices Hughes and Taft he considered himself restrained. Burger did not acknowledge any impropriety and his only reference to the visit story was to call it "totally false," although he and Kirks had corroborated important parts of it, and to label as "misinformed reporting" stories based on the Anderson column. Perhaps the most regrettable part of this episode was Burger's failure to make known that he saw a distinction, if he did see one, between informing Congress and improper lobbying in the company of a highly interested party.

Legislative statesmanship, as some Washington lobbyists make bold to call their craft, took other forms as well. In June 1971, Burger filed dissents in two search-and-seizure cases that did not stop at disagreement with his brethren but went beyond even an aside suggesting that Congress ought to look into the problem of excluding from criminal trials evidence seized in violation of the Constitution. Burger in fact wrote a five-point outline of the legislation Congress might consider. It left little for Senator Lloyd M. Bentsen, Jr., an opponent of the exclusionary rule, to improve upon, so the Texas Democrat submitted a bill following the Burger blueprint. It was considered of dubious constitutionality despite its parentage, and even the House of Delegates of the American Bar Association disapproved it and reaffirmed their support for the exclusionary rule. For the time being, at least, the bill was scuttled.

To be sure, a certain amount of discourse with Congress is often conducted through written Supreme Court opinions. Occasionally the Court will express its dissatisfaction with the way certain procedural laws governing its jurisdiction are working out in practice, as with the Expediting Act by which most antitrust suits reach the High Court on direct appeal from a trial court without being reviewed by an intermediate court of appeals. The justices reason that Congress should be told about the workings of such a law by those who are forced to deal with it. No question of social policy is involved; presumably the United States government would not stand to win any more cases under changed procedures, nor would the private companies defending themselves against antitrust charges stand to benefit. Frequently, also, the Court will comment in passing that a party has raised significant problems or stands to suffer an injustice at the hands of the law, flagging the issue for Congress if Congress wishes to notice it. But just as frequently the Court will conclude by saying that the solution lies with the policy-making body, the legislature, not the courts. The preceding example is not in that class of cases, nor is the one that follows.

Still more alarming was a move Burger made on March 27, 1972, when he filed an opinion in one of the more celebrated legal disputes in the nation's capital involving whether the Three Sisters Bridge should be built across the Potomac River. The legal issue, knotty enough even if there had been no political overtones, was whether the project was exempt from the procedural hurdles, such as scrutiny for environmental impact, that Congress had established for other highway construction. It was clear what the reigning members of the House Committees on Appropriations and Public Works wanted done. They not only pushed through a law specifying that the bridge be built "notwithstanding any other provision of law or any court decision or administrative action to the contrary," but they also refused to release funds for Washington's subway unless opponents capitulated. The final statute, however, also said the project "shall be carried out in accordance with all applicable provisions" of the existing highway code, which complicated the task of the United States Court of Appeals in grasping the "will of Congress" as distinguished from the will of some congressmen. The court of appeals, voicing misgivings about the congressional pressure on administrative officials, held that the bridge could not be built unless the secretary of transportation made new findings not based on any extraneous influence but in accordance with laws governing other projects.

This so enraged key congressmen that President Nixon, in order to regain subway appropriations, had to promise publicly to petition the Supreme Court for review. This promise—the president could not assure success—temporarily satisfied the congressmen. Unfortunately for Mr. Nixon and the petitioning Departments of Transportation and Justice, there was almost no way to make the case attractive from the standpoint of Supreme Court review under the High Court's standards familiar to lawyers. Even if wrongly decided, the case was local in nature and raised no general or national legal issues. Few thoughtful persons expected the Supreme Court to grant review of the decision and call for full briefing and oral argument. On March 24 the Court confirmed these estimates and simply issued a routine order that said, "Certiorari [review] denied." It was to this order that Burger appended his remarkable opinion.

The label Burger gave to it, an opinion "concurring" in the denial of certiorari, was itself all but unprecedented. The High Court does not explain why it refuses to hear cases and while the

practice of filing dissenting opinions has grown in recent years
and the dissents sometimes reveal the majority's reasoning, the
justices simply do not have the time to explain themselves in most
cases. Burger began:

I concur in the denial of certiorari in this case, but solely out of
considerations of timing. Questions of great importance to the
Washington, D.C., area are presented by the petition, not the least of
which is whether the Court of Appeals has . . . unjustifiably frustrated
the efforts of the Executive Branch to comply with the will of Congress
as rather clearly expressed in Section 23 of the Federal Aid Highway
Act of 1968.

Thus inclined on the merits of the case, he went on:

If we were to grant the writ, however, it would be almost a year before
we could render a decision in the case. It seems preferable, therefore,
that we stay our hand.

This observation, of course, assumed a great deal about what
"we" justices would do if the merits of the case were reached.
Then came the most remarkable statement of all:

In these circumstances Congress may, of course, take any further
legislative action it deems necessary to make unmistakably clear its
intentions with respect to the project, *even to the point of limiting or
prohibiting judicial review of its directives.*" [Emphasis supplied.]

Here, then, was advice to Congress from the judiciary to go
ahead and legislate, plus an advance opinion from one justice
that cutting off opponents' access to the courts would be
constitutional. Amazing as it was in the context of the bridge, it
was even more startling in the context of a hot issue of truly
national proportions: the Nixon administration's bill to remove
school busing questions from the federal courts.

A busing foe, Senator James B. Allen, Democrat of Alabama,
promptly took the Senate floor to declare with approval that
there was "a straw in the wind—an indication of the attitude of
the U.S. Supreme Court on the question of congressional power
to limit the exercise of discretionary powers by U.S. district court
judges." Allen read too much into the opinion of one justice, but
from the senator's perspective it was not an unreasonable guess

about Burger's own attitude as stated in the opinion. Before the official print of the Supreme Court's action was published, Burger added three words, "in this respect," to the end of the last quoted sentence, which was taken by some as a disengagement from the busing fight. It tended to confirm estimates by Washington lawyers that Burger was more concerned with two things: saving face for President Nixon by giving greater weight to the petition than the Court as a whole was disposed to give it and renewing old battles with some of his former associates on the court of appeals with whom he had often disagreed. But it was a curious performance for a "strict constructionist" dedicated to judicial restraint. As with the episode involving Tommy the Cork, it did not bode well for public confidence in an independent judiciary.

This time Burger's open letter to Congress evoked the intended response. That fall the House of Representatives went so far as to pass a provision to cut off judicial review of the bridge, but in the election year rush the highway supporters were unable to get the same provision through the Senate.

Thus it was that Burger, strict constructionist and judge's judge, was able to contain the reformist zeal that was at work in the waning days of the Warren regime and embark upon a new program of his own, setting his own model of judicial and extrajudicial conduct. Like it or not, Burger was setting an ethical tone for judicial life, a tone of permissiveness for business as usual and for lobbying by judges. There was cause for concern over where the judiciary would find ethical leadership.

8

☆ ☆ ☆

THE NEW ETHICS

"The place of justice is a hallowed place, and therefore, not only the Bench, but the foot place and precincts and purprise thereof ought to be preserved without scandal and corruption."

Francis Bacon, OF JUDICATURE

These words embellished the Canons of Judicial Ethics approved by the American Bar Association in 1924. Nobody seems to know why. When Bacon wrote them toward the end of his life he had been impeached as Lord Chancellor for accepting bribes; he had served three days in the Tower of London before receiving the equivalent of a suspended sentence and a forgiveness of a fine of £40,000; and he was exiled from London. The committee that set out to modernize the judiciary's ethical rules in 1969 had no idea, either, why the 1924 committee headed by William Howard Taft had embroidered the canons with quotations from Deuteronomy, the Magna Charta, or Abraham Lincoln, but they were determined not to emulate the earlier draftsmen. No, the body of rules from the 1970s forward would be in the spirit of the times—tightly worded and practical—with a minimum of "pious platitudes" that were out of fashion for a judiciary that had been through so much.

More than literary style distinguished the 1924 code from the revision begun in 1969. The entire setting was changed. Not long before the Taft committee was appointed the very notion that lawyers should write rules for judges had been widely doubted, and it was no simple matter to overcome the ABA's own reluctance to enter the judicial thicket. In 1969, by contrast, the ABA was so solidly entrenched as "officers of the court"—high-ranking officers at that—that the U.S. Judicial Conference itself treated the private organization of lawyers with deference and even Congress hesitated to write an ethics law while the bar association's experts were at their labors.

The canons will not be judged for their literary craftsmanship alone, nor by the prestige of the ABA, which is always subject to ups and downs. But it is illuminating to review the history, seeing how greatly the concept of private lawmaking has changed and why, before examining the men who did the revising of the rules and their work. As the story unfolds, it becomes clear that the lawyers and the judges are closer together than ever. Whatever the merits and demerits of the new ethical norms—and there are plentiful examples of both—there remains a serious question whether the standards are good enough for the ultimate satisfaction of the public, which did not have much to do with the process. "The ethical expectations of the public," Dean Robert B. McKay of the New York University School of Law has written, "have risen even more rapidly than have the perceptions of the judges of what is expected of them." As a result, although the quality and integrity of the American judiciary is at its highest so far and is still rising, "the public seems almost more mistrustful of the legal system in general, and the judiciary in particular, than ever before."

☆

Most lawyers have forgotten it if they ever knew, but it was baseball's "Black Sox" scandal of the 1919 World Series that fathered the first Canons of Judicial Ethics. As so often happens in a crisis of public confidence, the scandal involving bribes to members of the Chicago White Sox for throwing the series to the Cincinnati Reds caused organized baseball to turn to the judiciary for leadership and a return to respectability. Kenesaw Mountain Landis, the outspoken judge from the U.S. District

Court of Chicago, was hired as "czar" of the national pastime. Nationally famous for the fine of $29 million he slapped on Standard Oil of Indiana and for presiding over World War I subversion trials, Landis had been favorably noticed by the major leagues for his friendly handling of one of the earliest attacks on the game as a violation of the federal antitrust laws.

What shook the bar, especially the Chicago bar, was that Landis began serving simultaneously as judge and czar at an annual compensation rate of $50,000—$42,500 from baseball and $7,500 as his regular judicial pay. One of the most indignant lawyers was John M. Harlan of Chicago, son of one Supreme Court justice and father of another, who led a censure movement at the ABA's 1921 convention. Said Harlan to the ABA's House of Delegates, "Now, I wish to say right here and now that the American Bar Association, if we are to have any esprit de corps as an association, if professional honor and dignity means anything, ought to tell the American public whether we countenance such an act." The delegates then resolved that Landis's behavior "meets with our unqualified condemnation, as conduct unworthy of the office of judge, derogatory to the dignity of the Bench, and undermining public confidence in the independence of the judiciary."

Actually, independence was a quality Landis possessed in abundance. He had a reputation as a judicial tyrant, frequently given to taking a case over from counsel in mid-trial by joining fully in the questioning of witnesses, a practice that is acceptable in moderation but that some jurists take to extremes. Often a bully to defendants and their lawyers, he made his own contribution to the law of judicial behavior at about the same time his sports venture was maturing. He refused to disqualify himself from the espionage trial of Victor L. Berger, the Milwaukee socialist who was twice elected to Congress and twice excluded from the House, and four others of German nationality or extraction. The defendants filed affidavits charging that Judge Landis, while meting out a stiff sentence to a German-American a few months before their trial, had said of German-Americans: "Their hearts reek with disloyalty. . . . I prefer the safeblower." According to the affidavits, the jurist had declared, "If anybody has said anything worse about the Germans than I have, I would like to know it so I could use it." Judge Landis produced a transcript that portrayed him as referring to the kaiser, not Germans, and complaining that the German leader had given his people a bad name. There was nothing in this official record about "reeking with disloyalty." The judge refused to disqualify himself but in 1921 the Supreme Court, by a six to three vote, reversed. Perhaps skeptical about their ability to review the actions of a judge who held control over the official transcript, the majority justices refused to decide which version of the record was true. Instead, they held that under the 1910 federal disqualification law then being interpreted and still in effect today, a trial judge must step aside when a "legally sufficient" affidavit of prejudice is filed against him, without weighing the merits of the charges. The jurist need not admit the accuracy of the charges, courts have held, but neither may they dismiss them out of their own certainty of rectitude.

Landis defied the critics and vowed that he would not run from a fight or resign under an attack that included moves toward impeachment. A year later when the attacks subsided, Landis did quit the bench and ascended the baseball throne as full-time czar. It was a sensible change of occupation since baseball felt the need of a dictator and the judiciary was better off with one less autocrat.

The ABA censure seemed to release the inhibitions the bar association had felt since 1908, when it issued the first ethical guidelines for lawyers with only a suggestion for future study of the question of judicial canons. More than humility had prompted the caution. As Charles A. Boston, a New York lawyer who spoke out for judicial canons and who became the principal draftsman of the 1924 canons, observed, there was in 1908 "the agitation for a recall of the judiciary and for the recall of judicial decisions," a popular movement to strike back at perceived judicial oppression, and to the organized bar "it was not deemed wise to add fuel to that flame by intimating through the adoption of Canons of Judicial Ethics that the judiciary were in fault."

Boston seized the moment to follow up on the Landis resolution with a letter to the ABA's ruling executive committee.

"The time is now ripe" for judicial canons, he advised the committee. "The agitation for the recall appears to have diminished, and, perhaps, to have spent its force." The executive committee dusted off some old and unused resolutions, found authority to study judicial ethics, and appointed a committee headed by Chief Justice William Howard Taft to draft the canons. Taft, a former president of the United States and past president of the ABA, was a logical man for the task, a symbol of public correctness whose stature as a jurist and bar organization man would ensure acceptance of the canons. To counteract possible criticism that lawyers were judging judges, the committee of five was dominated by judges. Flanking Taft were the chief justices of two states, Robert von Moschzisker of Pennsylvania and Leslie C. Cornish of Maine. Boston, who was to become ABA president a decade later, was one of the lawyer members. The other lawyer was George Sutherland, the former U.S. senator from Utah whose appointment to the Supreme Court in the fall of 1922 required him to withdraw after a few months on the committee in favor of another lawyer member. That lawyer, Garret W. McEnerney of San Francisco, did little for the committee; Frank M. Angellotti of the same city succeeded him. Angellotti, too, had the judicial perspective. Although he was in private practice, he had been a justice of the California Supreme Court from 1903 to 1915 and its chief justice from 1915 to 1921, when he left the bench.

These were men who knew each other. Overwhelmingly Republican, Masonic, and very conservative, they hardly had to discuss what was proper in the courthouse and in fact they did very little discussing. Nor did they often meet with the public during their two years of work. When the committee first gathered in New York in May 1922, only two relative outsiders joined their deliberations: Henry Taft, brother of the chief justice, and John W. Davis, who was the president of the ABA. Though a Democrat and the 1924 challenger to the Republican incumbent in the White House, Davis had Taft's admiration. Relieved that such a sound lawyer was the Democratic nominee, Taft wrote to Chief Justice von Moschzisker, "I agree with you in felicitating ourselves that John Davis was named by the Democrats. I don't think he is going to be elected, but we can go to bed now with comfort that in all probability either Coolidge or Davis will be the President, and that he will set his face like flint against any change of our form of government or the power of the courts." Boston enjoyed the confidence of Taft, who as president had urged him to accept a federal judgeship only to be met by the familiar cry that the successful Manhattan lawyer could not afford it.

It was not hard to guess who on the committee would do the work. "You and I will have to put the work on to Boston," said the chief justice of Pennsylvania to the chief justice of the United States. "Boston is a hard worker and a very effective one." Plunging right in after the initial meeting, Boston produced within a month a proposed first draft that was to undergo innumerable small adjustments but few fundamental changes at the hands of the committee and the ABA. When after two meetings in December the draft was floated in the February 1923 issue of the *American Bar Association Journal*, Boston was the designated receiver of criticisms and suggestions. At von Moschzisker's urging, he was told to screen out the frivolous suggestions and fend off much of the criticism.

Boston's initial draft did not contain the embroidery from a Francis Bacon essay with which this chapter begins, nor the quotations from Deuteronomy and the Magna Charta that also precede the Taft canons. It did include an admonition that "it is no sufficient justification or excuse for a judge, who has accepted gratuities, or bounties, or favors calculated to warp or influence the judgment or action of a normal man, that he has not been influenced thereby." This caution did not survive later revisons of the canons.

The committee imposed other economies of language, notwithstanding the insinuations of latter-day critics that the draftsmen exercised no self-discipline. Killed also was a Boston canon on "unpopularity with the bar," reflecting the view of many lawyers that

while intimacy or popularity with the Bar is not a necessary equipment for judicial office, the approval won by distribution of patronage or marked favoritism to its individual members is not an index of judicial ability, nevertheless if a judge is generally unpopular with members of the Bar, it may properly be taken by him as an admonition that he is falling into ways that do not make for confidence in the court, or its judgments, and as indicating a probability that there is some substantial departure from those standards which should guide a judge in his official administration.

Justice Russell Benedict, a member of New York's state trial bench, unsuccessfully beseeched the committee to add yet another "ancient precedent" atop the canons, from the eighteenth-century law lectures of Justice James Wilson, proclaiming that "a judge is the blessing, or he is the curse of society. His powers are important; his character and conduct can never be objects of indifference." The phrase did find its way into the preamble. Another Benedict suggestion was adopted, adding to canon 2 that a judge "should avoid falling into the attitude of mind that the courts are made for his benefit instead of for the benefit of the litigants."

If the "ancient precedents" were mostly window dressing, the preamble at least was a fair indication of what the canons were, and were not:

In addition to the Canons for Professional Conduct of Lawyers which it has formulated and adopted, the American Bar Association, mindful that the character and conduct of a judge should never be objects of indifference, and that declared ethical standards tend to become habits of life, deems it desirable to set forth its views respecting those principles which should govern the personal practice of members of the judiciary in the administration of their office. The Association accordingly adopts the following Canons, the spirit of which it suggests as a proper guide and reminder for judges, and as indicating what the people have a right to expect from them.

A 1921 draft had called the canons "a proper guide of conduct for judges," but the final version called them "a proper guide and reminder for judges." The distinction was made clear by the canons themselves, which drew some criticism because they were not "enforceable." Others who criticized the proposed code said the canons were obvious, too idealistic, or unnecessary for good judges and likely to be ignored by bad ones. Undeterred, Boston urged the ABA's executive committee to move the canons favorably through the association's machinery toward final approval. "It has been suggested," he acknowledged,

that this declaration will be inefficacious without a sanction; this is not a law, nor a penal announcement. Its true purpose is stated in the preamble. It is for the enlightenment of others, as well as for a guide and reminder to the judiciary. It is designed not only to promote correct habits, but to dissuade the ill-informed from expected incorrect conduct. It will, we feel certain, prove to be a beneficent force.

From Maine, Chief Justice Cornish expressed satisfaction, writing Taft:

I have been somewhat amused by the various criticisms which Mr. Boston has been kind enough to condense and analyze. I suppose that if Moses, when he came down out of the mountain, had submitted the Ten Commandments to the populace, or if the Master, when he gave the Beatitudes, had adopted that method, just as many criticisms, pro and con, would have been made as have been made upon our joint efforts along the line of judicial ethics.

The work took longer than the Decalogue or the Beatitudes, but it progressed swiftly by bar association standards. Like any large organization, the ABA has long worked through committees and sections. Bases must be touched, and the ABA's Judicial Section had to be consulted. Since the final code could not be ready for the August 1923 convention, the entire code lay dormant for one year before final approval in August 1924 at Philadelphia. During that entire twelve months only one change was made, but the change stirred the committee's members more than any action they had taken previously. The subject was "kinship," and it proved to be a touchy one with some judges.

Boston felt strongly about the practice of judges hearing cases in which relatives served as counsel. A proposed canon declared that a judge "should not, unless it is unavoidable, sit in litigation where a near relative is a party or counsel." At a meeting in the spring of 1924 Taft encountered the chief justice of the Massachusetts Supreme Judicial Court, Arthur P. Rugg, who complained about the canon and followed it up with a letter to Taft.

Justice Rugg said he had no objection to the rule as applied to judges sitting alone, but that members of his multimember tribunal "back as far as any of us have memory" had never withdrawn from such cases when heard by the full bench. He cited five of his colleagues who had sons or other relatives argue before the state's high court without raising an ethical doubt, and added that his own son had done the same. Taft agreed with Rugg and wrote Boston that the restrictions on counsel were unnecessary since they had grown "out of a few abuses" in instances of judges sitting alone at the trial level. Boston argued for retaining the notion with the proviso that the judge might sit in unavoidable circumstances. He said the Second U.S. Circuit Court of Appeals, before which he practiced, had recently gone through a *cause célèbre* over just this kind of issue, to the embarrassment of bench and bar. A lawyer had been brought into a case already being handled by eminent counsel for no apparent reason other than his kinship to a judge. Taft was firm, but illness prevented him from attending the Philadelphia convention and maintaining his point in person. His ally, Chief Justice von Moschzisker, reported what happened at a meeting with a committee of judges from the Judicial Section on the eve of the code's presentation to the ABA membership:

We had a meeting in Boston's room. . . . Our friend Boston died a little hard, but die he did, and we have eliminated the part that should go out. Both Allread and Crane [of the Judicial Section] had the same idea as Boston at the start of the consultation, but the first two came around to our thought in the end. Boston asked me to make the report to the Convention, but I stepped aside and allowed him to make it; for he likes that sort of thing. At any rate, he read it and did it very well. Neither your name nor that of Judge Rugg was mentioned in connection with the elimination.

The final version of the canon said that a judge "should not act in a controversy where a near relative is a party" but said nothing about counsel. That problem apparently was covered by the next sentence, which read, "He should not suffer his conduct to justify the impression that any person can improperly influence him. . . ."

The episode illustrates one of the judiciary's most common foibles: the inability to accept judicial reform that might somehow imply incorrect behavior in the past. The dangers from kinship of counsel, even on a multijudge court, are obvious to the mind of today, the clearest danger being that the lawyer's relative may cast the deciding vote. So widely understood is this principle now that companies are sometimes suspected of hiring certain law firms for the base purpose of *disqualifying* a judge thought to be hostile to their position, rather than with the notion of winning a case through kinship.

Oddly, Taft himself became embroiled in an ethical controversy during his chairmanship of the ethics committee. The Hearst newspapers in 1922 bannered a story that he was receiving a $10,000 annuity from the Carnegie Corporation. The money, income from U.S. Steel mortgage bonds, had been willed to Taft by steel baron Andrew Carnegie for use during Taft's lifetime and thereafter for his widow. Unlike Justice Fortas a half-century later, Taft was to do nothing in return for the money. Alpheus T. Mason, a Taft biographer, found that "the press rallied strongly to the Chief Justice's support. Much gratified, he observed 'that no other newspapers took any part in the attack, and those which have spoken have noted its injustice.' "

Nevertheless, Taft assigned the annuity to Yale University, telling its president, "I am profoundly concerned that the usefulness and influence of the court should not be lessened on this account." The Carnegie bequest had been designed to ease the financial burden of former presidents—the widows of ex-Presidents Cleveland and Theodore Roosevelt had similar bounties—but simply would not do for an ex-president who had become chief justice. Whether Taft agreed with this appraisal or whether the Hearst attack blinded him to the correct ethical judgment, he handled the matter with appropriate dispatch and the issue vanished.

Understandably, the Taft canons did not condemn all outside income for judges. Nor did they prohibit, in so many words, a judge from taking an outside job as commissioner of baseball. Canon 25, "Business Promotions and Solicitations for Charity," enjoined judges from exploiting the prestige of office to drum up business for an outside enterprise but did not ban the enterprise. Canon 24 frowned on "Inconsistent Obligations," pecuniary or otherwise, "which will in any way interfere or appear to interfere with [the judge's] devotion to the expeditious and proper administration of his official functions." To many readers that would preclude a judge's taking on an assignment like running baseball, but a jurist might be free to interpret the canon otherwise.

Nor did the canons fly in the face of Taft's off-the-bench activism in what he considered judicial reform. Canon 23 took notice of the judge's "exceptional opportunity to observe the operation of statutes, especially those relating to practice . . . and he may well contribute to the public interest by advising those having authority to remedy defects of procedure, of the result of his observation and experience." As biographer Mason has noted, the code declared that partisan politics was off limits, which was "difficult to square" with Taft's own involvement in White House and congressional politics. The Taft brand, however, was decidedly upon canon 19, which urged appellate judges to be sparing in their resort to dissenting opinions in the interest of the law's clarity, a point Taft pressed within the Supreme Court's councils and addressed especially to the great dissenters Holmes and Brandeis. Judges were told in canon 11 that they were free, indeed had a duty, to criticize unprofessional conduct of lawyers brought to their attention and to relay the most serious complaints to court grievance bodies. Unsurprisingly, judges were encouraged in canon 33 to maintain their "interest in or appearance at meetings of members of the Bar." These were, after all, the ABA's own canons for judges. The ABA, and especially its most prominent member, Taft, did not want to scare judges away from the association. "It is not necessary to the proper performance of judicial duty that a judge should live in retirement or seclusion," said the canon.

Judges were told to run their courts efficiently (canons 6, 7, 8, 18), with courtesy and civility (canons 9, 10), fearlessly (canon 3), and independently (canon 14), but without idiosyncrasies or sensationalism (canon 21 and after 1937 canon 35, which banned courtroom radio and television); but beyond these predictable subjects there were few specific "thou shalts" or "thou shalt nots." On this point modern-day critics are correct when they speak of the breadth and generality of the Taft canons, but it does not follow that the critics correctly found them obsolete for contemporary life. The canons held firmly to one useful and durable theme: judges must not only do justice, it must *appear* that they do justice.

Canon 4: "A judge's official conduct should be free from impropriety *and the appearance of impropriety;* he should avoid infractions of law; and his personal behavior, not only upon the Bench and in the performance of judicial duties, but also in his everyday life, should be beyond reproach."

Canon 13: "A judge should not . . . suffer his conduct *to justify the impression* that any person can improperly influence him or unduly enjoy his favor, or that he is affected by the kinship, rank, position or influence of any party or other person."

Canon 24: "A judge should not accept inconsistent duties, nor incur obligations, pecuniary or otherwise, which will in any way interfere *or appear to interfere* with his devotion to the expeditious and proper administration of his official functions."

Canon 25: "A judge should avoid giving ground for any *reasonable suspicion* that he is utilizing the power or prestige of his office to persuade or coerce others to patronize or contribute, either to the success of private business ventures, or to charitable enterprises. He should, therefore, not enter into such private business, or pursue such a course of conduct, as would *justify such suspicion* . . . nor should he enter into any business relation which, in the normal course of events *reasonably to be expected,* might bring his personal interest into conflict with the impartial performance of his official duties."

Canon 26: "A judge should abstain from making personal investments in enterprises which are *apt* to be involved in litigation in the court. . . . It is desirable that he should, *so far as is reasonably possible,* refrain from all relations *which would normally tend to arouse the suspicion* that such relations warp or bias his judgment, or prevent his impartial attitude of mind in the administration of his judicial duties. . . ."

Canon 27: While a judge may hold executorships or trustee-ships, he should stay out of any position which would interfere "*or seem to interfere* with the proper performance of his judicial duties. . . ."

Canon 31: Where permitted to practice law on the side, the judge "must be scrupulously careful to avoid conduct in his practice whereby he utilizes *or seems to utilize* his judicial position to further his professional success." He may act as an arbitrator or law teacher and writer unless it interferes with his job of judging.

Canon 32: A judge should accept no gifts or favors from litigants, lawyers "or from others whose interests are *likely* to be submitted to him for judgment."

Canon 33: Though not obliged to live in seclusion or forswear relationships with the organized bar, the judge must be careful to avoid such action "*as may reasonably tend to awaken the suspicion* that his social or business relations or friendships, constitute an element in influencing his judicial conduct."

Italicized above are the phrases that stress the "appearance" of propriety, a stricter standard than mere obedience to ethical rules. In some passages the strictness is tempered by such words as "reasonably" or "justify," an indication that certain conduct need not be bad merely because somebody says it looks suspicious to him. To be sure, there were flaws in the old canons, but the high standard expected of judges was not one of them, and not all the shortcomings were corrected by the ABA committee that worked from 1969 to 1972.

The 1924 canons were rarely heard from again until the ABA was ready to revise them. Notably lacking was any immediate move to make the canons binding in the courts of the states. By the end of World War II, the canons of the post–World War I period were binding by the bar associations or supreme courts of only eleven states. After the war, states began adopting judicial codes with more frequency so that by 1968, when the ethics of Justice Fortas first became an issue, the ABA rules or variants of them governed in forty states. In some of those states the old canons, vague as they were in some respects, did become the basis for disciplining and even removing judges.

☆

By 1969, when the ABA turned to the revision of the Taft
canons, several things had changed. The question now was not so
much whether lawyers should set judicial standards—though the
legitimacy of the bar association, a private group, was not
universally conceded—but rather how fast the bar could update
standards that some had thought inadequate for contemporary
use. Thus there was no need that the revision committee be
dominated by judges, though it was appropriate to have a judge
as chairman. Nor could the task be entrusted to a tiny committee
of five. There simply were too many constituent interests within
the organized bar. After the chairmanship was established, it
remained for those interests to be represented. Although larger in
number than the Taft committee, this band of lawyers, fourteen
at maximum membership, was nearly as homogeneous. It was a
group of men from various regions but for the most part
accustomed to working together on projects familiar to the
organized bar. While it was accurate to say that the committee
had variety—a Supreme Court justice, state judges, federal
judges, big-city lawyers and small-city lawyers, and a smattering
of legal educators—it could hardly be said that it mirrored the
broadest legal community imaginable. The group was un-poor,
almost by definition; un-young, average age sixty-one; un-black
and totally male; well connected in the bar and public life but,
like much of the organized bar's leadership, not broadly based in
a social sense. It was a group far more capable than the Taft
committee of divining what "the people" expected of their
judges, but not a group necessarily in touch with all the people.
Though there were representatives of the judiciary, it was a
special part of the judiciary—judges who liked to work in bar
associations with lawyers, just as the lawyer members enjoyed the
company of judges off the bench. It would have been foolish to
expect the final version of the new canons to caution judges
against getting too "palsy" or informal with the bar.

Without doubt the chairmanship was given to the most logical
choice available, probably the outstanding state judge in the
land, retiring Chief Justice Roger J. Traynor of the California

Supreme Court. Leader of the country's most interesting and innovative court, Traynor had been a liberalizing influence in criminal law, civil law, and civil rights. Having weathered vicious attacks on his court's work by Governor Ronald Reagan and his state's conservatives, Traynor understood profoundly the necessity for an independent judiciary. Quiet of manner but tough under stress, articulate and witty, Traynor was both deeply respected and popular with the bar.

Vice-chairman of the committee was Whitney North Seymour, Sr., of New York, a former ABA president, for decades the personification of the "establishment lawyer," an advocate of commanding courtroom presence, skilled in personal diplomacy and possessing decades of experience in bar politics. From the Supreme Court, ABA president Bernard G. Segal was able to persuade Justice Potter Stewart to join the committee. Segal saw Stewart, then fifty-four, with a decade of High Court service behind him, as a "balance wheel" among jurists, one who had not been involved in the previous spring's controversy over ethical rules, friendly though not intimate with the organized bar.

Turning to the federal appellate bench, Segal chose Judge Irving R. Kaufman of the Second U.S. Circuit Court of Appeals, whose relationships with the bar included the presidency of the Institute of Judicial Administration, a body of lawyers and judges whose work to upgrade the judiciary was heavily dependent on the participation of judges. "The Institute, I suppose, could be considered a prime stimulator of outside activities of judges," its director, Delmar Karlen, conceded at a Senate inquiry into judicial moonlighting. Judge Kaufman—able, articulate, active, and activist—had spoken out during the previous spring against what he feared would be a retreat to "monasticism." Chosen to represent the federal district court judges was Edward T. Gignoux, the personable Maine jurist who had gone on the bench only after receiving assurances that he could sit elsewhere when his own court was typically quiet.

A state judge who had been chairman of the ABA's Section of Judicial Administration, Ivan Lee Holt, Jr., of St. Louis, rounded out Segal's choices from the bench, although Robert A. Leflar, former dean of the University of Arkansas Law School and the legal educator member, had been chief justice of his state's highest court. Like Judge Kaufman, Leflar had a keen interest in judge-lawyer cooperation, having served for the previous fifteen years as director of the Appellate Judges' Seminar that meets each summer at New York University. Chief Justice Burger, an alumnus and frequent participant in the New York seminars, said in a testimonial that Leflar's career "exemplifies the value of the 'great partnership' of lawyers, judges and law teachers."

William L. Marbury of Baltimore was another lawyer in the Seymour category of prominence. Conservative yet a prime mover in the drive to involve blue-chip law firms in public interest and antipoverty law, Marbury gave the committee added prestige and class. For a lawyer from the deeper South, Segal chose E. Dixie Beggs of Pensacola, Florida, a past president of the Fellows of the American Bar Foundation, the ABA's tax-exempt legal education and research arm.

These nine men rounded out the initial choices made by Segal. Gaps were purposely left so that succeeding presidents could make their appointments in keeping with what some bar officials consider to be patronage. (Segal, who was unopposed for the presidency in his year and felt free of bar political debts, rejected the term "patronage" as inapplicable to his choices.) Chosen later for the committee were Colorado Supreme Court justice James K. Groves, chairman of the ABA's legislature, the House of Delegates; Judge George H. Revelle of the Superior Court in Seattle, Washington; Walter P. Armstrong, Sr., of Memphis, chairman of the ABA's Standing Committee on Ethics and Professional Responsibility; W. O. Shafer of Odessa, Texas, past president of his state's bar; and Edward L. Wright of Little Rock, former ABA president and chairman of the committee that revised the association's Code of Professional Responsibility from 1964 to 1969.

Chairman Traynor chose as his reporter or chief draftsman E. Wayne Thode, a professor at the University of Utah College of Law. Later Geoffrey C. Hazard, Jr., a Yale law professor, was added as a consultant, in part because bar leaders thought his writing ability was needed. Hazard, who was born in 1929, was the only one who was in his forties.

The makeup of the 1969 committee was not the only contrast to 1924. Another change was the design of the just completed revisions of the lawyers' ethical code, which had been purposely written in such a way that what the ABA called "ethical considerations," which were statements of broad principle, would be separate and clearly distinct from action-oriented "disciplinary rules" thought to flow from those broad principles. (One example would be the ethical consideration that a lawyer should conduct his practice in a dignified manner and its companion disciplinary rule flatly forbidding advertising his services in newspapers or other media.) This format for the lawyers' code seemed destined to assure that the judicial code as well would contain some mandatory rules, not merely what Traynor called "a sampler of mottoes." Another change was atmospheric: the ABA had become accustomed to more than adoption of written rules; it was geared to a state-by-state lobbying effort to attempt to make its pronouncement on legal professional matters the policy of courts and legislatures throughout the land. The association cut its lobbying teeth with a campaign that led to the ratification of the Twenty-fifth Amendment on presidential inability and improved its techniques with state-by-state campaigns for adoption of the new lawyers' code and the ABA's Standards of Criminal Justice. This capability existed, its existence was an inducement to its use, and the likelihood that it would be used helped set the committee's mental framework. These were to be "the highest possible standards of conduct that would be realistically applicable to diverse conditions" across the legal landscape.

The first thing that was not "realistically applicable," in the Traynor committee's opinion, was the June 10 resolution of the U.S. Judicial Conference, with its sharp curbs on outside activity and its financial reporting requirement. As reported in more detail in the previous chapter, the committee asked the federal judiciary to suspend—a euphemism for abandon—the June resolution, and the judiciary acquiesced, if indeed it did not heartily welcome the request.

Underlying the committee's request was a basic assumption— a questionable one—that it was important for one code of conduct to be written for both state and federal judges and that the federal system should shift into neutral to await the expertise of the private bar committee and the ABA as a whole.

Although Segal was overly optimistic in predicting that the code could be drafted in a year's time, it did not take long for the committee to reach agreement on basic principles, particularly the principles involved in the hottest issues of the time. The clearest signal, announced in the committee's initial report of June 1970, was that judges had no ethical duty to disclose their off-the-bench income unless it was for services rendered. "A judge has a right to privacy like everybody else," Chairman Traynor explained later. He said the public has "a right to know, and a deep interest in, everything a judge does while a judge and particularly any money he makes out of it," but not his private investments. Rejected, if it had ever been seriously entertained, was the thought that a listing of a judge's financial interest would enable lawyers and parties to lawsuits to assess the need to ask the judge to step aside. Instead, the report said there would be disclosure of a judge's financial holdings only in one limited instance: when a particular stock or other interest was such that it ordinarily would disqualify him from a case before him. The judge, at the same time that he disqualified himself, would issue an accounting of the particular interest. Both sides in the case then could consider waiving the disqualification and asking the judge to sit because they thought he could be fair despite his interest. The Velvet Blackjack had returned in a new form, more subtle but no less coercive in its pressure on lawyers to waive their clients' right to a disinterested judge. The disclosure was a broad invitation for a waiver. The committee's report said the disclosure and waiver procedure should be handled through court clerks in such a way that if one side or the other withheld the waiver, the judge would not be aware of which side it was. For a group of men so seasoned in litigation, the committee's assumption that the judge would remain ignorant on such a matter was, to be as charitable as possible, naive. Nevertheless, the report proposed a bold form of public disclosure even for a small part of a judge's financial holdings. It was soon abandoned by the committee in favor of a still more subtle and still more coercive procedure, as we shall see.

Another major proposal, a marked departure from the Taft canons, was that disqualification should follow automatically from the ownership of any financial interest in a party "no matter how small," as small as one share of stock. No longer would there be haggling over whether a judge's interest was "substantial." Instead, a clear, bright line would be drawn.

Why so stringent? Aside from its eminent sensibility, there was another design. Even this apparently drastic measure was tailored to the judges' desire to protect their investment "privacy." Traynor explained that the then-current "substantial interest" standard probably would not be "manageable without full disclosure" of the judge's portfolio to enable the parties to test just how substantial the financial interest might be. The "one share of stock" test cut off any such inquiry at the threshold.

There was no mention of privacy for a judge's debts in the initial report, but this proved to be an oversight and the committee later made clear that there was no need to publicize debts.

Off-bench income for services would be made public every six months. Judges were told to shed nonfamily trusteeships, a major improvement. They were told to stay out of businesses and not serve as officers, directors, or advisers of any business organization, a very important tightening of the code. As could be predicted, bar activities were blessed and judges were told they could teach, write, and speak on legal subjects provided they did not appear to be prejudging some case. The spirit of the old canons was carried forward into political activity, disapproving it for all except those unfortunate judges forced to run for their offices. Appearing as a character witness was discouraged and so was service on nonjudicial commissions; but judges were urged to work with legislatures to improve the law.

Missing from the new principles, but not missed, was any concept of a judge's "duty to sit," the doctrine that a judge should participate, rather than disqualify himself, in cases where the propriety was unclear. This was the concept that had been so bitterly debated during the Haynsworth fight and claimed by Haynsworth's supporters as a clinching argument for the propriety of his actions. Putting aside that debate, the committee chose as its clear policy for the future that the "appearance of propriety" standard should govern so that a judge would not preside when to do so was questionable.

Making its first appearance was a "grandfather clause" that would permit sitting judges to keep trusteeships and positions in family businesses they held on the date the code became binding in their jurisdictions.

This, then, was the first phase of the committee's work, the completion of a set of basic principles as a prelude to the drafting of new canons. Nearly a year passed during which the committee held public hearings (but not public internal debate), received hundreds of letters of inquiry and suggestion (which the committee refused to make available to the press although no pledge of confidentiality had been given to the correspondents), and, in May 1971, produced a printed tentative draft of the code for further dissemination and study.

Predictably, the tentative draft reaffirmed the insistence on judicial privacy of the year before. "A judge has the rights of an ordinary citizen except to the extent required to safeguard the proper performance of his duties," the committee said. "The ownership of investments and receipt of income therefrom does not as such affect the performance of a judge's duties, *and should not be permitted to be the occasion for groundless attacks on his integrity.*" The emphasized phrase (the emphasis is supplied) was both surprising and illuminating—surprising because the committee studying the most judicious of subjects appeared to be taking sides on the question of whether attacks on a judge's integrity, and particularly attacks based on stock holdings, were ever justified. Indeed, the implication was that an examination or discussion of a judge's holdings necessarily was an attack on the jurist's integrity, groundless or not. In the context of the time, the special source of concern was clear enough. The integrity of judges and the validity of the whole legal system were under attack from many quarters, but the organized bar folk were most fretful about attacks from the New Left. Here was a curious and unfortunate display of anxiety over the system. Why not opt for disclosure and let the attackers of integrity attack to their heart's content (in an orderly manner)? A judge who was challenged could in the first instance decide whether he was somehow disqualified by reason of a disclosed financial interest, and that would be subject to review by a court of appeals on the basis of a full record of evidence. Not only would there be more certainty as to whether an attack on the judge's integrity was justified, but in addition the scrutiny of financial interests could be undertaken without overtones of questioned integrity. The outcome would be a system that vindicated itself in every case, whether or not the courts found that a judge had conflicting interests. The italicized phrase did not survive the final draft of the code, but it was indelibly printed in the tentative draft and perhaps in the minds of many of the drafters.

The Velvet Blackjack also underwent a subtle change in the tentative draft. The committee's initial report had called upon the judge, when disqualifying himself because of an economic conflict such as stock ownership, to make an automatic, full, and public statement of the disqualifying factors, such as the amount of stock he owned in a company whose case was before him. This was to have been the only disclosure of a judge's investments, a limited exposure designed to permit the parties to initiate a waiver request if they desired the judge to sit notwithstanding his economic interest. But even this modest disclosure proved too much for the draftsmen. They now provided instead that the judge would make such a report only if he chose to do so. He would choose to do so in cases in which *in his opinion* the financial interest was "insubstantial." He would make the disclosure at the same time that he stepped out of the case. The judge would not thereafter return to the case unless the lawyers and clients on both sides agreed with him that his interest was indeed insubstantial.

"This procedure is designed to minimize the chance that a party or lawyer will feel coerced into an agreement," the draft declared. A recommended procedure was to have a court clerical official available to handle the requests initiated by both sides, transmitting them to the judge only when all sides had applied for the judge to reinstate himself. The whole procedure, even after this revision, seemed absurd to anyone familiar with courthouses. Where was this detached clerk to be found? Could

anyone seriously argue that coercion had been minimized? The
system, called "remittal of disqualification," *could not even begin*
until the judge had determined for himself, and communicated
to counsel, that he was willing to sit and felt qualified to do so.
The original idea of automatic disclosure was flawed enough
because of its potential for coercing waiver, but at least under the
initial proposal the judge would not be communicating his
willingness to sit and his personal judgment that he should sit. It
is fanciful to claim that a judge who makes such a discretionary
disclosure and then hears nothing from either side will not know
which side withheld its waiver. The judge normally will suppose
that the company in which he held stock was willing to have him
sit and the opponent withheld the waiver. It would at least be
human of him to suppose or speculate along those lines and it
would be natural for the lawyer in question to expect such
speculation and worry about the possible consequences to his
local practice at a later date. The situation would be no more just
nor less coercive if the judge guessed wrongly which party was
the holdout.

Incredibly, the committee not only determined that a judge
need not report his debts, but also made it possible for a judge to
sit in a case involving the bank to which he owes his money. Lest
it be thought that a judge who was a debtor to one of the parties
could be disqualified for financial interest, the committee's
reporter, Professor Thode, explained in his appendix to the code
that "an ordinary loan to a judge from a lending institution
should not be prohibited, although the lending institution may
sometimes be a litigant in proceedings before the judge." How a
judge who owes money to a bank can be disinterested when the
bank is involved in a case before him is a proposition that must
baffle a mere layman. If the layman happens to be locked in a
lawsuit with that bank, it might do more than baffle him; it
might outrage him if the judge-debtor presides in his case.

According to the committee, the bank loan was to be "from a
lending institution in its regular course of business on the same
terms generally available to persons who are not judges." But
judges, like other community leaders, are known to receive the
prime lending rate wherever they are, a circumstance that makes

the warning about equal terms something less than a full safeguard. It is unrealistic to insist that the terms be the same as for a nonjudge. It is also difficult to determine in most cases whether any particular judge would get the same rate if he were not a judge. No mention was made of the size of loans, which could be immense in terms of the *judge's* assets.

In place of an earlier inhibition on mutual fund relationships —the initial report said the judge was disqualified if the mutual fund's portfolio included a substantial interest in a party—the committee relented and said there would be no disqualification unless the mutual fund itself was a party. The theory here was that a judge should not have to keep track of every shift in a fund's investments. The reports now were to be made at least yearly, rather than twice a year.

Elaborating on the desirability of joining in bar and other public affairs, the tentative draft said, "Separation of a judge from extrajudicial activities is neither possible nor wise; he should not become isolated from the society in which he lives." In its final form the code said "complete separation" was bad.

On a more stringent note, the committee held that a judge should not act as an outside arbitrator—an easy rule to lay down since few judges were doing it anyway. It decreed that though judges may work with foundations they may not (as Justice Douglas had done) give investment advice to them. The unarticulated reason may have been that a judge runs too high a risk of seeming to be practicing law in this situation. The draft made crystal clear that outside service on even worthy commissions was disapproved, partly because it tended to make the judiciary appear part of the political process.

But the great achievement of the May 1971 draft was one of tone, epitomized in the canon, "A judge should avoid impropriety and the appearance of impropriety in all of his activities." This was followed by the commentary: "He must expect to be the subject of constant public scrutiny. He must therefore accept restrictions on his conduct that might be viewed as burdensome by the ordinary citizen, and he should do so freely and willingly."

The mold of the new canons had been mostly cast by now; the

ensuing year produced many changes of style but few of substance. One, which became relevant in subsequent controversy over Justice William H. Rehnquist, was the committee's attempt to clarify whether a judge's previous association with a government agency had the same disqualifying effect as when a lawyer from his former private firm was involved. Even an agency of lawyers such as the Justice Department could not be equated with a law firm, the committee decided, so it declared that a judge formerly employed by a government agency "should disqualify himself in a proceeding if his impartiality might reasonably be questioned because of such association."

One rejected proposal would have specially admonished judges to be more patient and courteous to indigent litigants and their lawyers as well as persons in the "alienated" category. The committee said such a provision was "unnecessary. The standards of patience, dignity and courtesy are the same in every proceeding." Compliance with the general provision for behavior, the committee said, "will go far toward changing the image of our courts in the minds of a substantial segment of the public." Failure to acknowledge this problem was regrettable in view of the notorious fact that some judges are more patient and tolerant toward some kinds of litigants than to others.

Another damper was placed on progress when the committee flatly ruled out a "blind trust" as a possible way out of disqualification problems for judges with sizable investment portfolios. This is an arrangement by which the judge or other public official is shielded from knowledge of certain investments because he has turned over their management to a trustee without any supervision of the trustee's day-to-day investment decisions. Such an arrangement could not prevent a judge from having an actual financial interest in the outcome of a case or in one of the parties to it, but it would prevent him from knowing what his interest was and thus, the theory goes, he stands just as unbiased in the eyes of the litigants as though he had no interest. There are difficulties with the blind trust concept, but the idea seemed worth exploring to Lewis F. Powell, Jr., the successful corporation lawyer from Richmond, when he was nominated to the Supreme Court in 1971, just when the ABA committee was drawing up its final pronouncements on the subject. In apparent disappointment, Powell told the Senate Judiciary Committee that the new canon seemed to preclude that solution to his considerable stock problems.

The canon provided pointedly that "a judge should inform himself about his personal and fiduciary financial interest." The command to judges to be aware of their portfolios was part of the committee's response to the Haynsworth controversies, specifically the judge's failure to keep abreast of his own broker's activity and its impact on pending cases. This was sound enough as a means of helping a judge cope with potential financial conflicts, but the committee treated it as an end in itself rather than merely as a means to the end. To say that a judge without a blind trust should know what he owns hardly answers the question of whether a blind trust might be a workable idea for some judges. It was anomalous that the ABA, rather than being in a position to direct the conduct of the respected Supreme Court nominee, did not ask Powell whether his research showed that a blind trust was more feasible than the committee had thought.

Indeed, the committee never said that a "true" blind trust would not be a good idea. Rather, it questioned whether there was such a thing—a good and fair question, but one the committee answered for itself without examination. The committee gave three reasons for rejecting blind trusts. One was that the complexity and cost "would make it unavailable to most judges." (No one had suggested that all judges be required to put their stock in blind trusts; rather it was considered a promising idea for some judges.) Second, "There was doubt as to how blind the blind trust would be," since the judge, for example, had to sign his income tax returns complete with reports of investment income. (The committee did not ask how this is accomplished by those who do have blind trusts.) Third and "most important was the doubt that the public and litigants would believe that the trust was blind" if certain holdings became known. (Again, there was no attempt to explore whether safeguards were available that would make the device credible to the public.) None of these reasons disclosed any serious study of the question. Perhaps,

being men of affairs, the members of the committee were entitled
to rely on their own expertise; but that only raises again the
question of why only Justice Powell had an open mind about the
concept.

Otherwise, the final proposed draft of May 1972 was ready for
the home-stretch drive for approval by the ABA's House of
Delegates at the August convention in San Francisco. When it
reached there, a last-minute flurry of opposition, ineffectual but
typical of the kind of antipathy to change the committee had
encountered previously, developed with a resolution condemning
the code as discriminating against judges. The resolution was the
work of the National Conference of State Trial Judges, one of
the groups whose existence was encouraged by the canons. The
judges objected bitterly to the disclosure requirement, limited
though it was. They complained that sitting judges who must
stand for reelection could be at an unfair disadvantage to
challengers who did not have to disclose. A dissent by Judge
James A. Noe, a member of a Seattle trial court already bound
by disclosure rules, pointed out that the solution in Washington
State had been simple: a requirement that the challenger make
similar disclosure. "At a time when the judicial system is under a
cloud of suspicion if not outright attack, a national judges'
conference refusing to accept such a code on such a limited
argument cannot help but detract from the image of the
judiciary in the mind of the public," said Judge Noe.

Somehow the Traynor committee persuaded the judges to stay
off the House of Delegates floor with their objections. As it
happened, only two amendments were offered. One, requiring a
judge to pursue disciplinary measures against a fellow judge as
well as against a fellow lawyer, was agreed to. The second
amendment, a bid by Attorney General Andrew P. Miller of
Virginia to eliminate the "remittal of disqualification" rule, was
rejected. Miller argued that the waiver section "clearly sets up a
race to the courthouse" between lawyers hastening to assure the
judge that he is "a pretty good old boy after all" and urging him
to sit. Chairman Traynor, citing the problem in the state of
Maine where Judge Gignoux of the committee was for many
years the only federal judge, said the plan minimized coercion

while avoiding the inconvenience to the parties and the judges that results because of disqualification, where the case is delayed to summon a new judge from elsewhere. The committee prevailed easily. House approval by unanimous voice vote soon followed.

☆

The customary campaign for adoption by the states was launched immediately by a bar committee. Within a year eight states and the District of Columbia had adopted the code. One would have expected that the U.S. Judicial Conference, which had nominally "suspended" its own rules to await the rulings of the ABA, would have rushed to embrace the new code at its fall meeting, but it was not until the following spring that the conference was moved to take its own action. The official reason was that there had been sentiment favoring a still longer waiting period for the federal judges—to see how the state courts, bars, and legislatures reacted to the code! Once again, the federal judiciary, where so much of the ethical trouble lay, was taking a back seat.

But the moment of truth for the federal bench could not be put off indefinitely. On an afternoon in early April 1973, the judges of the secret conference met, wrestled verbally for several hours, and produced the first code of ethics ever adopted by the federal judiciary. It was a toughened version of the ABA code, stipulating that wherever federal law or previous conference rule was more restrictive of the judge, the stronger provision should govern. There was no "grandfather clause." Rather there was a grace period: one year for judges to relinquish their executorships and trusteeships for clients outside their own families, a concession designed more for fairness to those relying on the jurist's services than to the judge himself. After one year, a judge still worried about a special hardship could continue to work as fiduciary for a nonfamily interest—but without compensation. For federal judges, the "duty to sit" was now out, the "appearance of propriety" was in, if the conference rules were valid. True, the 1924 canons had set the "appearance" standard, but federal judges had not adopted it as their standard. Still to be resolved some day was whether the rule-making power of the conference could withstand a legal or constitutional challenge, and whether Congress would now proceed to enact a disqualification statute that would clearly govern the Supreme Court as well as the lower bench.

A peculiar flaw marred the conference action, historic and sweeping as it was. The judges were unable to decide, and so left to "further study," the odd question of the propriety of a federal judge's candidacy for an elective seat on the state judiciary. Thus the conference was forced to suspend decision on whether the new code's prohibition of political activity should apply to federal judges. The impasse was forced by friends and supporters of Judge Jack B. Weinstein of the U.S. District Court in Brooklyn, who at the time was a candidate for the Democratic nomination for chief judge of the Court of Appeals of New York, the state's highest and one of the country's most important courts. Some judges thought it obvious that a federal judge, enjoying life tenure and other emoluments and safeguards, should never run for any political office without first resigning, as Charles Evans Hughes had done in 1916 to run for president. Others said that the revered Learned Hand had run for the same court from the bench as a Teddy Roosevelt "Bull Moose" candidate back in 1913. Weinstein supporters argued that any conference action would plunge the judges into New York's political thicket by siding with the candidate's opponents. That argument prevailed; the conference stayed its hand. Weinstein then lost the primary by a handful of votes, and the conference adopted a canon against all political candidacy the following autumn.

In the final analysis, what was the exercise over judicial norms of ethics all about? What did it accomplish? Are judges going to be more honest or be so perceived? Before assessing these questions, we must first turn to an episode of early disobedience to the canons, since to be effective a code must be obeyed.

9

☆ ☆ ☆

A JUDGE AND HIS CAUSE

"Although a judge has been appointed by imperial power yet because it is our pleasure that all litigations should proceed without suspicion, let it be permitted to him, who thinks the judge under suspicion, to recuse him before issue joined, so that the cause go to another."

Justinian Code

"No man can be a judge in his own cause."

Sir Edward Coke (1614)

Just as the independence and the impartiality of a court seem to go together, so is it hard to separate an attack on a court's independence from an attack on its ability to be fair. Any time a president of the United States—be he Nixon, Roosevelt, or whoever—makes a political issue of his determination to "turn the Supreme Court around," there is an attack on the court's independence that is fraught with danger for justice and the appearance of justice. Some conservatives may smack their lips at the hope for change, liberals may quail at the prospect of lost civil liberties; but thoughtful persons of left and right and middle will be concerned over the politicization of the highest court. The concern will be no less when the Court is conservative and its attackers are liberal.

Periods of such marked and conspicuous change put a heavy

strain on judicial ethics. Failure of a jurist to abide by high ethical standards can exacerbate the tensions that already run high when the courts are confronted by highly emotional, somewhat political, and deeply divisive issues. Observance of ethical restraints can ease tension and produce judicial decisions that are not only more fair, but that are also perceived as such.

Even under fairly normal circumstances, the changes in Supreme Court personnel can be unsettling to the law. Justice Felix Frankfurter, in a 1950 dissent from the Court's third change of direction in search-and-seizure law in three years, complained: "Especially ought the court not reenforce needlessly the instabilities of our day by giving fair ground for the belief that Law is the expression of chance—for instance, of unexpected changes in the court's composition and the contingencies in the choice of successors." In the spring of 1971, Justice Hugo L. Black dissented from an overruling made possible by the replacement of two justices by Nixon appointees. "This precious fourteenth amendment American citizenship should not be blown around by every passing political wind that changes the composition of this court," said Black. "While I remain on the court I shall continue to oppose the power of judges, appointed by changing administrations, to change the Constitution from time to time according to their notions of what is 'fair' and 'reasonable.' "

In the fall Black was gone, and with him John Marshall Harlan, and the winds of change were stirring anew. After a period of surveying a field of unqualified candidates, a period that itself was disquieting to those who appreciated the loss of the two judicial giants, the Nixon administration at last came up with two qualified nominees, Lewis F. Powell, Jr., and William H. Rehnquist. Both men were aptly classified as "conservatives," and even allowing for some slippage between a president's expectations and a justice's performance, the third and fourth Nixon nominees were certain to have a profound effect on the Supreme Court's future course. Powell's prestige and the moderation that for the most part had tempered his philosophy enabled him to sail through Senate confirmation with but a single dissenting vote. Rehnquist, however, had been the cutting edge of Nixon's major differences with Congress, civil libertarians, and civil rights advocates. His confirmation on December 11, 1971, by a vote of sixty-eight to twenty-six, followed a bitter battle during which senators—both those who opposed him and some who ended up voting for him—were frustrated in their efforts to question Rehnquist about his views because he invoked the "attorney-client" privilege as the president's "lawyer's lawyer."

This chapter deals with how Rehnquist responded to the ethical issues raised by his sitting in judgment on matters deeply affecting his former client, the president. The sad conclusion— sad because it must be made of a jurist with brains, ability, and dedication to the Court—is that Rehnquist's performance was one of the most serious ethical lapses in the Court's history. Sad, too, because his behavior, documented in his own extraordinary memorandum justifying his conduct, came at an ethical water- shed when the distress of past scandals was supposed to be behind us. The memorandum, the only one ever published by a justice in response to a motion to disqualify himself (such motions are themselves almost as rare), is itself a monument both to Rehnquist's technical ability and to his ethical shortsightedness. If the standards set forth in the memorandum are allowed to stand for Supreme Court justices or for the lower federal judiciary, we shall have learned nothing for all our anguish.

Rehnquist had been through much of the anguish himself, first in giving advice to Attorney General John N. Mitchell during the Fortas episode in the spring of 1969, later that year as the lawyer trying to usher the Haynsworth nomination through the Senate, and in 1970 while performing similar functions for both the Carswell and Blackmun nominations. Indeed, he appeared to have learned from the Haynsworth fight that whatever might be said in judgment of that unfortunate nominee, the Senate had opted for a stricter ethical standard for the present and future. The Justice Department's correspondence with the Senate Judi- ciary Committee over Justice Blackmun's finances carried a notation that perhaps the old disqualification statute itself had been given a stricter modern meaning by the way the Senate interpreted it in the Haynsworth vote. And Rehnquist, quite possibly the author of that comment, testified at his own hearing that as a justice "my own inclination would be, applying the standards laid down by [the disqualification law] and to the extent there is no conflict between them and the canons of judicial ethics, to try to follow that sort of stricter standards that I think the Senate, by its vote, indicated should prevail."

Senators had been anxious to know whether Rehnquist would consider himself qualified to sit in the forthcoming test of the president's power to wiretap, in the name of national security and without court authorization, individuals classified by the executive branch as domestic subversives. After many questions on the subject, Rehnquist assured the Judiciary Committee that since he had given key legal advice in the preparation of the Justice Department's position before the Supreme Court, he would not sit in the case although he did not personally sign the government's legal brief. Similar anxieties were expressed about Powell's participation in the same case, in view of his strong published statements that opponents of wiretapping were exaggerating its dangers. (Justice Rehnquist did indeed recuse himself in the case as the Court rejected the Justice Department's position by an eight to zero vote in an opinion by none other than Justice Powell.) Rehnquist indicated also that he would not sit in another important case, testing the power of prosecutors, grand juries, and even congressional committees to give only limited or "use" immunity from prosecution rather than total immunity when coercing them into giving self-incriminating testimony. In that case Rehnquist had actually signed the brief and had been prepared to argue for the government in support of such power. (The decision, which incidentally upheld the constitutionality of the procedures later used to squeeze testimony from many Watergate suspects, was by a five to three vote, with Justice Powell again writing the majority opinion.)

The most ethically sensitive cases that faced Rehnquist were the *Branzburg* and *Tatum* cases. The *Branzburg* case pitted much of the newspaper industry against the government's claimed power to subpoena unpublished and sometimes confidential information from newsmen Paul M. Branzburg of the *Louisville Courier-Journal*, Earl Caldwell of the *New York Times*, and Paul Pappas of television station WTEC-TV in New Bedford, Massachusetts. The *Tatum* case, which would ultimately produce the famous Rehnquist memorandum, raised the question of whether peace workers and antiwar groups could take the government to court over the army's program of surveillance, infiltration, intelligence gathering, and dissemination to other federal agencies of information about law-abiding civilians.

Another case with a lurking though perhaps a more tenuous ethical question was the *Gravel* case, involving the government's attempt to elicit grand jury testimony about the source of the copy of the Pentagon Papers that came into the hands of Senator Mike Gravel, Democrat of Alaska, and that he published after unsuccessfully trying to make it a part of Congress's official record. Rehnquist as assistant attorney general had fired the first volley in the Pentagon Papers fight by telegraphing editors at the *New York Times* and *The Washington Post* to ask voluntary suspension of publication, a request that, when refused, was converted into a demand and a court complaint to enjoin publication. So far as anyone knew, Rehnquist had little to do with the Pentagon Papers after dealing with the issue of prior restraint on their publication by the press (decided in the newspapers' favor in June 1971) and before his Supreme Court nomination the following October. While the *Gravel* case also involved the Pentagon Papers and whether they could be lawfully disclosed to the public, the legal issues were different. While Justice Rehnquist clearly would have been disqualified from the prior restraint case, it is harder to insist on the basis of known facts that he should have stayed out of the *Gravel* case.

Although it was not a surprise to see Justice Rehnquist on the bench taking part in the *Gravel* hearing, it was a shock to see him there when the *Branzburg* and *Tatum* cases were called for oral argument. Assistant Attorney General Rehnquist had been the Justice Department's chief public spokesman, second only to the attorney general himself, for the Justice Department's controversial policy of subpoenaing newsmen for investigations of Black Panthers and other groups. On one occasion immediately recalled by newsmen, Rehnquist had appeared in the role of administration spokesman to defend the department's 1970 subpoena guidelines, which his Office of Legal Counsel had helped to prepare. He played the apologist's role on a panel of commentators that included critics of administration policy. The guidelines were instructions to United States Attorneys' offices across the land, and they served as "litigating" material that the government cited in every court case to show the reasonableness of Mitchell's policy. Justice Rehnquist, from the outset of his Supreme Court service an active questioner from the bench, showed no consciousness of impropriety in his frequent give-and-take discussions with counsel for the three newsmen. He said nothing, however, during the entire oral argument in the *Tatum* case, perhaps signaling that it did involve an ethical question on which he was reserving judgment. This unaccustomed reticence only added confusion to the stunned surprise of counsel for Arlo Tatum, director of the Central Committee for Conscientious Objectors, and the other political dissenters who were trying to maintain their suit against the army. Did Rehnquist actually intend to vote in the case or was he merely sitting to hear the case out of interest? Was he there on some sort of provisional basis to determine for himself whether his previous involvement was disqualifying? Unlikely as this was, did not this possibility counsel caution to anyone tempted to move to strike the justice from the case? If the justice were inclined against participating, a move to recuse him might offend not only him but perhaps others on the Court as well. Senator Sam J. Ervin, Jr., the North Carolina Democrat whose outspoken defense of privacy rights and First Amendment freedoms later entered millions of American households through televised coverage of the Watergate hearings, was more sensitive than most to why Justice Rehnquist should not sit; but sitting alongside lawyers from the American Civil Liberties Union in the High Court's hearing room, he quietly counseled the cautious approach. Ervin, who joined the argument as a friend of the court on the side of the civilian plaintiffs, was unwilling to assume the worst. He recalled that when he argued in the *Darlington* labor cases, Justice Potter Stewart sat on the bench but dropped out when something said at the hearing reminded him of a close association with a textile official.

Broadly, Rehnquist was considered disqualified because of his role as principal administration defender and witness at extensive hearings on military surveillance held before Ervin's Subcommittee on Constitutional Rights. There Rehnquist stated that the Pentagon program, however unwise or regrettable, did not violate anyone's constitutional rights. Specifically and crucially, he had testified that the *Tatum* lawsuit, which was pending in lower courts while the Ervin hearings were under way, was not "justiciable"; that is, it was the kind of lawsuit that courts should and would dismiss as judicially unmanageable. This was the very issue in the case when it reached the Supreme Court.

Furthermore, Rehnquist had made clear to Ervin the department's determined resistance to any legislation attempting to control the military practices—which he said had stopped anyway—or to any attempt to impose a judicial remedy by statute. The problem was best left to the "self-discipline" of the executive branch, Rehnquist testified in a vein that later became so much more familiar to Americans when the war and Watergate were aired publicly.

Central to the administration's position that there was no violation of constitutional rights was its contention that nobody had been hurt. It was not enough, in this view, that there was no congressional authorization for the program, or even that the military exceeded its constitutional bounds by intruding into the civilian sector of American life. The program would have been unconstitutional not because of its mere existence, but only if it actually infringed the rights of specific plaintiffs who went to court. According to the *Tatum* complaint, the surveillance did just that by threatening the privacy of political dissidents and hindering their exercise of First Amendment rights of free speech, assembly, and political association. But, said the Justice Department, Tatum and his friends were not hindered; they continued meeting, marching, protesting the war, and they even went to court to assert their rights to do so. Tatum countered by pointing to that portion of his complaint that specified that other less hardy souls were indeed inhibited from associating with the Tatums and other protesters. It was not denied—indeed, it could not be denied under the rules of pleading. When a party moves to dismiss a lawsuit without undergoing a trial, it must accept every charge in the complaint as true, at least for the sake of argument, and then go on to show the court that there is no case under the law even if all the charges are true.

In large measure the case came down to how one viewed First Amendment rights and the measures necessary to safeguard them. To civil libertarians, First Amendment rights are not only basic, they are also very fragile. They need the solicitude of courts—what Justice William J. Brennan, Jr., calls "breathing space"—to survive. Government conduct that discourages free expression may defy precise measurement, since the identities of those discouraged are often by definition unknown and unknowable. When the federal government or a state is challenged on these grounds, it conventionally argues that there is nobody in the case with the requisite injury, no one with the kind of legal standing to make the case judicially manageable.

This description of the issues might seem weighted on the side of the *Tatum* plaintiffs, but it is their perspective that must be appreciated when considering their ethical complaint. The rest of the ethical issue is whether the complaint was grounded on a reasonable fear that the jurist was biased against them. They said that they felt just such a fear about a jurist who not only was out of sympathy with their cause but also had publicly stated his opinion that they had no case.

On June 29, 1972, the Supreme Court ruled against the newsmen. Three days earlier the Court had ruled that the *Tatum* lawsuit should be dismissed without a trial to examine the Pentagon practice or to demonstrate the alleged injuries. Each time the vote was five to four and each time the four Nixon appointees—Chief Justice Burger and Justices Blackmun, Rehnquist, and Powell—were joined by Justice White to make the majority. In each case the dissenters were Justices Douglas, Brennan, Stewart, and Marshall. By the same margin and by the same lineup the Court rejected the contention of Senator Gravel, which the Senate itself had supported, that the senator and his aide were constitutionally immune from inquiry into the acquisition of the Pentagon Papers. On these highly contested issues at least, the Supreme Court had indeed been turned around, the result swung by appointees of a different philosophy.

With little hesitation, both the American Civil Liberties Union on behalf of the *Tatum* plaintiffs and Senator Gravel decided to seek a rehearing and disqualification of Justice Rehnquist. Although the newsmen and their lawyers appeared to have a stronger claim than Gravel to an ethical challenge, it was not in their strategic interest to file a protest and they did not. In two of the three cases the withdrawal of Justice Rehnquist would not have made a difference, since a four to four vote would only affirm their contempt convictions for refusing to cooperate with grand juries; the third newsman, Caldwell, by this time was no longer sought by the grand jury. Some counsel privately expressed reluctance to appear to join a cabal of dissatisfied litigants in moving against Justice Rehnquist in so personal a manner. Unquestionably the course of moving to disqualify a justice would be a disagreeable, abrasive process, but the ACLU deemed the legal issue clear enough. If they had been silenced by a Velvet Blackjack, they would remain silent no longer.

"This motion is not made lightly," the ACLU told Justice Rehnquist, "but only after careful consideration by counsel and their colleagues in full knowledge of its unprecedented nature." The only precedent the ACLU could cite for such an action by a party was that unhappy episode in 1945 when the losing party in a celebrated miners' wage dispute had called for a rehearing on the ground that Justice Black, whose law partner of two decades earlier had argued for the labor union, should not have participated. The Court rejected this motion, however, with a most unusual separate concurrence by Justice Robert H. Jackson, joined by Justice Felix Frankfurter, pointing out that a justice's colleagues lacked power to judge the propriety of his action. Two years later, in a bitter open letter, Justice Jackson made clear that he indeed disapproved of Justice Black's role in the case. (Current canons support Justice Black and call for disqualification only where the case was in the law firm when the jurist and lawyer were partners.) That regrettable precedent did not augur well for the ACLU or for the Court's ability to handle the new motion dispassionately.

Accompanying the motion asking Justice Rehnquist to step aside was a petition for rehearing addressed to the entire Court.

The petition pointed to five separate instances in which the ACLU claimed that the five-member majority had accepted as though proven critical facts that underlay the decision, including the unproven assertion that the government had destroyed key surveillance records whose existence had been part of the complaint. In addition, the petition contended, the majority opinion had ignored numerous assertions of fact by the plaintiffs that, under the previously mentioned pleading rules governing motions to dismiss, must be accepted by the courts. It was needless to add that none of these alleged errors could have been committed by the Court if there had been no majority, since the consequences of a four to four tie vote are an affirmance of the lower court's judgment, which was that the case should go to trial rather than be dismissed, and no written opinion of any kind. The petition seemed correct in all respects and was most temperately worded. There was no opportunity for the government to dispute these points since the Supreme Court's rules do not call for an answer to a rehearing request unless the Court is considering granting it.

The motion to recuse Justice Rehnquist was based in part on the same federal disqualification statute, Section 455 of Title 28 of the U.S. Code that had been debated during the Haynsworth fight: "Any justice or judge of the United States shall disqualify himself in any case in which he has a substantial interest, has been of counsel, is or has been a material witness, or is so related to or connected with any party or his attorney as to render it improper, in his opinion, for him to sit. . . ."

The second prong of the ACLU motion, more telling as a matter of policy though not based on any yet-recognized law, was the new ABA Code of Judicial Conduct. The code had been published in final draft form and was then scheduled for final ABA approval at the summer convention. Approval took place on schedule and the code was ABA policy by the time the Supreme Court convened again in the fall.

The motion said Rehnquist had been a self-styled Justice Department "spokesman" on the broad question of the constitutionality of surveillance and had appeared twice as a witness before Ervin's subcommittee. On one occasion the witness said he did not agree that "there are any serious constitutional problems with respect to collecting data on or keeping under surveillance persons who are merely exercising their rights of peaceful assembly or petition to redress a grievance." The witness did not limit himself to such generalities, the petition continued, but instead, "the concrete factual setting which he chose to discuss was the surveillance of civilians by the United States Army as depicted in the pleadings and the District Court decision in *Tatum v. Laird*, the very lawsuit" he voted on as a justice. A second statement had been even more pointed as Assistant Attorney General Rehnquist told Ervin:

My point of disagreement with you is to say whether in the case of *Tatum v. Laird* that has been pending in the Court of Appeals here in the District of Columbia that an action will lie by private citizens to enjoin the gathering of information by the executive branch where there has been no threat of compulsory process and no pending action against any of those individuals on the part of the Government.

Besides speaking publicly in the same vein, Rehnquist also complied with a request from Senator Roman L. Hruska, Republican of Nebraska, for a legal memorandum supporting his constitutional thesis. The memorandum denied that there had been any interruption in robust debate as a result of the program of surveillance. In addition, Rehnquist during the hearings had been the government's custodian of large amounts of computerized evidence that the ACLU had been trying to get.

As for the new ABA code, the motion emphasized the broad admonitions of canon 2 that a judge "should avoid impropriety and the appearance of impropriety in all his activities" and canon 3C requiring disqualification when "his impartiality might reasonably be questioned." The ACLU said it was by no means questioning the good faith of Rehnquist's pre-judicial expression of views. "Indeed, it was precisely because of the clarity and finality of his testimonial views and the intimacy of his knowledge of the evidentiary facts at issue in this case that the respondents [the *Tatum* plaintiffs] were convinced that Mr. Justice Rehnquist would not participate in the Court's deliberation and decision. . . ."

The disqualification statute, strictly construed, was indeed severe, the ACLU admitted, but it argued that, in the language of an important 1955 Supreme Court decision, it "may sometimes bar trial by judges who have no actual bias and who would do their very best to weigh the scales of justice equally between contending parties. But to perform its high function in the best way 'justice must satisfy the appearance of justice.' " There was no need to get into the question of actual bias, the ACLU said, when the judge has merely the normal concern about a case he had started before going on the bench. Citing a decision disqualifying then federal trial judge G. Harrold Carswell from a case that had been handled in his office when he had been United States attorney, the ACLU described it as "the interest that any lawyer has in pushing his case to a successful conclusion." This was a broad definition of the term "case" suggested by the fact that the Ervin hearings and the *Tatum* lawsuit were parallel proceedings going on in different forums.

Under the circumstances, said the ACLU,

> Mr. Justice Rehnquist's impartiality is clearly questionable because of his appearance as an expert witness for the Justice Department in Senate hearings inquiring into the subject matter of the case, because of his intimate knowledge of the evidence underlying the respondents' allegations, and because of his public statements about the lack of merit in respondents' claims.

The answer came from the Court and the justice on October 10, 1972, the first decision day of the new term: "Motion to withdraw opinion of this Court denied. Motion to recuse, *nunc pro tunc,* presented to Mr. Justice Rehnquist, by him denied." There followed a sixteen-page memorandum by the justice that was as unusual for its content as it was unprecedented in law.

First the memorandum disposed of the ABA code as a separate and distinct basis for decision on the motion. "Since I do not read these particular provisions as being materially different from the standards enunciated in the congressional statute, there is no occasion for me to give them separate consideration," Justice Rehnquist said. This was a startling statement in light of the universally acknowledged fact that the new canons set a much stricter disqualification standard than the existing federal statute. As discussed in the previous chapter, the new canons applied the "appearance of justice" test that would disqualify a judge in a doubtful case in place of the "duty to sit" concept that federal judges had evolved so that they would sit in the doubtful cases. For his legal authority in support of this remarkable conclusion, the justice cited none other than the 1969 report of the Senate Judiciary Committee majority supporting the Haynsworth nomination, which argued that the old canons then in effect should be read to harmonize with the federal statute in judging that nominee's ethical conduct. That this was dubious authority indeed was underscored by Rehnquist's own confirmation hearing testimony, quoted earlier in this chapter, that the full Senate's vote against Judge Haynsworth, which had of course *rejected* the Judiciary Committee's views, inclined him, in applying the federal disqualification law, "to the extent there is no conflict between them and the canons of judicial ethics, to try to follow that sort of stricter standards that I think the Senate, by its vote, indicated should prevail."

Having reduced his problem to the dimensions of the less restrictive federal law, Justice Rehnquist proceeded to take the narrowest possible view of the word "case." Said he: "I never participated, either of record or in any advisory capacity, in the District Court, in the Court of Appeals, or in this Court in the government's conduct of the case of *Laird v. Tatum.*" He added, "Since I have neither been of counsel nor have I been a material witness in *Laird v. Tatum*, these provisions are not applicable. . . . I did not have even an advisory role in the conduct of the case of *Laird v. Tatum.* . . ."

Turning to the statements made before the Ervin subcommittee, Rehnquist said there were two. One, in his prepared statement, was simply that the government had retained one printout from the army's computer for inspection by the court in the *Tatum* case. Justice Rehnquist quoted this statement in his memorandum. He did not quote the second statement, however, the one set out in full on page 217. If he had, he might have faced the disqualification issue more squarely. This was the remark of witness Rehnquist disagreeing with Chairman Ervin over

whether "an action will lie" in the case of *Tatum* v. *Laird*. Justice
Rehnquist called this exchange "a discussion of the applicable
law." But this, as all lawyers will recognize and most lawyers will
freely state, is not a mere discussion of the "applicable law." It is
a statement of how the law should be applied to a particular
case. Time after time throughout the memorandum's sixteen
pages, Justice Rehnquist repeated that characterization of his
Senate testimony. Time after time he refused to treat the ACLU
charge that he had commented on the merits—or, as witness
Rehnquist had testified, lack of merits—of the lawsuit itself.

For example, the memorandum said that since most justices
come to the bench no earlier than their middle years, "It would
be not merely unusual, but extraordinary, if they had not at least
given opinions *as to constitutional issues* [emphasis supplied] in their
previous legal careers. Proof that a Justice's mind at the time he
joined the Court was a complete *tabula rasa* in the area of
constitutional adjudication would be evidence of lack of qualification, not lack of bias." The ACLU had not contested this
truism.

Later in the memorandum the justice said that since no jurist
starts from dead center on such issues, "it is not a ground for
disqualification that a judge has prior to his nomination
expressed his then understanding *of the meaning of some particular
provision of the Constitution.*" [Emphasis supplied.] This, too, was not
contested as a general proposition.

Although the ACLU pitched that part of its argument based
on the federal statute on the so-called mandatory clauses of
section 455—those that require disqualification if a judge has a
substantial interest, has been of counsel, or is or has been a
material witness—Justice Rehnquist devoted most of his memorandum to the so-called discretionary clause—"so related to or
connected with any party or his attorney as to render it
improper, in his opinion, for him to sit"—on which the ACLU
apparently had deemed it useless to rely. Much of his argument
here had to do with the historic practices of different justices,
some of whom sat in close cases. He noted that Justice Black had
been criticized for sitting in Fair Labor Standards Act cases but
not, to Rehnquist's knowledge, because he had been the legisla-

tion's floor manager while a senator from Alabama. Frankfurter wrote about the evils of the antilabor injunction and helped sire the 1933 federal law against it, then wrote the Court's opinion in a major 1941 case involving the law. Justice Jackson voted in a 1950 case based on an issue he had decided as attorney general before he joined the Court in 1941. Charles Evans Hughes criticized a decision in a law lecture a few years before becoming chief justice and nine years later wrote the Court's opinion in another case overruling the decision. Justice Harlan felt free in 1961 to join with the Court in rejecting a view he had expressed while a judge on the Second U.S. Circuit Court of Appeals. And Justice Holmes sat on no fewer than eight cases in which he had taken part while chief justice of the Massachusetts Supreme Judicial Court (this at a time when the federal law on such matters, enacted in 1891, did not apply to members of the U.S. Supreme Court). But all of these examples, except possibly the Holmes cases, were irrelevant, since they did not involve a justice sitting in a *case* about which he had already publicly commented while it was pending.

Justice Rehnquist's final reason for sitting was based on supposed problems in judicial administration posed by an equally divided Court and the doctrine, developed in several federal circuits but repudiated in the new ABA code and perhaps by the Senate's Haynsworth vote, that a jurist had a "duty to sit" unless clearly disqualified. He deemed it undesirable that a case heard by the Supreme Court should be nondecided by a deadlocked vote. It should not be left "unsettled" in that fashion. This concern, which is a valid concern as a general proposition, scarcely applied to the *Tatum* case, which might have been quite effectively resolved by a four to four affirmance. A tie vote would have sustained the court of appeals and required a trial on the complaint. How much preferable such a result, rather than having it decided by the vote of a disqualified justice, fresh from the ranks of the Nixon administration where he had made something of a cause out of defending the challenged surveillance practice from legal attack.

Justice Rehnquist said the "duty to sit" doctrine impelled him to sit even though "I would certainly concede that fair-minded judges might disagree about the matter." In addition to the doctrine's abandonment in the new ABA code, another code provision seemed to apply with special relevance to his situation: the section that said a judge formerly employed by a governmental agency "should disqualify himself in a proceeding if his impartiality might reasonably be questioned because of such association." That test would seem to call for disqualification under the justice's own concession that his judgment might indeed reasonably be questioned. But of course Justice Rehnquist had already rejected any argument based on the new code since he saw them as not "materially different" from the standards he was applying.

Admittedly, some close questions, intriguing to lawyers and scholars, may arise when a judge sits in a case with a trace of past involvement. Often the proper response is a matter of degree. For example, Justice Thurgood Marshall's participation in civil rights cases sometimes stirs discussion, despite the fact that jurists of the white race decided civil rights cases without challenge for generations. Justice Marshall has recused himself when the National Association for the Advancement of Colored People is a party in a case before him but understandably does not sit out every new case brought by lawyers for the NAACP Legal Defense Fund, Inc., where he served as director-counsel before 1962. Justice Byron R. White repeatedly declines to sit in some criminal cases, apparently because they involve a law he lobbied through Congress as deputy attorney general under Attorney General Robert F. Kennedy. Others on the Supreme Court constantly confront ethical problems with subtle features. But there was nothing subtle about the *Tatum* case and Justice Rehnquist's relationship to it. Try as he might to restate the matter, Rehnquist judged the rights of parties after giving his view that one of the parties had no rights and after working to defeat that party's claim to rights.

Even when the Supreme Court has been taken over and reconstituted by a series of new appointments, justice is not administered by lining up the Court's members and simply polling them on controversial questions. The Court sits to decide cases, and unless its work is done judicially and judiciously it is not a court, it is only supreme, and that not for long if its credibility erodes. The civil libertarians who were so heavily engaged in the *Tatum* case could not expect to win on the issue in the long run, given the High Court's makeup, but they had a right to expect that they would not lose the issue except in a case decided by disinterested justices.

10

☆ ☆ ☆

APPEARANCE, REALITY,
AND PERSPECTIVE

"One of the toughest problems we have in this life is in seeing
the difference between the apparent and the real, and in basing our
actions only on that which is real. We all must do that more than we
do. I have confidence in the ultimate prevalence of truth; I intend to do
what I can to speed truth's discovery."

John D. Ehrlichman,
letter of resignation to President Nixon,
April 30, 1973

"[T]he problem inheres in institutional arrangements. That is
why we have conflict-of-interest laws, not that someone appointed
Secretary of the Treasury or Attorney General cannot be trusted, but
that he must be above suspicion and that his judgment must not be
deflected one way or the other by being put in what may appear to be a
compromising position of conflicting loyalties. It is just as bad for a man
of honor to lean over backwards to avoid the imputation of bias as it is
to be actually biased so far as these important functions in the
administration of justice are concerned. . . . The problem is to arrive at
an institutional arrangement that is not dependent on confidence in the
individual."

Paul A. Freund, testifying on legislation
to protect the independence of the special
Watergate prosecutor, November 7, 1973

No one can sensibly say, after Watergate, that the
scandals in judicial ethics from Fortas to Rehnquist amount to

the moral crisis of the age. By hindsight they were perhaps only contributing factors to the growth of cynicism about the quality of the nation's leadership. While the lapses of judges and justices threatened only one branch of the three, Watergate, as Senator Lowell Weicker, Republican of Connecticut, put it, involved the near theft of the entire country through the capture of its democratic election processes. Yet it is no small thing to sap the moral strength of the judicial branch. If the people's ultimate hope is the exercise of political rights, surely they are in grave danger when the judiciary, whose function it often becomes to preserve those very rights, is stripped of public confidence, the source of so much of the judiciary's actual power. Indeed, some of the disease that infected the judiciary was the same kind of ethical confusion that plagued the Johnson and Nixon White House: the inability to keep the branches of government distinct, from Fortas's role as part-time member of Lyndon Johnson's general staff to Rehnquist's refusal to see that his roles as Richard Nixon's lawyer's lawyer had become incompatible with the job of being his administration's judge.

In this ethical climate, some of which he had inherited and some of which he had helped create with his attacks on the Court, President Nixon dangled directorship of the Federal Bureau of Investigation before federal judge W. Matt Byrne while the judge presided over the trial of the administration's chosen prime foe, Daniel Ellsberg. John D. Ehrlichman, Nixon's agent in the Byrne transaction, later swore that he had "scoured the canons of ethics" in a fruitless attempt "to find if I had in any way infringed upon them." Among the canons Ehrlichman overlooked or found inoperative was canon 9 of the American Bar Association's 1969 Code of Professional Responsibility, which states in italics, *"A lawyer should avoid even the appearance of professional impropriety."* The canon writers never dreamed that they would have to state specifically in black letter text that no member of the bar acting for a lawyer-president, and no lawyer-president, should offer one of the most coveted positions in government to a judge handling such a case. Ehrlichman, whose resignation letter stressed the need for distinguishing between appearance and reality, should have applied imagination—enough to ask how such a move would have appeared had it been made by the Ellsberg defense.

It was fully as indecorous for Judge Byrne to entertain Ehrlichman's inquiry as to whether he was interested in such a post, but one may seriously doubt whether any official ethical judgment will be placed upon the judge's conduct unless an attempt is made to promote him. The entire question of ethical controls for the federal bench is both intriguing and, as we have seen in the Douglas and other episodes, constitutionally unsettled. The very immunities federal judges enjoy from outside discipline can only heighten the dismay when so much of the ethical problem lies with the federal bench. Nowhere in the public sector are the conditions for independence and high standards more favorable: appointment for life (or during "good behavior" as those who would create federal disciplinary bodies emphasize); a salary that, while not enormous, could easily satisfy anyone with a grain of desire for public service; the opportunity to decide some of the most fascinating questions known to the law; usually comfortable working facilities and a small office staff at no cost; and not least a courtroom where he is treated like a king if he demands it. If this book is at all accurate about the trouble at the federal level, what is the state of the judiciary generally? What is to be done?

Though it may seem naive to say it, the best hope for an honest judiciary may lie in the establishment of rather high-sounding ethical guidelines, statements of lofty norms of morality that are so often denounced by realists. To a code of principles on this plane, one ingredient must be added, that of disclosure—public courts publicly accessible and judicial behavior amenable to public scrutiny. Like the conviction three decades ago of Judge Martin T. Manton of New York, exposure of secret activity by some judges may injure the reputations of courts and judges in the minds of some persons, but it should reassure many more that something is being done. Judge Manton actually argued in his unsuccessful petition for Supreme Court review that "from a broad viewpoint it serves no public policy for a high judicial officer to be convicted of a judicial crime. It tends to destroy the confidence of the People in the Courts." One must wonder what confidence would have remained had Manton's conviction been overturned. We are dealing with lapses by highly located and visible personages at a time of rising demands for propriety by a wider range of the populace.

We have indeed come a long way from the relatively simple society in which a handful of giants—the same political geniuses who created the marvelously balanced and checked system of American government—could like John Jay hold down simultaneously a position at the top of the federal judiciary, a key ambassadorship, and the candidacy for a prestigious governorship. Ethical questions, never without a political tinge, could for a time cripple even the superindependent Justice Douglas, could help cost Fortas the chief justiceship, and could provide the pivotal votes to deny a seat on the Supreme Court to Judge Haynsworth. Frequently, otherwise estimable federal judges have behaved as though the rising public demands did not exist. Many judges continued, and continue, to coerce the bar into acquiescence in unnecessarily low ethical standards. Some judges, pushing their powers to the point of autocratic behavior, have been ill equipped to cope with new problems of justice to which the judiciary must constantly address itself. Institutions like the Judicial Conference of the United States do not protect the judges from their own excesses so much as they help to isolate them still further from public supervision and criticism while encouraging them to feel that they can engage in legislative lobbying with impunity. The organized bar, a complicated institution hindered in reform work by its own clubbiness with judges, has taken the first steps for ethical betterment in the form of a modern, though not necessarily up-to-date, code of judicial conduct. That the new code could not induce proper conduct by Justice Rehnquist at the ethical watershed of his first term on the Supreme Court is simply another indication that action by Congress is essential and overdue.

Congressional action should take the form of legislating a standard at least as high as that set by the ABA and the Judicial Conference. The U.S. Senate passed legislation along these lines on October 4, 1973, and passed the problem to a House of Representatives whose Judiciary Committee was beginning to become bogged down in a more pressing ethical study, that of possibly impeaching the president of the United States. As is often the case, legislation critical to the effective operation of the federal courts was in danger of being lost in the political shuffle. Certainly there was little time for Congress to focus on ways in which the standards were not yet tight enough. Before examining the standards that need tightening, it is appropriate to ask how the code, described in its key particulars in chapter 8, might have avoided some of the recent tragedies.

Fortas was denied elevation to chief justice, and his further downfall began, when senators zeroed in on his White House contacts and the $15,000 fee he accepted for conducting the series of American University law seminars. It is doubtful that any ethical canon would have deterred Fortas and President Johnson from getting together in councils over the war and such matters as urban riots, since Fortas has persisted in his position that no *case* was compromised thereby. But an ethical rule might have deterred Fortas and the law school from setting the compensation level so overreachingly high, since the code requires that such outside earnings be reported. As for the $20,000 fee from Louis Wolfson that unseated Justice Fortas, this arrangement also might have been discouraged by the public reporting requirement. The code would not, unfortunately, require reporting the total deal, whereby Fortas was to perform the same social justice research each year for life for the same compensation, with later lifetime support for his widow.

Would the crusty Douglas have behaved differently? Perhaps not, in view of his stand on federal judicial immunity from legislative controls, but Douglas did for a time comply with a Judicial Conference standard of reporting outside earnings. The code would have blessed his work for a private foundation— though some would have interpreted the Parvin Foundation as violating appearances—and even his $12,000 compensation would have been all right if reported. One canon would have forbidden his giving investment advice to the foundation but not his votes as a director on investment matters, but the canon does not support critics' claims that the investment advice amounted to the illegal "practice of law."

Earl Warren would have been spared the task he sought to spare himself, the chairmanship of the committee to investigate the Kennedy assassination.

Surely the code would have saved a lot of grief for Judge Haynsworth. It would have forbidden his acting as a director for the vending company whose dealings with nonunion textile mills triggered organized labor's sharpest charges of conflict of interest for participation in the case that tested unionism in the middle South. It would not have forced him, however, to disclose the size of his interest in the company (one-seventh), its monetary value ($450,000 when he sold it), its relationship to the rest of his personal wealth (sizable), nor the scope of the company's dealings with nonunion textile plants (extensive and exclusive). Such detailed disclosures, which are not currently required by any code, might have precipitated an earlier showdown on the proprieties and settled the matter long before his nomination to the Supreme Court. Quite possibly the new canons would have exonerated Haynsworth completely, since they say nothing about holdings in companies "doing business with" parties before the courts. There would remain an argument over total appearances, however, including the question of whether, in terms of the code, "his impartiality might reasonably be questioned," and particularly whether he had a financial or other interest "that could be substantially affected by the outcome of the proceeding." Labor unions argued that the judge stood to lose business for his firm. The code's command that a judge "inform himself" of his own investments would have warned Judge Haynsworth to keep a closer watch on his portfolio. This might have enabled him to answer more quickly and with less criticism for delay the Senate demands for information on his investments. He also might have been better organized to avoid buying the Brunswick Corporation stock until that case was totally over. The code's disqualification standard of a single share of stock confirmed Judge Haynsworth's own opinion that the Brunswick purchase was regrettable. A canon calling for investment disclosure might have been still more helpful in limiting Judge Haynsworth's intense stock-trading activity.

An unfortunate and subtle change from the 1924 canons would have given Judge Haynsworth the victory in his quarrel with Senator Bayh over whether it was ethical to hold $50,000 worth of J. P. Stevens stock. Whereas old canon 26 told judges not to invest "in enterprises which are apt to be involved in litigation in the court," the new canon says only that he "should manage his investments and other financial interests to minimize the number of cases in which he is disqualified." Judge Haynsworth's position, fortified by the ABA committee's most authoritative interpretation of the new canon, was that it was all right to hold the Stevens stock, notwithstanding the frequent judgments of labor law violation his court had been called upon to render against the company, since as a former lawyer for the company he was disqualified anyway from any Stevens case. One can only hope that the chief judge of the textile circuit can find other investment opportunities. While the new code does not settle all the Haynsworth controversies, it would have avoided many of them and would have cleared the air of the pestilential "duty to sit" doctrine that infested the judicial scene.

What of our wayward Fifth Circuit judges with their oil holdings and their unpleasant duty of passing on the conduct of their deceased colleague Judge Cecil? Clearly, Mrs. Cecil's ownership of Humble stock would have been sufficient to win a new trial for our self-styled inventor, Kinnear. The totality of other "appearances" might in themselves have been enough once the "duty to sit" doctrine was out of the way. Notably and regrettably, the ABA committee omitted completely any specific sanctions to help a litigant like Clarence Kinnear who belatedly finds out about a judge's disqualification, so the precise outcome of such a case is still somewhat uncertain.

As for the oil-interested judges themselves, they of course would have to surrender those stock holdings or sit out the cases. They also would have to relinquish the paid trusteeships in which some of those oil stocks were assets. Although the ABA code would give "grandfather clause" sanctuary for sitting judges (allowing them to continue in their old practices while new judges would obey the rules), this cushion fortunately is not

available to federal judges abiding by the modifications adopted
by the U.S. Judicial Conference when it made the code binding
on the district and appellate judges.

This is a decidedly mixed picture, but with much happy news
for those desirous of uplifting judicial standards. What of the
future? The ABA code already adopted by the U.S. Judicial
Conference should be widely accepted by courts, state legislatures, and Congress—as minimum standards, which is what they
are, especially for federal courts. Then the code or law should be
tightened still further, the precise form depending on the forum
involved.

To give proper credit for genuine advances and to establish
where further reform should begin, let us first consider the major
accomplishments already made by the 1972 ABA code:

1. The burial of the "duty to sit" doctrine and its replacement
with the "appearance of justice" standard by which judges stay
out of doubtful cases.

2. The rule that one share of stock suffices to disqualify, which
liberates the bench and bar from fruitless and irritating inquiries
into how much is a disqualifying "substantial interest."

3. The public, periodic reporting of outside earnings for work.

4. The rule that judges and business enterprise activity don't
mix.

5. The rules that discourage judges from appearing as
character witnesses and protect the bench against raids even for
"worthy" public service on Warren Commissions and Pearl
Harbor inquests.

But some of these rules do not go far enough and there are
other rules and more action needed:

CONGRESS SHOULD SPEEDILY ENACT A CONTEMPORARY DISQUAL-
ICATION STATUTE. This is urgent if for no other reason than that
the Supreme Court is still uncovered by the more stringent
provisions of the ABA code. Justice Rehnquist's disheartening
memorandum indicated that he might not have acted differently
if the new code were law, but there is hope that having a law in
concrete form, perhaps against a clear legislative history covering

the principles governing the *Tatum* case, the result might be different, and surely other justices would be so guided. A statute would avoid any uncertainty growing out of doubts about the rule-making power of the U.S. Judicial Conference.

ANY LEGISLATION SHOULD ELIMINATE THE POSSIBILITY OF WAIVER OF DISQUALIFICATION BY COUNSEL AND THE PARTIES. This would free lawyers from the threat of the Velvet Blackjack and place the responsibility for decision squarely where it belongs, with the judge.

THE FEDERAL STATUTE SHOULD SPECIFY REMEDIES FOR VIOLATIONS OF ETHICAL RULES. At a minimum, a litigant who demonstrates that a judge sat improperly should be guaranteed the right to a new trial. Some litigants, especially those from whom disqualifying facts have been concealed, should have a chance to reopen their cases. Disciplinary consequences for the judge involve harder questions for longer-range study, which should not delay enactment of the law.

JUDGES AND JUSTICES SHOULD BE REQUIRED TO REPORT MOST OF THEIR DEBTS. The only exemption from disclosure should be a mortgage on the house the judge lives in. Even if there is some room for the argument the ABA makes against disclosure of what a judge owns, there should be no quarrel over disclosure of who owns the judge. It is no use to say, as the 1972 code says, that the only hazards involve a loan not from a lending institution and not on the same terms available to nonjudges. "Judges always get the prime rate," says Joseph Borkin. Judge Manton had an unsecured loan from the Bank of the United States at the outset of the ethical trouble that eventually sent him to jail. Judicial insolvency is a breeding ground for corruption, even more serious than the ethical shortfalls of the late 1960s and early 1970s.

JUDGES AND JUSTICES SHOULD BE REQUIRED TO REPORT THEIR INVESTMENT INCOME. No badge of suspicion need be attached to this requirement, cries of "second-class citizenship" notwith-standing. To be sure, some jurists have been guilty of unethical activity in connection with their stock holdings, and this would be exposed and thus deterred by reporting. But even without this history, Congress has a right to know whether some judges are making as much as the government pays them by playing the stock market. The public has a right to know whether pleas for salary increases are warranted and whether judges are spending significant amounts of judicial time dealing in the market. The same right to know applies to whether judges are complying with the command that they arrange their affairs to minimize their disqualifications. If the code drafters are correct that a judge of a federal circuit court of appeals may own stock in the most litigious corporation in one of his region's dominant industries, as with J. P. Stevens and Judge Haynsworth, then at least the public ought to *know* that the judge has those holdings. And if Congress should permit the Velvet Blackjack type of waiver, at least counsel should have access to enough information about the judge's *overall* financial condition to weigh intelligently whether the disqualifying interest is a significant part of the jurist's own assets.

JUDGES AND JUSTICES SHOULD BE REQUIRED TO REPORT THEIR REAL ESTATE HOLDINGS BEYOND THE LAND THEY LIVE ON. It may be proper, as the new code indicates, for a judge to hold real estate; but in an era of increasing scarcity of land and natural resources—an era in which allocation of these resources is one of the prime judicial issues—the public and potential litigants should know which jurists have such interests. The parties are often in a better position than even a very conscientious judge to identify a disqualifying interest.

JUDGES AND JUSTICES, WHEN REPORTING THEIR OUTSIDE EARNINGS, SHOULD BE REQUIRED TO REPORT ANY EARNED EQUITY IN FUTURE INCOME, NOT MERELY CURRENT INCOME. Thus, Justice Fortas would have been required to disclose not only his $20,000 fee for one year, but also the earned right to compensation for his widow after his death. The report should also state whether the compensation is a one-time fee for piecework, or part of a continuing arrangement.

THE PUBLIC REPORTS SHOULD BE AVAILABLE FOR INSPECTION AT A CENTRAL LOCATION. It is not enough to have public reports filed only in the judge's own courthouse. For federal judges copies should be available for inspection centrally in Washington. In state court systems, a newsman or citizen should be able to go to one location, his state's supreme court, to inspect a copy of the report filed by any judge in the state. Meaningful public scrutiny, which apparently is contemplated by the ABA committee, is a practical impossibility if the monitors must pedal from courthouse to courthouse to gather their data. The filings should be identical at every place where the judge files. Does this sound nit-picking and overly suspicious? After a brief experience with its income-reporting system, the U.S. Judicial Conference found it necessary to adopt just such a rule. Apparently some judges were filing confidential addenda in their secret reports to Washington that were not available to the public at the judge's own courthouse.

A GENERAL "OPEN COURTS" POLICY IS IN ORDER. A 1924 canon, discarded by the "modern" draftsmen, carried the worthwhile message that the judge "should avoid unconsciously falling into the attitude of mind that the litigants are made for the courts instead of the courts for the litigants." Some working arrangements must be developed whereby an inquiry, by a reporter or interested citizen, about a judge's action in the general realm of ethics, can be made without triggering a defensive reaction by the judge.

JUDGES AND JUSTICES SHOULD GIVE REASONS WHEN THEY DISQUALIFY OR REFUSE TO DISQUALIFY THEMSELVES. Some feel that jurists, especially Supreme Court justices, should be free to decide the disqualification issue for themselves without the encumbrance of concern over precedent or even the requirement of internal consistency. But the controversies of recent years have shown how little we know about why judges sit and do not sit. Those not on the bench are making increasing demands for consistency and some rule of law in this area. It would not hurt a judge to *have* a reason for stepping aside or for rejecting a motion that he do so. It should be a reason he can articulate, and if he can articulate it he ought to do so. Again, this would provide a check on whether judges are minimizing their disqualifications.

Congress, which should develop some oversight on the ethical issue after passing a fresh disqualification law, should have a basis for knowing how the law is working. One serious objection to this proposal must be faced. Occasionally a judge is moved to disqualify himself because someone inadvertently or otherwise talks to him about a pending case. The judge might well hesitate to record this reason publicly for fear of inviting other episodes triggered by someone with an interest in disqualifying that particular judge. On the other hand, perhaps the broad rule should be that such an episode ordinarily would not be grounds for disqualification.

MUCH MORE CLARITY IS NEEDED ABOUT WHAT A JURIST MAY PROPERLY SAY OFF ɪHE BENCH ABOUT PUBLIC ISSUES. No intelligent person believes a judge should come to his job as a cipher on law and public policy, nor is he rendered speechless and without First Amendment rights on ascending the bench; but the judge's spoken and written words may either betray a bias or solidify it, either way making the litigant and ultimately the public uneasy. The new code is not self-explanatory on the matter and the clarifying commentary of Professor E. Wayne Thode, the principal draftsman, is unsatisfactory. According to Thode,

> There is a significant difference between the statement, "I will grant all divorce actions that come before me—whatever the strength of the evidence to support the statutory ground for divorce—because I believe that persons who no longer live in harmony should be divorced," and the statement, "I believe that limited statutory grounds for divorce are not in the public interest. The law should be changed to allow persons who no longer live in harmony to obtain a divorce."

It is true that the way a thing is said is very important, but the moderate tone of the second judge is not very reassuring.

JUDGES AND JUSTICES SHOULD KEEP THEIR ORGANIZED BAR ACTIVITIES TO A DISCREET MINIMUM. It is far from self-evident that, as the ABA committee says without explanation, judges should be "encouraged" to take part in bar association activities. Certainly a note of caution is in order lest jurists slip into the lobbying practices so familiar in the organized bar. That canon on bar activities is the bar's canon, not the public's canon. What would one expect the organized bar to say on the subject? Attendance at bar meetings is not necessarily a way to maintain contact with the "real world" and surely it is not the exclusive way. Why not declare, for instance, that attendance at bar meetings shall be denied to any judge who has failed to make at least one visit to a prison within his jurisdiction since the last bar meeting?

JUDGES AND JUSTICES SHOULD CLARIFY WHAT OUTSIDE ACTIVITIES INTERFERE WITH JUDICIAL DUTIES. Does the concept of interference with judicial work not have some relationship to how hard a judge is working and how burdened his colleagues are? We are not told by the code. Ironically, the same U.S. Judicial Conference that suspended the Warren rules on outside activities voted a resolution that a "judicial emergency" existed whenever a federal criminal indictment had been pending without trial for one year. May a judge in such a district, who is not himself working overtime, teach a law course (however edifying for him and his students) without interfering with his judicial duties? No.

JUDGES AND JUSTICES SHOULD NOT BELONG TO CLUBS OR ORGANIZATIONS THAT DISCRIMINATE ON THE BASIS OF RACE, SEX, RELIGION, OR NATIONAL ORIGIN. Would such a rule impinge on the judge's "privacy"? Yes, in the sense that the rest of us are free to discriminate in our affiliations. Some might even say it would be an overkill cure for G. Harrold Carswell's leadership role in converting a public golf course to a private country club to avoid desegregation. Precise line drawing can await the time when judges actually face up to the fact that they do not shed their judgeships when they lend their prestige to discriminatory causes. The perspective to keep in mind is that of the minority litigant who knows that the judge belongs to a club he cannot join because of human cruelty. If the bench were purged of judges who lend their personal efforts and official prestige to private discrimination—and conversely if discriminatory clubs were bereft of judges as members—one would feel better about the ABA committee's rejection of a canon admonishing judges to give special care to the underdog.

JUDGES AND JUSTICES SHOULD NOT BE FORBIDDEN TO DEVELOP, IF THEY WISH TO AND CAN, EFFECTIVE "BLIND TRUST" ARRANGEMENTS FOR SECURITIES. The ABA committee was content to express unsupported fears that no blind trust was workable or would be seen to be workable. No one can be confident that the opposite is true, but why not permit exploration of the idea? Not every jurist is interested in such schemes and not every portfolio would be suited to them, but what of that?

JUDGES AND JUSTICES SHOULD NOT LEAVE THE FEDERAL BENCH FOR POLITICAL CAREERS OR POLITICAL CHORES. They should undertake a federal judgeship with sufficient solemnity to have renounced political ambition. Let them resign if they become bored, but forbid their taking up politics for a period of, say, two to five years after resignation. At a minimum, let no sitting judge run for office. Like Charles Evans Hughes in 1916, he must at least resign first.

ETHICS SHOULD BE REQUIRED LEARNING IN THE LAW SCHOOLS, AND JUDICIAL ETHICS SHOULD BE INCLUDED. The current place of ethics in law school curricula—usually nonexistent or blended into other courses—is eloquent testimony of the priority now afforded ethics in the law. For those who think there is not enough to do in law school to justify spending three years there, ample time would seem available to schedule a required course providing the attention ethics deserves. Watergate is but the most dramatic example of a legal profession untutored in ethics, which surely can take its place alongside the full instruction now given in the law of property, contracts, commercial transactions, taxation, accounting, and creditors' remedies.

These recommendations do not include the creation of a federal disciplinary commission despite its endorsement by many thoughtful persons. As discussed more fully in chapter 2, the idea is not politically feasible, not solely for reasons that are subject to change in the foreseeable future but chiefly because it would trespass on territory that many senators have set aside for themselves. The constitutional obstacles are also impressive and a strong case, including strong prospects that the remedy would be very effective, would be needed to surmount them. This reform has not yet proved itself in the nonfederal courts of the District of Columbia, which could be an important laboratory. In any event, legislation of this sort should take a back seat to higher priority matters.

The same certain Senate resistance is one of the factors that make prescribing a popular remedy of improved selection methods unrealistic. It may be, as historian Irving Brant contends, that "the worst blight in our entire structure of government" is the treatment of federal district judgeships "as political patronage for members of Congress or as refuges for congressional lame ducks." Nevertheless, many another blight will be removed before that one is.

The measures proposed here would not cure all of the ills afflicting the federal judiciary, but they would increase the odds for justice without violating any rights of the judiciary. It is not hard to guess where the next judicial scandals will emerge—they will spring from violations of these principles—nor is it risky to predict that we will indeed have more scandals on the federal bench. They will come from the classic sources of judicial insolvency and human greed. Bankruptcy cases will continue to produce their share of corruption because so little attention is paid to their proceedings. New kinds of litigation may also challenge the judiciary and find it ethically inadequate, such as when a judge who tries to hold back the law or who decides a case unjustly turns out to be a slum lord or land speculator. Even without the temptations of outside wealth or political ambition or whatever it is that distracts the jurist from doing his honest best, the judges and justices will be hard pressed to do adequate justice. New laws and new forms of litigation will continue to bring more Americans into the legal system, and their demands and their interests will carry fresh ethical problems. As Professor David Mellinkoff of the UCLA Law School told the Senate Judiciary Committee during the Haynsworth fight, this perspective must be taken into account:

At best losing a lawsuit is disheartening, at worst a crushing experience to anyone convinced rightly or wrongly of the justice of his cause. The disappointment is endurable only under a system of justice in which the loser knows that the process by which he lost was a fair one. . . .

In the U.S. district court a jury awards an injured seaman $50 on a claim against Grace Lines—a claim which he thought was worth $30,000. Saddened, he takes his case to the U.S. Court of Appeals. It is not difficult to imagine the bitterness in the heart of this injured seaman when he learns that one of the judges to whom he appealed in vain was even a small owner of the company that owns Grace Lines.

Thus it will no longer do for the brotherhood of judges to be certain that none of them could be "bought off" or influenced by some trifling investment interest. The judiciary must look more deeply into the interests of the *consumers* of justice as perceived by them. In doing so, it is not unreasonable to ask that the judges use a little imagination and consider how mysterious and secretive the system is to the man on the street, so that an investment holding might loom as a symbol of deeper, though hidden, bias. Certainly to the litigant who has only debts, any investment by a judge looks big, just as a debtor might be bitter to learn that His Honor enjoys large amounts of credit at very favorable rates.

Does this mean that judges must yield to every imagined charge of conflict of interest, regardless of the merits, so long as there is a member of the public who believes it? No. Surely there can be some objective content to any inquiry into whether the "appearance of justice" has been compromised in a given case. The complaining party or the public must have a reasonable fear that judicial impartiality is in jeopardy. Courts can handle such an inquiry despite its subjective qualities, since they deal all the time with concepts of reasonableness—enforcing the Fourth Amendment's ban on unreasonable searches and seizures, for example, or basing civil liability on whether a driver or pedestrian behaved reasonably under the circumstances. But in weighing claims of conflicts of interest by litigants against their brother judges, the judges must appreciate how the litigants *feel*.

Meanwhile, the "appearance" standard will increasingly affect our daily lives, as the unraveling of Watergate and related scandals has demonstrated. The extraordinary replacement of normal Justice Department functions by Special Prosecutor

Archibald Cox was replete with expressions of confidence in the basic integrity of government institutions, such as the department's criminal division and its officials, but at the same time assertions that the appearance of things was the critical consideration and that an outsider could restore public confidence. Attorney General Elliot L. Richardson said he had repeatedly stressed "that it was not a matter of our not believing we would do it right," referring to the Watergate investigation. "We had to be concerned with the public confidence and therefore with appearances."

Expressions of the need for better appearances have been made for generations—no, for centuries. While cynics no less than zealous reformers are free to evoke the same refrain when it suits them, none can gainsay its basic truth. "The place of justice is a hallowed place," and this is no less true because corruption plagued the man who said it so eloquently. In an age when images—televised or conjured up by molders of public opinion and taste—often blend so confusingly with reality, does not the appearance of justice have something to do with the reality of justice? If justices and judges would pay more attention to appearances, would there not be more hope that they are performing their tasks justly? If the "consumers" of the judicial system perceive it as just, on the basis of fair disclosure of its actual operations, what more can they ask of the system? Justice Frankfurter said it for the Supreme Court in 1954: "Justice must satisfy the appearance of justice." To be sure, it is not enough that justice merely appear to be done; but the appearance of justice is an indispensable element of justice itself.

APPENDIX A

Code of Judicial Conduct

American Bar Association Special Committee on Standards of Judicial Conduct

Almost fifty years ago the American Bar Association formulated the original *Canons of Judicial Ethics.* Those Canons, occasionally amended, have been adopted in most states. In 1969 the Association determined that current needs and problems required revision of the Canons. In the revision process, the Association has sought and considered the views of the Bench and Bar and other interested persons. In the judgment of the Association this Code, consisting of statements of norms denominated canons, the accompanying text setting forth specific rules, and the commentary, states the standards that judges should observe. The canons and text establish mandatory standards unless otherwise indicated. It is hoped that all jurisdictions will adopt this Code and establish effective disciplinary procedures for its enforcement.

Canon 1
A Judge Should Uphold the Integrity and Independence of the Judiciary

An independent and honorable judiciary is indispensable to justice in our society. A judge should participate in establishing, maintaining, and enforcing, and should himself observe, high standards of conduct so that the integrity and independence of

Reprinted by permission of the American Bar Association and the American Bar Association Special Committee on Standards of Judicial Conduct.

the judiciary may be preserved. The provisions of this Code should be construed and applied to further that objective.

Canon 2

A Judge Should Avoid Impropriety and the Appearance of Impropriety in All His Activities

A. A judge should respect and comply with the law and should conduct himself at all times in a manner that promotes public confidence in the integrity and impartiality of the judiciary.

B. A judge should not allow his family, social, or other relationships to influence his judicial conduct or judgment. He should not lend the prestige of his office to advance the private interests of others; nor should he convey or permit others to convey the impression that they are in a special position to influence him. He should not testify voluntarily as a character witness.

COMMENTARY

Public confidence in the judiciary is eroded by irresponsible or improper conduct by judges. A judge must avoid all impropriety and appearance of impropriety. He must expect to be the subject of constant public scrutiny. He must therefore accept restrictions on his conduct that might be viewed as burdensome by the ordinary citizen and should do so freely and willingly.

The testimony of a judge as a character witness injects the prestige of his office into the proceeding in which he testifies and may be misunderstood to be an official testimonial. This Canon, however, does not afford him a privilege against testifying in response to an official summons.

Canon 3
A Judge Should Perform the Duties of His Office Impartially and Diligently

The judicial duties of a judge take precedence over all his other activities. His judicial duties include all the duties of his office prescribed by law. In the performance of these duties, the following standards apply:

A. Adjudicative Responsibilities.
   (1) A judge should be faithful to the law and maintain professional competence in it. He should be unswayed by partisan interests, public clamor, or fear of criticism.
   (2) A judge should maintain order and decorum in proceedings before him.
   (3) A judge should be patient, dignified, and courteous to litigants, jurors, witnesses, lawyers, and others with whom he deals in his official capacity, and should require similar conduct of lawyers, and of his staff, court officials, and others subject to his direction and control.

COMMENTARY

The duty to hear all proceedings fairly and with patience is not inconsistent with the duty to dispose promptly of the business of the court. Courts can be efficient and business-like while being patient and deliberate.

   (4) A judge should accord to every person who is legally interested in a proceeding, or his lawyer, full right to be heard according to law, and, except as authorized by law, neither initiate nor consider *ex parte* or other communications concerning a pending or impending proceeding. A judge, however, may obtain the advice of a disinterested expert on the law applicable to a proceeding before him if he gives notice to the parties of

the person consulted and the substance of the advice, and affords the parties reasonable opportunity to respond.

The proscription against communications concerning a proceeding includes communications from lawyers, law teachers, and other persons who are not participants in the proceeding, except to the limited extent permitted. It does not preclude a judge from consulting with other judges, or with court personnel whose function is to aid the judge in carrying out his adjudicative responsibilities.

An appropriate and often desirable procedure for a court to obtain the advice of a disinterested expert on legal issues is to invite him to file a brief *amicus curiae.*

(5) A judge should dispose promptly of the business of the court.

COMMENTARY

Prompt disposition of the court's business requires a judge to devote adequate time to his duties, to be punctual in attending court and expeditious in determining matters under submission, and to insist that court officials, litigants and their lawyers cooperate with him to that end.

(6) A judge should abstain from public comment about a pending or impending proceeding in any court, and should require similar abstention on the part of court personnel subject to his direction and control. This subsection does not prohibit judges from making public statements in the course of their official duties or from explaining for public information the procedures of the court.

COMMENTARY

"Court personnel" does not include the lawyers in a proceeding before a judge. The conduct of lawyers is governed by DR7-107 of the *Code of Professional Responsibility.*

(7) A judge should prohibit broadcasting, televising, recording, or taking photographs in the courtroom and areas adjacent thereto during sessions of court or recesses between sessions, except that a judge may authorize:

   (a) the use of electronic or photographic means for the presentation of evidence, for the perpetuation of a record, or for other purposes of judicial administration;

   (b) the broadcasting, televising, recording, or photographing of investitive, ceremonial, or naturalization proceedings;

   (c) the photographic or electronic recording and reproduction of appropriate court proceedings under the following conditions:

      (i) the means of recording will not distract participants or impair the dignity of the proceedings;

      (ii) the parties have consented, and the consent to being depicted or recorded has been obtained from each witness appearing in the recording and reproduction;

      (iii) the reproduction will not be exhibited until after the proceeding has been concluded and all direct appeals have been exhausted; and

      (iv) the reproduction will be exhibited only for instructional purposes in educational institutions.

COMMENTARY

Temperate conduct of judicial proceedings is essential to the fair administration of justice. The recording and reproduction of a proceeding should not distort or dramatize the proceeding.

B. Administrative Responsibilities.

(1) A judge should diligently discharge his administrative responsibilities, maintain professional competence in judicial administration, and facilitate the performance of the administrative responsibilities of other judges and court officials.

(2) A judge should require his staff and court officials subject to his direction and control to observe the standards of fidelity and diligence that apply to him.

(3) A judge should take or initiate appropriate disciplinary measures against a judge or lawyer for unprofessional conduct of which the judge may become aware.

COMMENTARY

Disciplinary measures may include reporting a lawyer's misconduct to an appropriate disciplinary body.

(4) A judge should not make unnecessary appointments. He should exercise his power of appointment only on the basis of merit, avoiding nepotism and favoritism. He should not approve compensation of appointees beyond the fair value of services rendered.

COMMENTARY

Appointees of the judge include officials such as referees, commissioners, special masters, receivers, guardians and personnel such as clerks, secretaries, and bailiffs. Consent by the parties to an appointment or an award of compensation does not relieve the judge of the obligation prescribed by this subsection.

C. Disqualification.

(1) A judge should disqualify himself in a proceeding in which his impartiality might reasonably be questioned, including but not limited to instances where:

(a) he has a personal bias or prejudice concerning a party, or personal knowledge of disputed evidentiary facts concerning the proceeding;

(b) he served as lawyer in the matter in controversy, or a lawyer with whom he previously practiced law served during such association as a lawyer concerning the matter, or the judge or such lawyer has been a material witness concerning it;

COMMENTARY

A lawyer in a governmental agency does not necessarily have an association with other lawyers employed by that agency within the meaning of this subsection; a judge formerly employed by a governmental agency, however, should disqualify himself in a proceeding if his impartiality might reasonably be questioned because of such association.

> (c) he knows that he, individually or as a fiduciary, or his spouse or minor child residing in his household, has a financial interest in the subject matter in controversy or in a party to the proceeding, or any other interest that could be substantially affected by the outcome of the proceeding;
>
> (d) he or his spouse, or a person within the third degree of relationship to either of them, or the spouse of such a person:
> > (i) is a party to the proceeding, or an officer, director, or trustee of a party;
> > (ii) is acting as a lawyer in the proceeding;

COMMENTARY

The fact that a lawyer in a proceeding is affiliated with a law firm with which a lawyer-relative of the judge is affiliated does not of itself disqualify the judge. Under appropriate circumstances, the fact that "his impartiality might reasonably be questioned" under Canon 3C(1), or that the lawyer-relative is known by the judge to have an interest in the law firm that could be "substantially affected by the outcome of the proceeding" under Canon 3C(1) (d) (iii) may require his disqualification.

> > (iii) is known by the judge to have an interest that could be substantially affected by the outcome of the proceeding;
> > (iv) is to the judge's knowledge likely to be a material witness in the proceeding;

(2) A judge should inform himself about his personal and fiduciary financial interests, and make a reasonable effort to inform himself about the personal financial interests of his spouse and minor children residing in his household.

(3) For the purposes of this section:

   (a) the degree of relationship is calculated according to the civil law system;

COMMENTARY

According to the civil law system, the third degree of relationship test would, for example, disqualify the judge if his or his spouse's father, grandfather, uncle, brother, or niece's husband were a party or lawyer in the proceeding, but would not disqualify him if a cousin were a party or lawyer in the proceeding.

   (b) "fiduciary" includes such relationships as executor, administrator, trustee, and guardian;

   (c) "financial interest" means ownership of a legal or equitable interest, however small, or a relationship as director, advisor, or other active participant in the affairs of a party, except that:

      (i)   ownership in a mutual or common investment fund that holds securities is not a "financial interest" in such securities unless the judge participates in the management of the fund;

      (ii) an office in an educational, religious, charitable, fraternal, or civic organization is not a "financial interest" in securities held by the organization;

      (iii) the proprietary interest of a policy holder in a mutual insurance company, of a depositor in a mutual savings association, or a similar proprietary interest, is a "financial interest" in the organization only if the outcome of the proceeding could substantially affect the value of the interest;

(iv) ownership of government securities is a "financial interest" in the issuer only if the outcome
of the proceeding could substantially affect the
value of the securities.

D. **Remittal of Disqualification.**

A judge disqualified by the terms of Canon 3C(1) (c) or
Canon 3C(1) (d) may, instead of withdrawing from the
proceeding, disclose on the record the basis of his disqualification. If, based on such disclosure, the parties and
lawyers, independently of the judge's participation, all agree
in writing that the judge's relationship is immaterial or that
his financial interest is insubstantial, the judge is no longer
disqualified, and may participate in the proceeding. The
agreement, signed by all parties and lawyers, shall be
incorporated in the record of the proceeding.

COMMENTARY

This procedure is designed to minimize the chance that a party or
lawyer will feel coerced into an agreement. When a party is not
immediately available, the judge without violating this section may
proceed on the written assurance of the lawyer that his party's consent
will be subsequently filed.

Canon 4

A Judge May Engage in Activities to Improve the Law,
the Legal System, and the Administration of Justice

A judge, subject to the proper performance of his judicial
duties, may engage in the following quasi-judicial activities, if
in doing so he does not cast doubt on his capacity to decide
impartially any issue that may come before him:

A. He may speak, write, lecture, teach, and particpate in other
activities concerning the law, the legal system, and the
administration of justice.

B. He may appear at a public hearing before an executive or
legislative body or official on matters concerning the law, the
legal system, and the administration of justice, and he may

otherwise consult with an executive or legislative body or official, but only on matters concerning the administration of justice.

C. He may serve as a member, officer, or director of an organization or governmental agency devoted to the improvement of the law, the legal system, or the administration of justice. He may assist such an organization in raising funds and may participate in their management and investment, but should not personally participate in public fund raising activities. He may make recommendations to public and private fund-granting agencies on projects and programs concerning the law, the legal system, and the administration of justice.

COMMENTARY

As a judicial officer and person specially learned in the law, a judge is in a unique position to contribute to the improvement of the law, the legal system, and the administration of justice, including revision of substantive and procedural law and improvement of criminal and juvenile justice. To the extent that his time permits, he is encouraged to do so, either independently or through a bar association, judicial conference, or other organization dedicated to the improvement of the law.

Extra-judicial activities are governed by Canon 5.

Canon 5
A Judge Should Regulate His Extra-Judicial Activities to Minimize the Risk of Conflict with His Judicial Duties

A. Avocational Activities. A judge may write, lecture, teach, and speak on non-legal subjects, and engage in the arts, sports, and other social and recreational activities, if such avocational activities do not detract from the dignity of his office or interfere with the performance of his judicial duties.

COMMENTARY

Complete separation of a judge from extra-judicial activities is neither possible nor wise; he should not become isolated from the society in which he lives.

B. Civic and Charitable Activities. A judge may participate in civic and charitable activities that do not reflect adversely upon his impartiality or interfere with the performance of his judicial duties. A judge may serve as an officer, director, trustee, or non-legal advisor of an educational, religious, charitable, fraternal, or civic organization not conducted for the economic or political advantage of its members, subject to the following limitations:

(1) A judge should not serve if it is likely that the organization will be engaged in proceedings that would ordinarily come before him or will be regularly engaged in adversary proceedings in any court.

COMMENTARY

The changing nature of some organizations and of their relationship to the law makes it necessary for a judge regularly to reexamine the activities of each organization with which he is affiliated to determine if it is proper for him to continue his relationship with it. For example, in many jurisdictions charitable hospitals are now more frequently in court than in the past. Similarly, the boards of some legal aid organizations now make policy decisions that may have political significance or imply commitment to causes that may come before the courts for adjudication.

(2) A judge should not solicit funds for any educational, religious, charitable, fraternal, or civic organization, or use or permit the use of the prestige of his office for that purpose, but he may be listed as an officer, director, or trustee of such an organization. He should not be a speaker or the guest of honor at an organization's fund raising events, but he may attend such events.

(3) A judge should not give investment advice to such an organization, but he may serve on its board of directors or trustees even though it has the responsibility for approving investment decisions.

COMMENTARY

A judge's participation in an organization devoted to quasi-judicial activities is governed by Canon 4.

C. Financial Activities.

(1) A judge should refrain from financial and business dealings that tend to reflect adversely on his impartiality, interfere with the proper performance of his judicial duties, exploit his judicial position, or involve him in frequent transactions with lawyers or persons likely to come before the court on which he serves.

*(2) Subject to the requirements of subsection (1), a judge may hold and manage investments, including real estate, and engage in other remunerative activity, but should not serve as an officer, director, manager, advisor, or employee of any business.

COMMENTARY

The Effective Date of Compliance provision of this Code qualifies this subsection with regard to a judge engaged in a family business at the time this Code becomes effective.

Canon 5 may cause temporary hardship in jurisdictions where judicial salaries are inadequate and judges are presently supplementing their income through commercial activities. The remedy, however, is to secure adequate judicial salaries.

[Canon 5C(2) sets the minimum standard to which a full-time judge should adhere. Jurisdictions that do not provide adequate judicial salaries but are willing to allow full time judges to supplement their incomes through commercial activities may adopt the following substitute until such time as adequate salaries are provided:

*(2) Subject to the requirement of subsection (1), a judge may hold and manage investments, including real estate, and engage in other remunerative activity including the operation of a business.

Jurisdictions adopting the foregoing substitute may also wish to prohibit a judge from engaging in certain types of businesses such as that of banks, public utilities, insurance companies, and other businesses affected with a public interest.]

(3) A judge should manage his investments and other financial interests to minimize the number of cases in which he is disqualified. As soon as he can do so without serious financial detriment, he should divest himself of investments and other financial interests that might require frequent disqualification.

(4) Neither a judge nor a member of his family residing in his household should accept a gift, bequest, favor, or loan from anyone except as follows:

   (a) a judge may accept a gift incident to a public testimonial to him; books supplied by publishers on a complimentary basis for official use; or an invitation to the judge and his spouse to attend a bar-related function or activity devoted to the improvement of the law, the legal system, or the administration of justice;

   (b) a judge or a member of his family residing in his household may accept ordinary social hospitality; a gift, bequest, favor, or loan from a relative; a wedding or engagement gift; a loan from a lending institution in its regular course of business on the same terms generally available to persons who are not judges; or a scholarship or fellowship awarded on the same terms applied to other applicants;

   (c) a judge or a member of his family residing in his household may accept any other gift, bequest, favor, or loan only if the donor is not a party or other

person whose interests have come or are likely to
come before him, and, if its value exceeds $100, the
judge reports it in the same manner as he reports
compensation in Canon 6C.

COMMENTARY

This subsection does not apply to contributions to a judge's campaign
for judicial office, a matter governed by Canon 7.

    (5) For the purposes of this section "member of his family
residing in his household" means any relative of a judge
by blood or marriage, or a person treated by a judge as a
member of his family, who resides in his household.

    (6) A judge is not required by this Code to disclose his
income, debts, or investments, except as provided in this
Canon and Canons 3 and 6.

COMMENTARY

Canon 3 requires a judge to disqualify himself in any proceeding in
which he has a financial interest, however small; Canon 5 requires a
judge to refrain from engaging in business and from financial activities
that might interfere with the impartial performance of his judicial
duties; Canon 6 requires him to report all compensation he receives for
activities outside his judicial office. A judge has the rights of an ordinary
citizen, including the right to privacy of his financial affairs, except to
the extent that limitations thereon are required to safeguard the proper
performance of his duties. Owning and receiving income from investments do not as such affect the performance of a judge's duties.

    (7) Information acquired by a judge in his judicial capacity
should not be used or disclosed by him in financial
dealings or for any other purpose not related to his
judicial duties.

D. Fiduciary Activities. A judge should not serve as the
executor, administrator, trustee, guardian, or other fiduciary, except for the estate, trust, or person of a member of
his family, and then only if such service will not interfere

with the proper performance of his judicial duties. "Member of his family" includes a spouse, child, grandchild, parent, grandparent, or other relative or person with whom the judge maintains a close familial relationship. As a family fiduciary a judge is subject to the following restrictions:

(1) He should not serve if it is likely that as a fiduciary he will be engaged in proceedings that would ordinarily come before him, or if the estate, trust, or ward becomes involved in adversary proceedings in the court on which he serves or one under its appellate jurisdiction.

COMMENTARY

The Effective Date of Compliance provision of this Code qualifies this subsection with regard to a judge who is an executor, administrator, trustee, or other fiduciary at the time this Code becomes effective.

(2) While acting as a fiduciary a judge is subject to the same restrictions on financial activities that apply to him in his personal capacity.

COMMENTARY

A judge's obligation under this Canon and his obligation as a fiduciary may come into conflict. For example, a judge should resign as trustee if it would result in detriment to the trust to divest it of holdings whose retention would place the judge in violation of Canon 5C(3).

E. **Arbitration. A judge should not act as an arbitrator or mediator.**

F. **Practice of Law. A judge should not practice law.**

G. **Extra-judicial Appointments. A judge should not accept appointment to a governmental committee, commission, or other position that is concerned with issues of fact or policy on matters other than the improvement of the law, the legal system, or the administration of justice. A judge, however, may represent his country, state, or locality on ceremonial occasions or in connection with historical, educational, and cultural activities.**

COMMENTARY

Valuable services have been rendered in the past to the states and the nation by judges appointed by the executive to undertake important extra-judicial assignments. The appropriateness of conferring these assignments on judges must be reassessed, however, in light of the demands on judicial manpower created by today's crowded dockets and the need to protect the courts from involvement in extra-judicial matters that may prove to be controversial. Judges should not be expected or permitted to accept governmental appointments that could interfere with the effectiveness and independence of the judiciary.

Canon 6
A Judge Should Regularly File Reports
of Compensation Received for Quasi-Judicial
and Extra-Judicial Activities

A judge may receive compensation and reimbursement of expenses for the quasi-judicial and extra-judicial activities permitted by this Code, if the source of such payments does not give the appearance of influencing the judge in his judicial duties or otherwise give the appearance of impropriety, subject to the following restrictions:

A. Compensation. Compensation should not exceed a reasonable amount nor should it exceed what a person who is not a judge would receive for the same activity.

B. Expense Reimbursement. Expense reimbursement should be limited to the actual cost of travel, food, and lodging reasonably incurred by the judge and, where appropriate to the occasion, by his spouse. Any payment in excess of such an amount is compensation.

C. Public Reports. A judge should report the date, place, and nature of any activity for which he received compensation, and the name of the payor and the amount of compensation so received. Compensation or income of a spouse attributed to the judge by operation of a community property law is

not extra-judicial compensation to the judge. His report should be made at least annually and should be filed as a public document in the office of the clerk of the court on which he serves or other office designated by rule of court.

Canon 7
A Judge Should Refrain from Political Activity Inappropriate to His Judicial Office

A. **Political Conduct in General.**
(1) A judge or a candidate for election to judicial office should not:
    (a) act as a leader or hold any office in a political organization;
    (b) make speeches for a political organization or candidate or publicly endorse a candidate for public office;

COMMENTARY

A candidate does not publicly endorse another candidate for public office by having his name on the same ticket.

    (c) solicit funds for or pay an assessment˙ or make a contribution to a political organization or candidate, attend political gatherings, or purchase tickets for political party dinners, or other functions, except as authorized in subsection A(2);
(2) A judge holding an office filled by public election between competing candidates, or a candidate for such office, may, only insofar as permitted by law, attend political gatherings, speak to such gatherings on his own behalf when he is a candidate for election or re-election, identify himself as a member of a political party, and contribute to a political party or organization.
(3) A judge should resign his office when he becomes a

candidate either in a party primary or in a general election for a non-judicial office, except that he may continue to hold his judicial office while being a candidate for election to or serving as a delegate in a state constitutional convention, if he is otherwise permitted by law to do so.

(4) A judge should not engage in any other political activity except on behalf of measures to improve the law, the legal system, or the administration of justice.

B. Campaign Conduct.

(1) A candidate, including an incumbent judge, for a judicial office that is filled either by public election between competing candidates or on the basis of a merit system election:

(a) should maintain the dignity appropriate to judicial office, and should encourage members of his family to adhere to the same standards of political conduct that apply to him;

(b) should prohibit public officials or employees subject to his direction or control from doing for him what he is prohibited from doing under this Canon; and except to the extent authorized under subsection B(2) or B(3), he should not allow any other person to do for him what he is prohibited from doing under this Canon;

(c) should not make pledges or promises of conduct in office other than the faithful and impartial performance of the duties of the office; announce his views on disputed legal or political issues; or misrepresent his identity, qualifications, present position, or other fact.

(2) A candidate, including an incumbent judge, for a judicial office that is filled by public election between competing candidates should not himself solicit or accept campaign funds, or solicit publicly stated support, but he may establish committees of responsible persons to secure and manage the expenditure of funds for his campaign and to obtain public statements of

support for his candidacy. Such committees are not prohibited from soliciting campaign contributions and public support from lawyers. A candidate's committees may solicit funds for his campaign no earlier than [90] days before a primary election and no later than [90] days after the last election in which he participates during the election year. A candidate should not use or permit the use of campaign contributions for the private benefit of himself or members of his family.

COMMENTARY

Unless the candidate is required by law to file a list of his campaign contributors, their names should not be revealed to the candidate.

[Each jurisdiction adopting this Code should prescribe a time limit on soliciting campaign funds that is appropriate to the elective process therein.]

(3) An incumbent judge who is a candidate for retention in or re-election to office without a competing candidate, and whose candidacy has drawn active opposition, may campaign in response thereto and may obtain publicly stated support and campaign funds in the manner provided in subsection B(2).

Compliance with the Code of Judicial Conduct

Anyone, whether or not a lawyer, who is an officer of a judicial system performing judicial functions, including an officer such as a referee in bankruptcy, special master, court commissioner, or magistrate, is a judge for the purpose of this Code. All judges should comply with this Code except as provided below.

A. **Part-time Judge.** A part-time judge is a judge who serves on a continuing or periodic basis, but is permitted by law to devote time to some other profession or occupation and whose compensation for that resason is less than that of a full-time judge. A part-time judge:

    (1) is not required to comply with Canon 5C(2), D, E, F, and G, and Canon 6C;

    (2) should not practice law in the court on which he serves or in any court subject to the appellate jurisdiction of the court on which he serves, or act as a lawyer in a proceeding in which he has served as a judge or in any other proceeding related thereto.

B. **Judge Pro Tempore.** A judge *pro tempore* is a person who is appointed to act temporarily as a judge.

    (1) While acting as such, a judge *pro tempore* is not required to comply with Canon 5C(2), (3), D, E, F, and G, and Canon 6C.

    (2) A person who has been a judge *pro tempore* should not act as a lawyer in a proceeding in which he has served as a judge or in any other proceeding related thereto.

C. **Retired Judge.** A retired judge who receives the same compensation as a full-time judge on the court from which he retired and is eligible for recall to judicial service should comply with all the provisions of this Code except Canon 5G, but he should refrain from judicial service during the period of an extra-judicial appointment not sanctioned by Canon 5G. All other retired judges eligible for recall to judicial service should comply with the provisions of this Code governing part-time judges.

Effective Date of Compliance

A person to whom this Code becomes applicable should arrange his affairs as soon as reasonably possible to comply with it. If, however, the demands on his time and the possibility of conflicts of interest are not substantial, a person who holds judicial office on the date this Code becomes effective may:

    (a) continue to act as an officer, director, or non-legal advisor of a family business;

    (b) continue to act as an executor, administrator, trustee, or other fiduciary for the estate or person of one who is not a member of his family.

Submitted by the Special Committee
on Standards of Judicial Conduct

Roger J. Traynor, *Chairman*	Robert A. Leflar
Walter P. Armstrong, Jr.	William L. Marbury
E. Dixie Beggs	George H. Revelle
Edward T. Gignoux	Whitney North Seymour
James K. Groves	W. O. Shafer
Ivan Lee Holt, Jr.	Potter Stewart
Irving R. Kaufman	Edward L. Wright

E. Wayne Thode, *Reporter*
Geoffrey C. Hazard, Jr., *Consultant*

April, 1972

APPENDIX B

Opinion of Mr. Justice Rehnquist

on Motion to Disqualify Himself

in *Laird* v. *Tatum*

(Issued October 10, 1972. Officially reported at 409 U.S. 824.)

No. 71-288. Laird, Secretary of Defense, et al. *v.* Tatum et al., 408 U.S. 1. Motion to withdraw opinion of this Court denied. Motion to recuse, *nunc pro tunc,* presented to Mr. Justice Rehnquist, by him denied.

Memorandum of Mr. Justice Rehnquist.

Respondents in this case have moved that I disqualify myself from participation. While neither the Court nor any Justice individually appears ever to have done so, I have determined that it would be appropriate for me to state the reasons which have led to my decision with respect to respondents' motion. In so doing, I do not wish to suggest that I believe such a course would be desirable or even appropriate in any but the peculiar circumstances present here.[1]

Respondents contend that because of testimony that I gave on behalf of the Department of Justice before the Subcommittee on Constitutional Rights of the Judiciary Committee of the United States Senate at its hearings during the 92d Cong., 1st Sess., on Federal Data Banks, Computers and the Bill of Rights (hereinafter Hearings), and because of other statements I made in speeches related to this general subject, I should have disqualified myself from participating in the Court's consideration or decision of this case. The governing statute is 28 U. S. C. § 455, which provides:

---

[1] In a motion of this kind, there is not apt to be anything akin to the "record" that supplies the factual basis for adjudication in most litigated matters. The judge will presumably know more about the factual background of his involvement in matters that form the basis of the motion than do the movants, but with the passage of any time at all his recollection will fade except to the extent it is refreshed by transcripts such as those available here. If the motion before me turned only on disputed factual inferences, no purpose would be served by my detailing my own recollection of the relevant facts. Since, however, the main thrust of respondents' motion is based on what seems to me an incorrect interpretation of the applicable statute, I believe that this is the exceptional case where an opinion is warranted.

"Any justice or judge of the United States shall disqualify himself in any case in which he has a substantial interest, has been of counsel, is or has been a material witness, or is so related to or connected with any party or his attorney as to render it improper, in his opinion, for him to sit on the trial, appeal, or other proceeding therein."

Respondents also cite various draft provisions of Standards of Judical Conduct prepared by a distinguished committee of the American Bar Association, and adopted by that body at its recent annual meeting. Since I do not read these particular provisions as being materially different from the standards enunciated in the statute, there is no occasion for me to give them separate consideration.[2]

Respondents in their motion summarize their factual contentions as follows:

"Under the circumstances of the instant case, Mr. Justice Rehnquist's impartiality is clearly questionable because of his appearance as an expert witness for the Justice Department in Senate hearings inquiring into the subject matter of the case, because of his intimate knowledge of the evidence underlying the respondents' allegations, and because of his public statements about the lack of merit in respondents' claims."

Respondents are substantially correct in characterizing my appearance before the Ervin Subcommittee as an "expert witness for the Justice Department" on the subject of statutory and constitutional law dealing with the authority of the Executive Branch to gather information. They are also correct in stating that during the course of my testimony at that hearing, and on other occasions, I expressed an understanding of the law, as established by decided cases of this Court and of other courts, which was contrary to the contentions of respondents in this case.

Respondents' reference, however, to my "intimate knowledge of the evidence underlying the respondents' allegations" seems to me to make a great deal of very little. When one of the Cabinet departments of the Executive Branch is requested to supply a witness for the congressional committee hearing devoted to a particular subject, it is generally confronted with a minor dilemma. If it is to send a witness with personal knowledge of every phase of the inquiry, there will be not one

---

[2] See Executive Report No. 91–12, 91st Cong., 1st Sess., Nomination of Clement F. Haynsworth, Jr., 10–11.

spokesman but a dozen. If it is to send one spokesman to testify as to the department's position with respect to the matter under inquiry, that spokesman will frequently be called upon to deal not only with matters within his own particular bailiwick in the department, but with those in other areas of the department with respect to which his familiarity may be slight. I commented on this fact in my testimony before Senator Ervin's Subcommittee:

"As you might imagine, the Justice Department, in selecting a witness to respond to your inquiries, had to pick someone who did not have personal knowledge in every field. So I can simply give you my understanding. . . ." Hearings 619.

There is one reference to the case of *Tatum* v. *Laird* in my prepared statement to the Subcommittee, and one reference to it in my subsequent appearance during a colloquy with Senator Ervin. The former appears as follows in the reported hearings:

"However, in connection with the case of *Tatum* v. *Laird*, now pending in the U.S. Court of Appeals for the District of Columbia Circuit, one printout from the Army computer has been retained for the inspection of the court. It will thereafter be destroyed." Hearings 601.

The second comment respecting the case was in a discussion of the applicable law with Senator Ervin, the chairman of the Subcommittee, during my second appearance.

My recollection is that the first time I learned of the existence of the case of *Laird* v. *Tatum*, other than having probably seen press accounts of it, was at the time I was preparing to testify as a witness before the Subcommittee in March 1971. I believe the case was then being appealed to the Court of Appeals by respondents. The office of the Deputy Attorney General, which is customarily responsible for collecting material from the various divisions to be used in preparing the Department's statement, advised me or one of my staff as to the arrangement with respect to the computer print-out from the Army Data Bank, and it was incorporated into the prepared statement that I read to the Subcommittee. I had then and have now no personal knowledge of the arrangement, nor so far as I know have I ever seen or been apprised of the contents of this particular print-out. Since the print-out had been lodged with the Justice Department by the Department of the Army, I later authorized its transmittal to the staff of the Subcommittee at the request of the latter.

At the request of Senator Hruska, one of the members of the Subcommittee, I supervised the preparation of a memorandum of law, which the record of the hearings indicates was filed on September 20, 1971. Respondents refer to it in their petition, but no copy is attached, and the hearing records do not contain a copy. I would expect such a memorandum to have commented on the decision of the Court of Appeals in *Laird* v. *Tatum*, treating it along with other applicable precedents in attempting to state what the Department thought the law to be in this general area.

Finally, I never participated, either of record or in any advisory capacity, in the District Court, in the Court of Appeals, or in this Court, in the Government's conduct of the case of *Laird* v. *Tatum*.

Respondents in their motion do not explicitly relate their factual contentions to the applicable provisions of 28 U. S. C. § 455. The so-called "mandatory" provisions of that section require disqualification of a Justice or judge "in any case in which he has a substantial interest, has been of counsel, is or has been a material witness. . . ."

Since I have neither been of counsel nor have I been a material witness in *Laird* v. *Tatum*, these provisions are not applicable. Respondents refer to a memorandum prepared in the Office of Legal Counsel for the benefit of Mr. Justice White shortly before he came on the Court, relating to disqualification. I reviewed it at the time of my confirmation hearings and found myself in substantial agreement with it. Its principal thrust is that a Justice Department official is disqualified if he either signs a pleading or brief or "if he actively participated in any case even though he did not sign a pleading or brief." I agree. In both *United States* v. *United States District Court*, 407 U.S. 297 (1972), for which I was not officially responsible in the Department but with respect to which I assisted in drafting the brief, and in *S&E Contractors* v. *United States,* 406 U.S. 1 (1972), in which I had only an advisory role which terminated immediately prior to the commencement of the litigation, I disqualified myself. Since I did not have even an advisory role in the conduct of the case of *Laird* v. *Tatum*, the application of such a rule would not require or authorize disqualification here.

This leaves remaining the so-called discretionary portion of the section, requiring disqualification where the judge "is so related to or connected with any party or his attorney as to render it improper, in his opinion, for him to sit on the trial, appeal, or other proceeding therein." The interpretation and application of this section by the various Justices who have sat on this Court seem to have varied widely. The leading commentator on the subject is John P. Frank, whose two articles, Disqualification of Judges, 56 Yale L. J. 605 (1947), and Disqualification of Judges: In Support of the Bayh Bill, 35 Law & Contemp. Prob. 43 (1970), contain the principal commentary on the subject. For a Justice of this Court who has come from the Justice Department, Mr. Frank explains disqualification practices as follows:

"Other relationships between the Court and the Department of Justice, however, might well be different. The Department's problem is special because it is the largest law office in the world and has cases by the hundreds of thousands and lawyers by the thousands. For the most part, the relationship of the Attorney General to most of those matters is purely formal. As between the Assistant Attorneys General for the various Departmental divisions, there is almost no connection." Frank, *supra*, 35 Law & Contemp. Prob., at 47.

Indeed, different Justices who have come from the Department of Justice have treated the same or very similar situations differently. In *Schneiderman* v. *United States*, 320 U.S. 118 (1943), a case brought and tried during the time Mr. Justice Murphy was Attorney General, but defended on appeal during the time that Mr. Justice Jackson was Attorney General, the latter disqualified himself but the former did not. 320 U.S., at 207.

I have no hesitation in concluding that my total lack of connection while in the Department of Justice with the defense of the case of *Laird* v. *Tatum* does not suggest discretionary disqualification here because of my previous relationship with the Justice Department.

However, respondents also contend that I should disqualify myself because I have previously expressed in public an understanding of the law on the question of the constitutionality of governmental surveillance. While no provision of the statute sets out such a provision for disqualification in so many words, it could conceivably be embraced within the general language of the discretionary clause. Such a contention raises rather squarely the question of whether a member of this Court, who prior to his taking that office has expressed a public view as to what the law is or ought to be, should later sit as a judge in a case raising that particular question. The present disqualification statute applying to Justices of the Supreme Court has been on the books only since 1948, but its predecessor, applying by its terms only to district court judges, was enacted in 1911. Mr. Chief Justice Stone, testifying before the Judiciary Commitee in 1943, stated:

"And it has always seemed to the Court that when a district judge could not sit in a case because of his previous association with it, or a circuit court of appeals judge, it was our manifest duty to take the same position." Hearings Before Comittee on the Judiciary on H. R. 2808, 78th Cong., 1st Sess., 24 (1943), quoted in Frank, *supra*, 56 Yale L. J., at 612 n. 26.

My impression is that none of the former Justices of this Court since 1911 have followed a practice of disqualifying themselves in cases involving points of law with respect to which they had expressed an opinion or formulated policy prior to ascending to the bench.

Mr. Justice Black while in the Senate was one of the principal authors of the Fair Labor Standards Act; indeed, it is cited in the 1970 edition of the United States Code as the "Black-Connery Fair Labor Standards Act." Not only did he introduce one of the early versions of the Act, but as Chairman of the Senate Labor and Education Committee he presided over lengthy hearings on the subject of the bill and presented the favorable report of that Committee to the Senate. See S. Rep. No. 884, 75th Cong., 1st Sess. (1937). Nonetheless, he sat in the case that upheld the constitutionality of that Act, *United States* v. *Darby*, 312, U.S. 100 (1941), and in later cases construing it, including *Jewell Ridge Coal Corp.* v. *Local 6167, UMW*, 325 U.S. 161 (1945). In the latter case, a petition for rehearing requested that he disqualify himself because one of his former law partners argued the case, and Justices Jackson and Frankfurter may be said to have implicitly criticized him for failing to do so.[3] But to my knowledge his Senate role with respect to the Act was never a source of criticism for his participation in the above cases.

Mr. Justice Frankfurter had, prior to coming to this Court, written extensively in the field of labor law. The Labor Injunction which he and Nathan Greene wrote was considered a classic critique of the abuses by the federal courts of their equitable jurisdiction in the area of labor relations. Professor Sanford H. Kadish has stated:

"The book was in no sense a disinterested inquiry. Its authors' commitment to the judgment that the labor injunction should be neutralized as a legal weapon against unions gives the book its energy and direction. It is, then, a brief, even a 'downright brief' as a critical reviewer would have it." Labor and the Law, in Felix Frankfurter The Judge 153, 165 (W. Mendelson ed. 1964).

---

[3] See denial of petition for rehearing in *Jewell Ridge Coal Corp.* v. *Local 6167, UMW*, 325 U.S. 897 (1945) (Jackson, J., concurring).

Justice Frankfurter had not only publicly expressed his views, but had when a law professor played an important, perhaps dominant, part in the drafting of the Norris-LaGuardia Act, 47 Stat. 70, 29 U. S. C. §§ 101–115. This Act was designed by its proponents to correct the abusive use by the federal courts of their injunctive powers in labor disputes. Yet, in addition to sitting in one of the leading cases interpreting the scope of the Act, *United States* v. *Hutcheson*, 312 U.S. 219 (1941), Justice Frankfurter wrote the Court's opinion.

Mr. Justice Jackson in *McGrath* v. *Kristensen*, 340 U.S. 162 (1950), participated in a case raising exactly the same issue that he had decided as Attorney General (in a way opposite to that in which the Court decided it). 340 U.S., at 176. Mr. Frank notes that Mr. Chief Justice Vinson, who had been active in drafting and preparing tax legislation while a member of the House of Representatives, never hesitated to sit in cases involving that legislation when he was Chief Justice.

Two years before he was appointed Chief Justice of this Court, Charles Evans Hughes wrote a book entitled The Supreme Court of the United States (Columbia University Press, 1928). In a chapter entitled Liberty, Property, and Social Justice he discussed at some length the doctrine expounded in the case of *Adkins* v. *Children's Hospital*, 261 U.S.. 525 (1923). I think that one would be warranted in saying that he implied some reservations about the holding of that case. See *id.*, at 205, 209–211. Nine years later, Mr. Chief Justice Hughes wrote the Court's opinion in *West Coast Hotel Co.* v. *Parrish*, 300 U.S. 379 (1937), in which a closely divided Court overruled *Adkins*. I have never heard any suggestion that because of his discussion of the subject in his book he should have recused himself.

Mr. Frank summarizes his view of Supreme Court practice as to disqualification in the following words:

"In short, Supreme Court Justices disqualify when they have a dollar interest; when they are related to a party and, more recently, when they are related to counsel; and when the particular matter was in one of their former law offices during their association; or, when in the government, they dealt with the precise matter and particularly with the precise case; otherwise, generally no." *Supra*, 35 Law & Contemp. Prob., at 50.

Not only is the sort of public-statement disqualification upon which respondents rely not covered by the terms of the applicable statute, then, but it does not appear to me to be supported by the practice of previous Justices of this Court. Since there is little controlling authority on the subject, and since under the existing practice of the Court disqualification has been a matter of individual decision, I suppose that one who felt very strongly that public-statement disqualification is a highly desirable thing might find a way to read it into the discretionary portion of the statute by implication. I find little to commend the concept on its merits, however, and I am, therefore, not disposed to construe the statutory language to embrace it.

I do not doubt that a litigant in the position of respondents would much prefer to argue his case before a Court none of whose members had expressed the views that I expressed about the relationship between surveillance and First Amendment rights while serving as an Assistant Attorney General. I would think it likewise true that counsel for Darby would have preferred not to have to argue before Mr. Justice Black; that counsel for Kristensen would have preferred not to argue before Mr. Justice Jackson;[4] that counsel for the United States would have preferred not to argue before Mr. Justice Frankfurter; and that counsel for West Coast Hotel Co. would have preferred a Court which did not include Mr. Chief Justice Hughes.

The Term of this Court just past bears eloquent witness to the fact that the Justices of this Court, each seeking to resolve close and difficult questions of constitutional interpretation, do not reach identical results. The differences must be at least in some part due to differing jurisprudential or philosophical propensities.

Mr. Justice Douglas' statement about federal district judges in his dissenting opinion in *Chandler* v. *Judicial Council*, 398 U.S. 74, 137 (1970), strikes me as being equally true of the Justices of this Court:

"Judges are not fungible; they cover the constitutional spectrum; and a particular judge's emphasis may make a world of difference when it comes to rulings on evidence, the temper of the courtroom, the tolerance for the proffered defense, and the like. Lawyers recognize this when they talk about 'shopping' for a judge; Senators recognize this when they are asked to give their 'advice and consent' to judicial appointments; laymen recognize this when they appraise the quality and image of the judiciary in their own community."

---

[4] The fact that Mr. Justice Jackson reversed his earlier opinion after sitting in *Kristensen* does not seem to me to bear on the disqualification issue. A judge will usually be required to make any decision as to disqualification before reaching any determination as to how he will vote if he does sit.

Since most Justices come to this bench no earlier than their middle years, it would be unusual if they had not by that time formulated at least some tentative notions that would influence them in their interpretation of the sweeping clauses of the Constitution and their interaction with one another. It would be not merely unusual, but extraordinary, if they had not at least given opinions as to constitutional issues in their previous legal careers. Proof that a Justice's mind at the time he joined the Court was a complete *tabula rasa* in the area of constitutional adjudication would be evidence of lack of qualification, not lack of bias.

Yet whether these opinions have become at all widely known may depend entirely on happenstance. With respect to those who come here directly from private life, such comments or opinions may never have been publicly uttered. But it would be unusual if those coming from policymaking divisions in the Executive Branch, from the Senate or House of Representatives, or from positions in state government had not divulged at least some hint of their general approach to public affairs, if not as to particular issues of law. Indeed, the clearest case of all is that of a Justice who comes to this Court from a lower court, and has, while sitting as a judge of the lower court, had occasion to pass on an issue that later comes before this Court. No more compelling example could be found of a situation in which a Justice had previously committed himself. Yet it is not and could not rationally be suggested that, so long as the cases be different, a Justice of this Court should disqualify himself for that reason. See, *e. g.*, the opinion of Mr. Justice Harlan, joining in *Lewis* v. *Manufacturers National Bank*, 364 U.S. 603, 610 (1961). Indeed, there is weighty authority for this proposition even when the cases are the same. Mr. Justice Holmes, after his appointment to this Court, sat in several cases which reviewed decisions of the Supreme Judicial Court of Massachusetts rendered, with his participation, while he was Chief Justice of that court. See *Worcester* v. *Street R. Co.*, 196 U.S. 539 (1905), reviewing 182 Mass. 49 (1902); *Dunbar* v. *Dunbar*, 190 U.S. 340 (1903), reviewing 180 Mass. 170 (1901); *Glidden* v. *Harrington*, 189 U.S. 255 (1903), reviewing 179 Mass. 486 (1901); and *Williams* v. *Parker*, 188 U.S. 491 (1903), reviewing 174 Mass. 476 (1899).

Mr. Frank sums the matter up this way:

"Supreme Court Justices are strong-minded men, and on the general subject matters which come before them, they do have propensities; the course of decision cannot be accounted for in any other way." *Supra*, 35 Law & Contemp. Prob., at 48.

The fact that some aspect of these propensities may have been publicly articulated prior to coming to this Court cannot, in my opinion, be regarded as anything more than a random circumstance that should not by itself form a basis for disqualification.[5]

Based upon the foregoing analysis, I conclude that the applicable statute does not warrant my disqualification in this case. Having so said, I would certainly concede that fair-minded judges might disagree about the matter. If all doubts were to be resolved in favor of disqualification, it may be that I should disqualify myself simply because I do regard the question as a fairly debatable one, even though upon analysis I would resolve it in favor of sitting.

Here again, one's course of action may well depend upon the view he takes of the process of disqualification. Those federal courts of appeals that have considered the matter have unanimously concluded that a federal judge has a duty to *sit* where *not disqualified* which is equally as strong as the duty to *not sit* where *disqualified. Edwards* v. *United States*, 334 F. 2d 360, 362 n. 2 (CA5 1964); *Tynan* v. *United States*, 126 U.S. App. D.C. 206, 376 F. 2d 761 (1967); *In re Union Leader Corp.*, 292 F. 2d 381 (CA1 1961); *Wolfson* v. *Palmieri*, 396 F. 2d 121 (CA2 1968); *Simmons* v. *United States*, 302 F. 2d 71 (CA3 1962); *United States* v. *Hoffa*, 382 F. 2d 856 (CA6 1967); *Tucker* v. *Kerner*, 186 F. 2d 79 (CA7 1950); *Walker* v. *Bishop*, 408 F. 2d 1378 (CA8 1969). These cases dealt with disqualification on the part of judges of the district courts and of the courts of appeals. I think that the policy in favor of the "equal duty" concept is even stronger in the case of a Justice of the Supreme Court of the United States. There is no way of substituting Justices on this Court as one judge may be substituted for another in the district courts. There is no higher court of appeal that may review an equally divided decision of this Court and thereby establish the law for our jurisdiction. See, *e. g.*, *Tinker* v. *Des Moines School District*, 258 F. Supp. 971 (SD Iowa 1966), affirmed by an equally divided court, 383 F. 2d 988 (CA8 1967), certiorari granted and judgment reversed, 393 U.S. 503 (1969). While it can seldom be predicted with confidence at the time that a Justice

---

[5] In terms of propriety, rather than disqualification, I would distinguish quite sharply between a public statement made prior to nomination for the bench, on the one hand, and a public statement made by a nominee to the bench. For the latter to express any but the most general observation about the law would suggest that, in order to obtain favorable consideration of his nomination, he deliberately was announcing in advance, without benefit of judicial oath, briefs, or argument, how he would decide a particular question that might come before him as a judge.

addresses himself to the issue of disqualification whether or not the Court in a particular case will be closely divided, the disqualification of one Justice of this Court raises the possibility of an affirmance of the judgment below by an equally divided Court. The consequence attending such a result is, of course, that the principle of law presented by the case is left unsettled. The undesirability of such a disposition is obviously not a reason for refusing to disqualify oneself where in fact one deems himself disqualified, but I believe it is a reason for not "bending over backwards" in order to deem one's self disqualified.

The prospect of affirmance by an equally divided Court, unsatisfactory enough in a single case, presents even more serious problems where companion cases reaching opposite results are heard together here. During the six months in which I have sat as a Justice of this Court, there were at least three such instances.[6] Since one of the stated reasons for granting certiorari is to resolve a conflict among other federal courts or state courts, the frequency of such instances is not surprising. Yet affirmance of each of such conflicting results by an equally divided Court would lay down "one rule in Athens, and another rule in Rome" with a vengeance. And since the notion of "public statement" disqualification that I understand respondents to advance appears to have no ascertainable time limit, it is questionable when or if such an unsettled state of the law could be resolved.

The oath prescribed by 28 U. S. C. § 453 that is taken by each person upon becoming a member of the federal judiciary requires that he "administer justice without respect to persons, and do equal right to the poor and to the rich," that he "faithfully and impartially discharge and perform all the duties incumbent upon [him] . . . agreeably to the Constitution and laws of the United States." Every litigant is entitled to have his case heard by a judge mindful of this oath. But neither the oath, the disqualification statute, nor the practice of the former Justices of this Court guarantees a litigant that each judge will start off from dead center in his willingness or ability to reconcile the opposing arguments of counsel with his understanding of the Constitution and the law. That being the case, it is not a ground for disqualification that a judge has prior to his nomination expressed his then understanding of the meaning of some particular provision of the Constitution.

---

[6] *Branzburg* v. *Hayes*, 408 U.S. 665 (1972). *Gelbard* v. *United States*, 408 U.S. 41 (1972). *Evansville Airport* v. *Delta Airlines Inc.*, 405 U.S. 707 (1972).

Based on the foregoing considerations, I conclude that respondents' motion that I disqualify myself in this case should be, and it hereby is, denied.[7]

---

[7] Petitioners in *Gravel* v. *United States*, 408 U.S. 606 (1972), have filed a petition for rehearing which asserts as one of the grounds that I should have disqualified myself in that case. Because respondents' motion in *Laird* was addressed to me, and because it seemed to me to be seriously and responsibly urged, I have dealt with my reasons for denying it at some length. Because I believe that the petition for rehearing in *Gravel*, insofar as it deals with disqualification, possesses none of these characteristics, there is no occasion for me to treat it in a similar manner. Since such motions have in the past been treated by the Court as being addressed to the individual Justice involved, however, I do venture the observation that in my opinion the petition insofar as it relates to disqualification verges on the frivolous. While my peripheral advisory role in *New York Times Co.* v. *United States*, 403 U.S. 713 (1971), would have warranted disqualification had I been on the Court when that case was heard, it could not conceivably warrant disqualification in *Gravel*, a different case raising entirely different constitutional issues.

NOTES

A wealth of basic background material on judicial behavior has been compiled by the Senate Judiciary Subcommittee on Separation of Powers as the result of 1969 and 1970 hearings under the chairmanship of Senator Sam J. Ervin, Jr., Democrat of North Carolina. One volume is entitled *The Independence of Federal Judges* (91st Cong., 2d sess., 1970), referred to in these notes as *Independence Hearings*. The other is called *Nonjudicial Activities of Supreme Court Justices and Other Federal Judges* (91st Cong., 1st sess., 1969), referred to here as *Nonjudicial Hearings*. Other Senate hearings and reports contain important testimony and documentation, especially the confirmation hearings on the Supreme Court nominations of Abe Fortas (to be chief justice, 90th Cong., 2d sess., 1968), Warren E. Burger (to be chief justice, 91st Cong., 1st sess., 1969), Clement F. Haynsworth, Jr. (91st Cong., 1st sess., 1969), G. Harrold Carswell (91st Cong., 2d sess., 1970), Harry A. Blackmun (91st Cong., 2d sess., 1970), and William H. Rehnquist and Lewis F. Powell, Jr. (92nd Cong., 1st sess., 1971), and the Senate Judiciary Committee reports associated with these confirmations. Basic to an understanding of the current standards of judicial ethics are the American Bar Association's 1924 Canons of Judicial Ethics and the ABA's 1972 Code of Judicial Conduct; the latter is reproduced as Appendix A. A useful adjunct to the new ABA code is the volume *Reporter's Notes to Code of Judicial Conduct* by Professor E. Wayne Thode, published by the ABA in 1973. Valuable scholarly discussions, rich with references to historical precedents and the more modern controversies, are contained in two law journals, *Law and Contemporary Problems*, vol. 35, no. 1 (Winter 1970), and *Utah Law Review*, no. 3 (Fall 1972). An important book, which deals with a different species of judicial misbehavior than is described in this book, is Joseph Borkin's *The*

Corrupt Judge; its author has a contagious zeal for judicial reform that had much to do with the undertaking of this work. A major event in the recent history of judicial behavior, Justice Rehnquist's opinion explaining his participation in a controversial 1971 case, is reproduced as Appendix B. An attempt is made here not to burden the reader with excessive citations. Much of the unattributed material is the result of personal observation as a newspaper reporter covering the most recent events, and when necessary the sources of confidential information are not identified.

1
Entanglements (pages 1–33)

1 *Jay to Washington: Correspondence and Public Papers of John Jay, 1782–1793* 3:487–88.

Fortas quotation: Fortas Hearings, p. 215.

2 *Justinian Code:* S. P. Scott, *The Civil Law* 12:270. (sixth century A.D.)

3 *rulings in 1927, 1955, and 1972: Tumey* v. *Ohio*, 273 U.S. 510 (1926); *In Re Murchison*, 349 U.S. 133 (1955); and *Ward* v. *Village of Monroeville*, 409 U.S. 57 (1972).

4 *Jay's letter: Jay Correspondence and Public Papers*, pp. 486–87.

5 *"mischievous and impolitic":* Charles Warren, *The Supreme Court in United States History* 1:119.

Ellsworth resignation: ibid., p. 275.

6 *Jay had been defeated:* ibid., p. 285.

Jay again confirmed: ibid., p. 173.

7 *the confusion of roles:* noted by Dean Acheson in his testimony, *Nonjudicial Hearings*, p. 123.

Jackson's "challenge": from transcript of recorded interview prepared for the Oral History Project of Columbia University, quoted in *The Justices of the United States Supreme Court* 4:2565–66.

8 *Frankfurter on Murphy:* Max Freedman, ed., *Roosevelt and Frank-furter*, p. 58.

Murphy disqualified himself: Ex Parte Quirin, 317 U.S. 1 (1942).

9–12 *Dred Scott episode:* Warren, *The Supreme Court in U.S. History* 2:279–303.

12 *Frankfurter to FDR on wiretapping:* Freedman, ed., *Roosevelt and Frankfurter*, p. 582.

Acheson commentary: Nonjudicial Hearings, p. 119.

13 *Stone's difficulties with executive invasion of judiciary:* Alpheus T. Mason, *Harlan Fiske Stone: Pillar of the Law,* especially pp. 698–720.

15 *Taft's lobbying:* see Alpheus T. Mason, *William Howard Taft: Chief Justice,* especially chapters 6 and 11.

17 *Hughes candidacy:* see Taft's letter attempting to persuade Hughes to run in Merloe J. Pusey, *Charles Evans Hughes,* vol. 1, p. 319. The other pressures on the unwilling justice are described in this chapter of the Hughes biography.

Goldberg's opportunity: Washington Post, July 21, 1965.

18 *Fortas's duty; Fortas Hearings,* pp. 124–25.

19 *Alsop column: Washington Post,* July 7, 1971.

20 *Fortas saw draft of LBJ message: Fortas Hearings,* p. 48.

Fortas on flag desecration and selective conscientious objection: Concerning Dissent and Civil Disobedience, pp. 16, 51–52; see also *Nonjudicial Hearings,* pp. 76–761. The flag desecration case was *Street* v. *New York,* 394 U.S. 576 (1969). The Supreme Court accepted the case for review on May 17, 1968; heard arguments October 21, 1968; and decided the case on April 21, 1969. The Court ordered a new trial for Street over separate dissents by Chief Justice Warren and Justices Black, White, and Fortas. It was the last dissenting opinion by Fortas before his resignation. The "selective C.O." issue remained open for two more terms after the Fortas pamphlet was published and was resolved in favor of the Selective Service System on March 8, 1971, in *Gillette* v. *U.S.,* 401 U.S. 437. A thoughtful review of the Fortas pamphlet by Tarrance Sandalow, a law professor at the University of

Michigan, appears in *Michigan Law Review* 67:599 (January 1969).

21 *"deepening their convictions without widening their experience"*: Sandalow book review, reprinted in *Nonjudicial Hearings,* p. 763.

Fortas's apparent need for outside experience: Washington Post, May 16, 1969.

22 *Thurmond's questions:* see John P. MacKenzie, "Thurgood Marshall," in *Justices of the United States Supreme Court* 4:3086–88.

Thornberry's first nomination by LBJ: see *Fortas Hearings,* p. 50.

23 *Griffin's testimony:* ibid., pp. 41–65.

23–24 *Dirksen on "gossamer":* ibid., p. 54.

24 *"of critical importance to the President":* ibid., p. 104.

"President always turns to me last": ibid., p. 106.

26 *"Mallory!":* ibid., p. 191.

27 *"an inadvertence":* ibid., p. 189.

28 *"full disclosure":* ibid., p. 106.

"personal hygeine": Washington Post, September 22, 1968.

29 *Solfisburg resignation:* see *Law and Contemporary Problems* 35:151–53.

30 *"I cannot and I will not be an instrument": Fortas Hearings,* p. 215.

31 *"a justice of the Supreme Court or a barber or a priest":* Victor S. Navasky, in *New York Times Magazine,* August 1, 1971, p. 32.

33 *Montesquieu: Spirit of the Laws* 1:152 (Nugent, ed., 1823), quoted by Senator Ervin in *Law and Contemporary Problems* 35:109.

no "cronyism": see John P. MacKenzie, "Warren E. Burger," in *Justices of the United States Supreme Court* 4:3114–21.

2
The Price of Independence (*pages 35–65*)

35 Bazelon quotation: *Independence Hearings,* p. 322.

Parker quotation: *Tennessee Law Review* 20:703, 705–6 (1949).

36–37 Ford on impeachable offenses: *Congressional Record,* April 15, 1970; Associate Justice William O. Douglas, *Final Report by the Special Subcommittee on H. Res. 920,* House Judiciary Committee, 91st Cong., 2d sess. (*Douglas Report*), p. 36. See also his November 1973 vice-presidential confirmation hearings, Senate Rules Committee, p. 65; House Judiciary Committee, pp. 72, 140.

37 McCloskey view: *Douglas Report,* pp. 367–84.

impeachments unreviewable: The fact that this is so clear to the author does not guarantee that the matter will not be bitterly litigated.

38 Chandler case: *Chandler* v. *Judicial Council,* 382 U.S. 1003 (1966), 398 U.S. 74 (1970).

39 Kerner case: *U.S.* v. *Isaacs and Kerner,* No. 73–1410, 7th Circuit, on appeal from the District Court for the Northern District of Illinois. Conviction affirmed, February 19, 1972.

40 Rehnquist advice: see Robert Shogan, *A Question of Judgment,* pp. 230–33.

41 Eastland view: see John H. Holloman III, "The Judicial Reform Act: History, Analysis and Comment," in *Law and Contemporary Problems* 35:128, by the chief counsel and staff director of the Senate Judiciary Committee.

Ervin volumes: *Independence Hearings* and *Nonjudicial Hearings.*

Rehnquist on Tydings bill: ibid., pp. 330–51.

42 Judge Hemphill's views: ibid., p. 510.

43 Ford's preparation of case against Douglas: Extensive questioning occurs throughout Ford's November 1973 vice-presidential confirmation hearings, particularly those before the House Judiciary Committee, about the campaign's origins and possible Nixon administration role.

44 *comments on Douglas disqualification:* see *New York Times* and *Washington Star*, December 9, 1970.

45 *the railroad rate case: Atlantic City Electric Co.* v. *U.S.,* 400 U.S. 73 (1970).

    Curious Yellow *case: Grove Press* v. *Maryland Board of Censors,* 401 U.S. 480 (1971).

46 *"not because . . . I relish obscenity": Byrne* v. *Karalexis,* 396 U.S. 976 (1969).

48 *Douglas and vice-presidency:* CBS News interview with Justice Douglas, September 6, 1972.

    Parvin's first letter to Douglas: Douglas Report, p. 86.

50 *Lansky finder's fee:* ibid., p. 300.

    Parvin's alertness to investment opportunities: ibid., p. 910.

    Douglas called it a "compulsion": ibid., p. 847.

51 *Parvin donated securities:* ibid., p. 875; *bought stock:* ibid., pp. 882, 884; *obtained loan:* ibid., p. 918; *sold short:* ibid., p. 104; *opened savings and loan account:* ibid., pp. 54, 395–96.

52 *Parvin reentered hotel business:* ibid., p. 907.

    Douglas to Parvin: ibid., p. 687.

55 *Douglas report to foundation board:* minutes of November 1, 1966, meeting, ibid., p. 907.

56 *Miss Agger's letter:* ibid., p. 96.

56–57 *"Honestly, Harry, what is wrong with me?":* ibid., pp. 101–2.

57 *Ashmore's summary:* ibid., pp. 104–5.

    Douglas to fellow justices: ibid., pp. 192–95.

58 *finance committee change:* ibid., p. 911.

59 *"Who will sit at the switchboard . . . ?": New York Times,* March 28, 1967, pp. 1, 71. The printed opinion is at 386 U.S 372, 438 (1967).

    "the King alone": Pierson v. *Ray,* 386 U.S. 547, 558, 565 (1967).

    "ceased to be private": Time v. *Hill,* 385 U.S. 374, 401 (1967).

60 meeting in Douglas's chambers: Douglas Report, p. 912.

Douglas on Pacem conference: ibid., pp. 335–36.

62 Silbert charged Douglas with neglect: ibid., pp. 861–67.

63 "I will not be brainwashed": ibid., pp. 865–66.

IRS case "is built on appearances": ibid., pp. 806–7.

"to get me off the Court": ibid., p. 110.

64 Parvin said Douglas drafted articles: ibid., p. 74.

3
Conflicts (pages 67–94)

68 corruption and business cycle: Joseph Borkin, The Corrupt Judge, p. 13.

69 Taft distrusted Manton: David J. Danielski, A Supreme Court Justice Is Appointed, pp. 44–45. For accounts of judicial involvement in oil companies, see chapter 4, pp. 109–17. A joint real estate venture by several justices and judges is described in Nonjudicial Hearings, pp. 811–13. The Detroit judge is described in George C. Edwards, Jr., "Judicial Ethics," Fordham Law Review 38:259 (1969). Another judge with similar confusion is described in Nonjudicial Hearings, p. 494.

71 The Nixon administration's slow response to ethical charges was noted ruefully by Haynsworth's leading Senate supporter, Senator Hollings, in The Washington Post, October 10, 1969.

72 "I do not think all mergers are bad": ibid., July 31, 1966, pp. K-1, K-3.

"economic destiny": 386 U.S. 372, 478 (1967).

74 Northeastern speech: Washington Post, May 9, 1969.

75 "Honest Abe!": ibid., May 11, 1969.

76 Fortas letter to Warren: reprinted in Shogan, A Question of Judgment, pp. 279–82.

77 *ABA report on Fortas:* Informal Opinion 1114, Formal Opinion 322, May 18, 1969.

81 *"duty to sit" doctrine:* memorandum by Assistant Attorney General Rehnquist dated September 5, 1969, reprinted in *Haynsworth Hearings,* pp. 19–25.

82 Commonwealth Coatings *case:* 393 U.S. 145 (1968).

84 *Bayh's position on Haynsworth: Washington Post,* September 17, 1969. Rehnquist's admission that he initially overlooked the case is described in *Rehnquist-Powell Hearings,* p. 61.

85 *"indicted rather than appointed": Haynsworth Hearings,* p. 37.

"Jeff and Mutt": ibid., p. 406.

86 *"You do not do business . . . in Greenville":* ibid., p. 226.

87 Haynsworth was *"very sorry":* ibid., p. 271.

88 *Haynsworth contributed to delay: Washington Post,* October 1, 1969.

Haynsworth offered trust idea: ibid., October 7, 1969.

90 *J. P. Stevens court record:* On October 28, 1969, the *Wall Street Journal* reported that the NLRB had upheld unfair labor practice charges against Stevens for the seventh time since 1966. In one of innumerable court reviews the Fifth U.S. Circuit Court of Appeals observed "the tenacity with which the employer [Stevens] persists in the exercise of deep seated anti-union convictions" and "the succession of formal cases culminating in the present one bearing five service stripes in which, except for minor variations, the Board's findings of spectacular employer violations of [federal labor law] have been upheld by three Courts of Appeals." *J. P. Stevens & Co., Inc.* v. *NLRB,* 417 F.2d 533, 534 (1969).

91 *stake in Vend-A-Matic: Judiciary Committee Report* (Individual Views of Senator Bayh), p. 33; *Washington Post,* October 9, 1969.

nonunion plants: ibid., October 1, 1969.

92 *business-getting duties: Judiciary Committee Report* (Individual Views of Senator Griffin), pp. 41–42.

Senator Hollings lamented: Congressional Record 116: 15110–12 (May 12, 1970).

93 Blackmun was lectured: Blackmun Hearings, p. 47.

94 Kleindienst view of Blackmun ethics: ibid., pp. 12, 17.

"times have changed": ibid., p. 41. For a subsequent expression of Justice Blackmun's view of an ethical problem, see his lay sermon at the prayer breakfast of the 1973 annual meeting of the American Bar Association, *Washington Post*, August 6, 1973.

4
The Velvet Blackjack (pages 95–117)

95 Walsh on Learned Hand: Haynsworth Hearings, p. 154.

97 John Frank on Velvet Blackjack: Law and Contemporary Problems 35:64.

106 The Washington Post reports on Four Seasons were published August 22 and 24, 1970.

107 multidistrict panel law: U.S. Code, Title 24, Section 1407.

108 panel's 1971 decision: In Re Four Seasons Securities Laws Litigation, 328 F. Supp. 221 (1971). The outcome of the battle over lawyers' fees is recorded at 59 Fed. Rules Decisions 657 (1973).

112 The race to court is recorded at 459 F.2d 1367 (January 11, 1972), in which the U.S. Court of Appeals for the District of Columbia Circuit transferred the case to the Fifth Circuit.

115 panel vacated: The court's order is not recorded in the published volumes of appellate cases.

116 Southern Louisiana Gas Rate Case: 428 F.2d 407 and 44 F.2d 125 (1970), *certiorari denied,* 400 U.S. 950 (1970). For a later phase in which Mobil Oil tried to disqualify Justice Douglas, see *U.S. Law Week* 42:2484 (February 25, 1974) and newspapers for February 26, 1974.

117 Kinnear case: see 150 F. Supp. 143 (E.D. Tex. 1956), 259 F.2d 398 (5th Cir. 1958), 296 F.2d 215 (5th Cir. 1961) 403 F.2d 437 (5th Cir. 1968, en banc), 324 F. Supp. 1371 (E.D. Tex. 1969), 441 F.2d 631 (5th Cir. 1971), *certiorari denied,* 404 U.S. 941 (1971).

5
Lions on the Throne (pages 119–34)

119 *"the Soldier and the Justice":* John Rushworth, *Historical Collections,* vol. 3, appendix 81 (1721–22).

120 *"glaring down":* Herman Schwartz, "Judges as Tyrants," *Criminal Law Bulletin* 7:129–30.

121 *a report of the 1971 conference action: New York Times,* October 31, 1971.

122 *civility "irrelevant":* Warren E. Burger, "The Necessity for Civility," *Federal Rules Decisions* 52:211–14 (May 1971).

Burke Marshall on "panic": Disorder in the Court, Report of the Association of the Bar of the City of New York Special Committee on Courtroom Conduct, pp. xiii–xiv.

123 *contempt decision from Communists' trial: Sacher* v. *U.S.,* 343 U.S. 1 (1952).

124 *Spock trial:* author's personal observations as reporter covering the trial.

127 *Seale should have been asked: U.S.* v. *Seale,* 461 F.2d 345, 358 (7th Cir., 1972). See also *Disorder in the Court,* p. 41.

"Did I say Feinglass?": Judy Clavir and John Spitzer, eds., *The Conspiracy Trial,* p. 356. See also p. 591 and elsewhere in the transcript.

"I nearly said Christian names"; ibid., p. 45.

128 *"do you no good":* ibid., p. xvi.

129 *Judge's calumny no excuse:* see *Disorder in the Court,* p. 112.

Seale's birthday cake: Clavir and Spitzer, eds., *Conspiracy Trial,* p. 122.

131 *Judge Gignoux's judgment and "sentencing":* see accounts in the *New York Times* and *The Washington Post* for December 5 and 7, 1973, and transcript of proceedings.

132 *Carswell's rude behavior:* see *Carswell Hearings,* especially pp. 149–205.

132 *"niggers" and "chimpanzees":* see Victor S. Navasky, *Kennedy Justice,* p. 245.

   prosecutors as judicial candidates: see Harold W. Chase, *Federal Judges: The Appointing Process,* especially pp. 107–8, 114.

133 *Judge Ford quoted:* see Jessica Mitford, *The Trial of Dr. Spock,* p. 162.

6
The Judges Lobby (*pages 135–52*)

135 *"propaganda organization":* Congressional Record 62:201 (1922), cited by David S. Myers in "Origin of the Judicial Conference," *American Bar Association Journal* 57:597, 599.

137 *criticism of federal courts:* see, for example, Felix Frankfurter and Nathan Greene, *The Labor Injunction* (1930), pp. 130–33.

138 *Taft to Daugherty:* July 3, 1921; see *Independence Hearings,* p. 3.

   "executive principle": Taft testimony is cited in Mason, *Taft,* p. 99; Myers in *ABA Journal,* p. 599, n. 12.

139 *"copying after the system in England":* Mason, *Taft,* pp. 101–2, quoting *Congressional Record* 67:4853, 4855.

143 Berger *v.* New York: 388 U.S. 41 (June 12, 1967).

146 *Jay's lecture:* discussed in chapter 1; see notes for pp. 1 and 4.

   "the Conference voted to adhere": Report of the Proceedings of the Judicial Conference, February 27–28, 1968, p. 33.

148 *Senator McClellan on the Senate floor:* Congressional Record 115: 33572–76 (November 10, 1969), quoted also in *Independence Hearings,* p. 1047.

149 *"Conference . . . deviated":* Washington Post, March 19, 1970.

150 *idea of an open conference: Independence Hearings,* p. 6.

   Ervin asked Judge Lumbard for views on constitutional amendment: Controlling Crime through More Effective Law Enforcement, Hearings before the Subcommittee on Criminal Laws and Procedures of the Senate Judiciary Committee, 90th Cong., 1st sess. (1967), pp. 170–98.

150 Judge Lumbard's testimony: Independence Hearings, especially pp. 57, 70, 73, 75.

151 Judge Bazelon's version: ibid., p. 316.

7
Earl Warren and Warren Earl (pages 153–77)

153 "A Semi-Revolution": The Poetry of Robert Frost, edited by Edward Connery Lathem (Holt, Rinehart & Winston, 1969), p. 363.

155 Warren on "decent society": Jacobellis v. *Ohio,* 378 U.S. 184, 199 (1964), Warren, C. J., dissenting, quoted by Burger in *Paris Adult Theatre* v. *Slayton,* 413 U.S. 49, 60, n. 10 (1973).

156 "Law floats on a sea of Ethics": see James E. Clayton, *The Making of Justice,* pp. 95–96.

Warren's misgivings about commission: television interview with Abram Sachar, chancellor of Brandeis University, May 3, 1972, taped and broadcast over Public Broadcasting Service stations, transcript pp. 19–21.

157 The *Wall Street Journal* article was reprinted in the *Congressional Record* for May 18, 1963, in extension of remarks by Senator Estes Kefauver, Democrat of Tennessee.

159 June 10 resolution: Report of the Proceedings of the Judicial Conference, June 10, 1969, pp. 42–43; also Judicial Reform Act, Hearings before the Senate Subcommittee on Improvements in Judicial Machinery, November 24, 1969, pp. 3–4.

163 Second Circuit resolution: New York Times, July 3, 1969.

164 "I am not your man": Washington Post, August 10, 1970.

169 Tydings grills conference officials: see Judicial Reform Act hearings mentioned in note for p. 159.

170 *ABA corrections commission advice not heeded:* compare ABA brief Amicus Curiae in *Preiser* v. *Rodriguez,* 411 U.S. 475 (1973), with the decision in that case.

171 *Burger on court overloads:* 1970 "state of the judiciary" speech is reprinted in *ABA Journal* 56:929.

172 *Jack Anderson column: Washington Post,* October 5, 1972.

Burger's response, including report of letter to Speaker Albert: ibid., October 14, 1972.

173 *Representative Eckhardt's criticism: Congressional Record* 118:H 10354 (October 18, 1972), daily edition.

Burger reasserted right: The Third Branch, vol. 4, no. 11, p. 1 (November 1972). (A Bulletin of the Federal Courts, published by the Administrative Office of the U.S. Courts and the Federal Judicial Center.)

Corroborated: that Kirks and Corcoran made the visit to the Speaker together. Denied: that Burger sent them (denied by Kirks but not specifically by Burger); that the "merits" of the legislation were discussed; and that there was any impropriety. Denied but not charged: that Kirks or Corcoran purported to speak for Burger or dropped his name.

174 *two search-and-seizure dissents: Coolidge* v. *New Hampshire,* 403 U.S. 433, 492 (1971); and *Bivens* v. *Six Narcotics Agents,* 403 U.S. 388, 411 (1971).

ABA rejects Bentsen bill idea: see, for example, *Washington Post,* February 13, 1973.

Burger opinion in Three Sisters Bridge case: Volpe v. *D.C. Federation of Civic Associations,* 405 U.S. 1030–1031 (1971). Compare text as initially delivered, *U.S. Law Week* 40:3468.

176 *Senator Allen sees "straw in the wind": Congressional Record,* March 28, 1972. For a commentary, see Frank R. Strong, "Three Little Words and What They Didn't Seem to Mean," *ABA Journal* 59:29 (January 1973).

8
The New Ethics (pages 179–206)

179 *Bacon's canon:* A "purprise" appears to have been related to a "purpresture," which is defined in the single-volume *Oxford Universal Dictionary* (1955), p. 1624, as ". . . an enclosure or building in royal, manorial or common lands. . . ."

For a poignant description of Bacon's punishment and exile during which *Of Judicature* was written see Catherine Drinker Bowen, *Francis Bacon: The Temper of a Man*, pp. 204–33.

180 *the public "more distrustful":* Robert B. McKay, "The Judiciary and Nonjudicial Activities," *Law and Contemporary Problems* 35:9.

181 *Landis friendly to baseball:* Allison Danzig and Joe Reichler, *Baseball; its Great Players, Teams and Managers,* p. 68. For the Landis resolution and preceding dialogue in ABA House of Delegates see *Reports of the American Bar Association,* vol. 46 (1921).

The case of *Berger* v. *U.S.* is reported at 255 U.S. 22 (1921).

183 *"The time is now ripe" for canons:* Charles A. Boston to ABA executive committee, September 24, 1921, Taft papers, Library of Congress.

Taft relieved by Davis nomination: Taft to von Moschzisker, July 10, 1924, ibid.; Taft to Horace P. Taft, same date, Mason, *Taft,* p. 163.

184 *Taft had urged judgeship for Boston:* author's interview with Lyon Boston, son of Charles Boston, August 1973.

Boston to do the work: von Moschzisker to Taft, April 21, 1922, Taft papers.

first draft produced in one month: Boston to committee members, June 8, 1922, ibid.

Boston urged to screen criticisms: von Moschzisker to Taft, February 2, 1923, ibid.

unused canon on popularity with bar: Boston to Taft, June 8, 1922, ibid.

186 Boston characterized the criticisms of the canons in a letter to the committee dated February 25, 1922, ibid.

canons "a beneficent force": draft of Boston report to ABA executive committee, May 1, 1923, ibid.

186 *canons likened to Commandments and Beatitudes:* von Moschzisker to Taft, April 28, 1923, ibid.

187 *"Boston died a little hard":* von Moschzisker to Taft, July 10, 1924, ibid.

188 *"the press rallied strongly":* Mason, *Taft,* pp. 274–75.

189 *"difficult to square" canon with Taft's involvement:* Mason, *Taft,* p. 283. Canon 28 covered partisan politics.

on dissenting opinions: Mason, *Taft,* chapter 9, especially p. 223.

191 *fate of the 1924 canons:* Susan Henderson, "The Origin and Adoption of the ABA Canons of Judicial Ethics," *Judicature* 52:387.

193 *"stimulator of outside activities":* Nonjudicial Hearings, p. 120.

194 *"great partnership":* Arkansas Law Review and Bar Association Journal, Spring 1971.

195 *"a sampler of mottoes":* Utah Law Review (1972), p. 335.

"highest possible standards": ibid.

197 *Traynor's explanation of the one-share standard:* see, for example, *Washington Post,* August 7, 1970.

200 *bank loans:* the language was adopted as canon 5C(4)(b).

201 *judges "should not become isolated":* canon 5A.

"appearance" canon: canon 2.

202 *disqualification:* canon 3C(1)(b), discussed by Thode in *Reporter's Notes,* p. 63.

canon on courtesy "unnecessary": Thode, *Reporter's Notes,* p. 52.

203 *Powell precluded from "blind trust":* Powell Hearings, pp. 203–4.

"A judge should inform himself": canon 3C(2).

204 *Judge Noe: Washington Post,* August 12, 1972.

205 *amendment approved:* The amendment inserted the words "judge or" before the word "lawyer" in canon 3B(3), which is reprinted here in Appendix B, p. 248.

floor action: ibid., August 18, 1972. The Judicial Conference adoption of the ABA code, with the exception noted, is described in *Judicial Disqualification*, Hearing before the Senate Subcommittee on Improvements in Judicial Machinery, 93d Cong., 1st sess. (To broaden and clarify the grounds for judicial disqualification), pp. 120–29. The conference action in the fall of 1973 is summarized in *Report of the Proceedings of the Judicial Conference*, September 13–14, 1973, pp. 52–53. The controversy over Judge Weinstein is discussed in *The Washington Post*, April 7, 1973.

9
A Judge and His Cause (*pages 207–23*)

208 *Frankfurter's dissent: U.S.* v. *Rabinowitz,* 339 U.S. 56, 86 (1950).

Black's dissent: Rogers v. *Bellei,* 401 U.S. 815, 837, 845 (1971).

209 *Rehnquist's advice on Fortas:* see Shogan, *A Question of Judgment.* pp. 230–33.

210 *Rehnquist on stricter standards: Blackmun Hearings,* pp. 12, 17; *Rehnquist-Powell Hearings,* p. 60.

Rehnquist recused himself: U.S. v. *U.S. District Court for the Eastern District of Michigan,* 407 U.S. 297 (1972); and *Kastigar* v. *U.S.,* 406 U.S. 441 (1972).

Branzburg *case: Branzburg* v. *Hayes,* 408 U.S. 665 (1972).

Tatum *case:* 408 U.S. 1 (1972).

211 Gravel *case: U.S.* v. *Gravel,* 408 U.S. 606 (1972).

212 *stunned counsel:* author's interviews with lawyers, Senator Ervin, and others, in addition to motions to recuse in *Tatum.*

215 *1945 case: Jewell Ridge Coal Co.* v. *Mine Workers,* petition for rehearing denied, 325 U.S. 897 (1945), discussed in John P. Frank, *Mr. Justice Black: The Man and His Opinions,* pp. 123–31.

217 *Rehnquist told Ervin: Hearings on Federal Data Banks, Computers and the Bill of Rights,* Senate Subcommittee on Constitutional Rights, 92d Cong., 1st sess., 1:864–65.

218 *1955 decision: In Re Murchison*, 349 U.S. 133, 136, discussed also in chapter 1.

Carswell disqualified: U.S. v. *Adams*, 302 F.2d 307 (5th Cir., 1962).

222 *canon covering former government attorney:* see canon 3C and commentary, Appendix A, p. 248.

Justice White: memorandum written for White's guidance as he left the Justice Department for the Court, reprinted in *Judicial Disqualification Hearings,* Senate Subcommittee on Improvements in Judicial Machinery, 93d Cong., 1st sess., p. 167.

223 *"credibility erodes":* For an indication that Justice Rehnquist has not retreated from his position on ethics, see his speech, "Sense and Nonsense about Judicial Ethics," delivered to the Association of the Bar of the City of New York, September 19, 1973. The text of the speech is in the association's publication, *The Record* 28:694.

10
Appearance, Reality, and Perspective (pages 225–41)

225 *truth's discovery:* Ehrlichman's April 30, 1973, resignation letter was not immediately followed by the discovery of truth. According to indictments returned on March 1 and March 7, 1974, Ehrlichman was accused of lying to the FBI on the following day, May 1, 1973; lying to a grand jury on May 3, May 9, and three times on May 14; and lying to the FBI again on July 21.

"institutional arrangements": Freund testimony is from *Special Prosecutor,* Hearings before the Senate Judiciary Committee, 93d Cong., 1st sess. (1973), p. 372.

226 *Senator Weicker on theft of country:* opening statement in *Presidential Campaign Activities of 1972,* Senate Resolution 60, Senate Select Committee on Presidential Campaign Activities (*Watergate Hearings*), bk. 1, p. 8 (May 17, 1973).

226 Ehrlichman "scoured the canons of ethics": his testimony, *Watergate Hearings*, July 27, 1973.

227 *Manton on public confidence:* Petition for Certiorari, *Manton* v. *U.S.*, No. 645, October Term 1939, denied by the Court, 309 U.S. 664 (February 26, 1940).

228 *Senate passed legislation:* Passage of the Judicial Disqualification Bill, S. 1064, 93d Cong., 1st sess., is recorded in the *Congressional Record* 119:S18681 (October 4, 1973) (daily edition). See also the interesting record compiled in the hearings on the bill, entitled "Judicial Disqualification," before the Senate Subcommittee on Improvements in Judicial Machinery in the same session of Congress.

229 *ABA code would have blessed work for private foundation:* canon 5.

     ban on investment advice: canon 5B(3).

230 *"impartiality might reasonably be questioned":* canon 3C.

231 *new canon and J. P. Stevens stock:* canon 5C(3) and Thode, *Reporter's Notes*, p. 83.

235 *Judicial Conference needed rule: Report of the Judicial Conference*, April 5–6, 1973, p. 9.

236 *Professor Thode on permissible commentary by judges:* Thode, *Reporter's Notes*, pp. 74–75.

237 *interfere with judicial duties:* This and similar phrases are used in canon 5A and elsewhere.

     "judicial emergency": Judicial Conference press release, November 1, 1969.

     Carswell and private club: see generally *Carswell Hearings*.

238 *renounce ambition:* Even the renunciation of ambition for higher judicial office may be becoming under certain circumstances. Although it apparently had no effect on the outcome, Justice Stewart called on President Nixon in April 1969 asking to be taken out of the running for chief justice if he indeed had been under consideration. See *Justices of the United States Supreme Court* 4:3118. One major reason: Stewart had vowed to have no further ambition than to be an associate justice. *The Washington Post*, May 28, 1969.

238 *a course in ethics:* For a description of where judicial ethics would fit in a course devoted primarily to the professional ethics of lawyers, see Robert C. Mathews, "Adjudicative Responsibility, Its Place in the Curriculum," *Utah Law Review*, no. 3 (Fall 1972), p. 421.

239 *"political patronage":* Irving Brant, *Impeachment: Trials and Errors,* p. 198.

240 *injured seaman's perspective:* Senate Report on Haynsworth Nomination, Executive Report No. 91–12, 91st Cong., 1st sess. (November 12, 1969), pp. 52 (Individual Views of Senator Tydings), 46 (Individual Views of Senator Bayh).

241 *Richardson on appearances:* see, for example, *National Journal,* July 14, 1973, p. 1016.

   Frankfurter on "appearance of justice": Offutt v. *United States,* 348 U.S. 11, 14 (1954).

INDEX

Page numbers in italics refer to notes